Pope Francis: The Last Pope?

T0164056

REVIEWS:

"Author Leo Lyon Zagami is a consummate Vatican insider."
—Alex Jones, *InfoWars*

"Leo Zagami tackles with courage and determination the difficult theme of secret societies and in particular the Western initiatic system, offering an avalanche of historical detail and valuable information. A titanic work, full of clarity and realism, indispensable for anyone who wants to understand thoroughly the occult scenario unknown to most people, but also an 'enlightening' guide to better cope with a world that is about to change radically in the delicate inscrutable relationship between earthly power and other unworldly powers."
—Varo Venturi, film director, *6 Days on Earth*

Exceptionally well-written, organized and presented, 'Pope Francis: The Last Pope?: Money Masons and Occultism in the Decline of the Catholic Church' *is an informed and informative as it is thoughtful and thought-provoking. Offering an iconoclastic perspective,* Pope Francis: The Last Pope? *will have an immense interest for seminary students and theologians, as well as non-specialist general readers with an interest in the Roman Catholic Church in general, and the future of the papacy in particular. Offering an iconoclastic perspective, this book is as informed and informative as it is thoughtful and thought-provoking."*
—*The Midwest Book Review*

Pope Francis: The Last Pope?

Money, Masons and Occultism
In the Decline of the Catholic Church

1st edition

Copyright © 2015 by Leo Lyon Zagami
Published by the Consortium of Collective Consciousness Publishing™

As is common in a historic and reference book such as this, much of the information included on these pages has been collected from diverse sources. When possible, the information has been checked and double-checked. Almost every topic has at least three data points, that is, three different sources that report the same information. Even with special effort to be accurate and thorough, the author and publisher cannot vouch for each and every reference. The author and publisher assume no responsibility or liability for any outcome, loss, arrest, or injury that occurs as a result of information or advice contained in this book. As with the purchase of goods or services, *caveat emptor* is the prevailing responsibility of the purchaser, and the same is true for those who study esoteric subjects.

Library of Congress Cataloging-in-Publication Data:

Zagami, Leo Lyon
  POPE FRANCIS: THE LAST POPE? / Leo Lyon Zagami
    p. cm.
    print ISBN 9781888729542 (Pbk.)

1. RELIGION / Christianity/Catholic. 2. SOCIAL SCIENCE / Conspiracy Theories. I. Title
  Library of Congress Catalog Card Number: 2015930353

Printed in the United States of America.

10 9 8 7 6 5 4 3 2

Pope Francis: The Last Pope?

Money, Masons and Occultism
In the Decline of the Catholic Church

Leo Lyon Zagami

Consortium of Collective Consciousness Publishing

LeoZagami.com ‡ CCCPublishing.com

TABLE OF CONTENTS

CHAPTER IV

Homosexuality and Child Abuse in the Vatican

CHAPTER V

Prophecies and More ...

CHAPTER VI

A "Black Pope" on the Papal Throne

EPILOGUE

FOREWORD

by Brad Olsen

On the weekend of my 49th birthday, something wonderful and something tragic happened … then something wonderful again. First the good news first. This same week just so happened to be when I was moving to the signed contract phase with bestselling Italian author Leo Lyon Zagami, including the option to publish five of his books. The first title in our publishing schedule is this book, which I have helped translate and edit, followed by Leo's *Confessions of an Illuminati,* volumes I, II, III, and the *Invisible Master.* The horizons of my next two years was looking to be filled with reissuing Leo's ground-breaking books into the English language. My decision to work with Leo was largely due to the urging of our mutual friend Sean Stone, son of film director Oliver Stone.

Everything was coming up roses when tragedy struck on Friday evening, the day before my birthday. My girlfriend, Jennifer, took a nasty fall on the pavement and shattered her elbow. She broke several bones in her left arm. Needless to say, our weekend plans were canceled. The day after her surgery, I went to bring her flowers and some other items that she needed. When I arrived, I said hello to Nora, an elderly woman who shared the hospital room with Jennifer. Nora had such a pleasant smile and disposition that I really took to her, and the three of us chatted for an hour before a Catholic priest arrived to administer her last rites, a communion, and absolution. Nora had been diagnosed with terminal cancer and she was going in for major surgery the next morning. A few months short of her 80th birthday, she was contemplating the possibility that she may not live through the operation, and wished to be forgiven for her sins.

Nora's priest happened to be a Jesuit. He was a kindly man, who I sensed had love in his heart. We had a discussion about the order, and I even told him about this book. As it turns out, both he and Nora were originally from Barcelona, Spain. The Father was attracted to the Jesuit order as a teenager, enrolled in seminary school, and in time became a priest. Eventually, he was assigned to deliver mass in one of the largest cathedrals in San Francisco, California, the city of "Saint Francis," the Patron Saint of Ecology, and the city where the four of us currently reside.

Pope Francis: The Last Pope?

As I left the hospital I was floored by the sheer synchronicity of the visit—my undertaking of a major publishing project that is both candid and critical of the Vatican and Jesuit authority, and at the same time, witnessing a deeply-moving Catholic religious ceremony I had not sought out, but was extremely grateful for the experience once it was over. My takeaway was to realize that there are exceptionally good Catholic people in the world. Both Nora and the Jesuit priest felt Pope Francis has been a positive change for the Catholic Church, and emphasized how much help the Church offers to so many people. But even the good Catholics need to understand the enormous changes taking place at the upper echelons of the Vatican. The main point is that groups such as organized religions are made up of people—some good, and others who might not be so well-intended.

ON PROPHECIES AND PROPHETS

Apart from being the first Jesuit pope in history, Pope Francis I has another form of notoriety. For over 900 years, historians have recognized that "the last pope" will arrive, around this time in history, and some propose that Francis himself is indeed the *Last Pope*. The most-popular prophecy is taken from Bishop Malachy's "Prophecy of the Popes." It is a list of verses predicting aspects of the reign of each Roman Catholic pope from Celestine II to the final pope, who is named "Peter the Roman," and whose reign would end with the destruction of Rome. Of course the Holy Father Pope Francis I, whose birth-name is Jorge Mario Bergoglio, does not have "Peter" nor "the Roman" in his name. But as the back-dating goes, Pope Benedict XVI was number 111 of the 112 popes prophesied by the later canonized Malachy. Since Pope Francis I reigns after Pope Benedict XVI, this makes him 112—Peter the Roman—*the last pope*—the pope who Malachy said would oversee the destruction of Rome—and this is consistent with biblical prophecy. Catholic prophecies also tell of an "Antipope" who will betray the faith. Could this really be the genial and popular Pope Francis?

Laying dormant for hundreds of years, the prophecies attributed to Saint Malachy were first published in 1595, by a Benedictine historian named Arnold de Wyon, who recorded them in his book called *Lignum Vitæ*. Tradition holds that Malachy had been summoned to Rome by Pope Innocent II, and while there, he experienced the profound vision of all future popes, including the last one, which he wrote down in a series of cryptic phrases identifying the reign of each pope. According to the prophecy, the pope following Benedict XVI will be the final pontiff, *Petrus Romanus* or Peter the Roman.

The idea by some Catholics that the next pope on Saint Malachy's list harkens to the dawn of a "great apostasy," followed by "great tribulation," sets the stage for the imminent unfolding of apocalyptic events. This would give rise to a false prophet, who, according to the book of Revelation, leads the world's religious communities toward embracing a political leader known as an "Antichrist." In recent history, several Catholic priests and pundits have been surprisingly outspoken on what they have seen as an inevitable danger rising from within the ranks of Catholicism—the result of secret and satanic "Illuminati-Masonic" influences. These critics claim to have secret knowledge of a multinational power-elite, an occult hierarchy that is operating behind world political machinations, and calling the shots on the global stage. The claims say that among this secret society are sinister false Catholic infiltrators who understand that, as the Roman Catholic Church represents one-sixth of the world's population—and over half of all Christians—control of the matters of church and state is indispensable toward the fulfillment of a *diabolical* plan they call the *New World Order.* It is through assuming control of the papacy that the False Prophet will deceive the world's Catholics and other religions into worshipping the Antichrist. As a case-in-point, during the final edits of this book, Pope Francis had recently met with Jewish and Muslim leaders to consider a new interfaith called "Chrislam," a mission that seems to be a unification of the Vatican's Roman Catholic system with the Islamic faith and other religions.

THE MESSENGER

Leo Lyon Zagami approaches the biggest issues facing the Roman Catholic Church in an entirely different manner. Rather than chronicling these issues in a public relations kind of way, he is an insider from Rome, a person with unprecedented access, and a member of a very influential Italian and British family. Leo's wife, Christy, also played an instrumental role in articulating this book from the Italian language into English, and even while the text of this book was being finalized, in Rome, the couple was witnessing, with a bird's eye perspective, major changes occurring on the other side of the Vatican walls. As far as I am concerned, no two other people could have been better situated to bring you this book, at this perfect time, than Leo and Christy Zagami. *Il mio cappello a voi i miei amici!*

And to our dear readers, please remember, do not be angry with the messenger. We bring this work to you as a service in the spirit of transparency and openness. In the final assessment, it is only the truth that will set us free.

Brad Olsen
CCC Publishing
San Francisco, CA

Translation: Brad Olsen, Christy Zagami, Leo Zagami
Editing: Mark Maxam, Brad Olsen
Cover and book design: Mark Maxam
Back cover photographer: Gerald Bruneau

Pope Francis: The Last Pope?

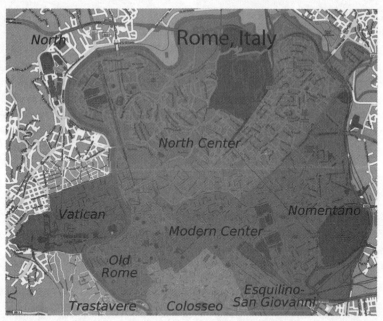

Modern Map of Rome Districts

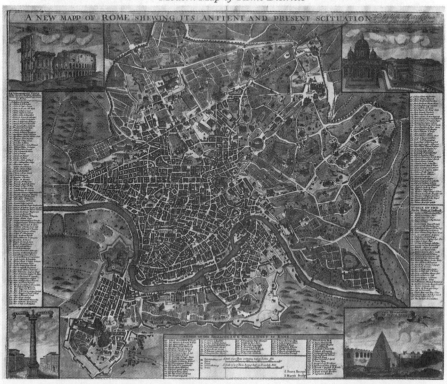

Above: Map of Rome, 1721, John Senex; Following, page 10: Vatican City Detail

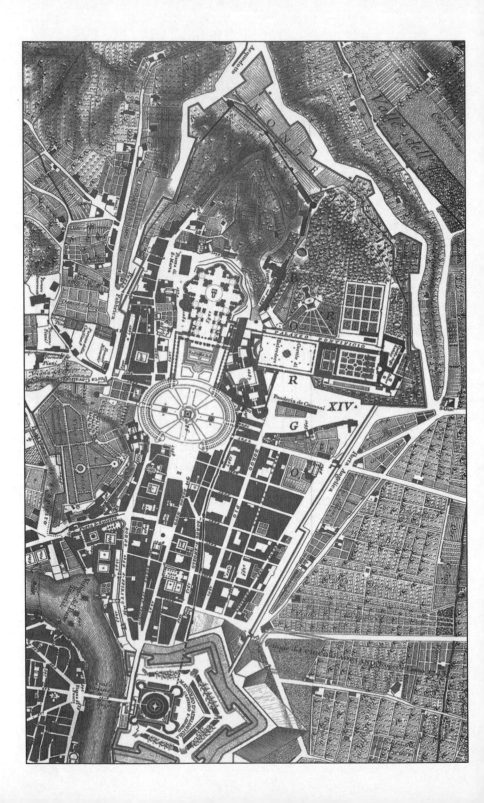

Introduction

THE SURRENDER

FROM A THRONE OF PETER RESIGNATION TO FRANCIS WHO WILL SAVE THE CHURCH FROM ORGIES AND LOBBIES

On June 21, 2013, the Italian journalist Francesco Antonio Grana broke a story in one of the best-known and most read newspapers in Italy, *il Fatto Quotidiano*[1] "the Daily Fact," the following exciting news announcing that Jorge Mario Bergoglio has resigned as Cardinal on the 17th of December, 2011. Upon completion of his seventy-fifth year of life, as expected in the Code of Canon Law, the then Cardinal Archbishop of Buenos Aires had written and sent to Benedict XVI, his letter of resignation. The German pope had set it aside, suggesting he had other plans. After a year, at the end of 2012, there was no signal yet from Rome to Cardinal Bergoglio, who was then seventy-six, on the appointment of his successor. Since that moment, what would have occurred on February 11, 2013, will remain in history. From the Catholic Church came the shocking announcement that Pope Benedict XVI would give up his position. Just a month later, on March 12th, Bergoglio entered into conclave. He did not enter as Archbishop Emeritus, as would have happened if Ratzinger had scrupulously respected the ecclesiastical bureaucracy and accepted his resignation. After a little more

1   Article by Francesco Antonio Grana June 21, 2013: *IOR, the Curia and Pedophilia. The first hundred days of Francis Pope in the Vatican*: http://www.ilfattoquotidiano. it/2013/06/21/ior-curia-e-pedofilia-primi-cento-giorni-di-papa-francesco-in-vati-cano/632454/ ‡ Archived from the internet on June 25, 2013.

than twenty-four hours, in spite of all the odds, Bergoglio would materialize, being named, Pope Francis.

"I came to Rome," confessed Bergoglio, *"with only a few clothes and washed them at night, and suddenly this ... but I thought I didn't have a chance! Betting in London I was at the forty-fourth place ... just imagine! Who has bet on me has earned a lot of money ..."* In fact, few outside the Holy See knew that he would be elected pope. A Jesuit seemed very farfetched, and many others hoped for a different solution. Who knew the gravity that revolved around this wicked choice that puts the Church for the first time in the hands of a member of the order created by St. Ignatius Loyola. Catechesis, the hearings, the angelus, homilies, speeches, almost everything embedded in the arms of Pope Francis contains up until now, only one key point: "the credibility of the Church."

This statement about the credibility of the Holy See is not only true for the journalists of *Il Fatto Quotidiano,* who are generally critical of the Vatican, but Rome-watchers worldwide. It is definitely a fact strongly emphasized by all the media, which show daily, and perhaps with excessive emphasis to be credible, the salvific capacity of the new Jesuit pontiff.

There is a rather heavy legacy left by Ratzinger to his successor. A legacy that has *obviously* pushed the German pope to his resignation, an unusual gesture that shocked Catholics around the world. A terrible legacy of secrets and shameful acts that only a few journalists and writers have had the courage to denounce in non-suspicious times. The information on such subjects has always been neglected or manipulated by the mainstream media.

I was among the first to go in a different direction with my publications, and prior to that, on the internet. The beginning of my internet divulgatory work in 2006 was made possible thanks to the collaboration of courageous journalists such as Greg Szymanski of *The Investigative Journal.* Published in the third volume of my *Confessions* trilogy,[2] I give ample space to the discussion on this mysterious lobby that only now is being mentioned openly by Pope Francis. The gay (and pedophile) lobby, which together with unscrupulous bankers from the financial world, use and abuse the Vatican Bank (IOR) by laundering dirty money, destroying, with their unscrupulous acts, the credibility of the Catholic Church, and joined by a secret pact—the one between the Church and the evil side of Freemasonry.

It would appear that Bergoglio's retirement was put on hold purposefully, because of something rotten going on in the Vatican. Something that goes far beyond the expectations of the most avid conspiracy theorists. Saving the good name of the church was something that only he, as a Jesuit, could

---

2   The trilogy *Confessions of an Illuminati* by the author (originally published in Italy) now available in the English language by CCC Publishing, San Francisco, CA.

handle. Here is a simple but efficient example that will illustrate the possible reason for his election to the throne of Saint Peter. It is similar to when the government of the newly created Russian Federation, implicated in a thousand scandals, appointed Vladimir Putin, the former head of the FSB (one of the agencies that succeeded the KGB), as Yeltsin's successor to become its president. Although perhaps a comparison that may seem risky, it perfectly reflects what is happening in the Vatican—the head of an intelligence agency assuming the top spot.

Do not be fooled by the humble gestures and "Good Shepherd" manners of Papa Francesco. This *lobby* has secrets that even *he* cannot make public. As revelations come to light, they may signify the end of the Church and its role as a representative of God on Earth. *But what secret could be so threatening?* First, despite the many criticisms inside and outside the Vatican, there are the infamous gay orgies and crimes of pedophilia practiced not only by the ordinary priests around the world, but in the "hallowed halls" of the Vatican itself, and by people at the highest level of the Catholic Church hierarchy. These individuals, with their perverse behavior and their wicked choices, are destroying, perhaps intentionally, what little is left in the sacredness of the Church of Rome. In June of 2013, a special witness finally emerged confirming these infamous stories of orgies and sordid affairs in the Vatican. It also confirmed what I have been saying for years at my own risk and peril. Those that have followed my work probably will not be surprised, but most people will be shocked at these claims.

Despite everything, the words and direct testimony of Francesco Zanardi, who has been fighting against sexual violence committed by the clergy for many years with his own association called "network abuse," has finally reached the shocked Italian media, and the Italian public in general. In this moment of time for the Church of Pope Francis, this information is heavy as bricks. Nonetheless, this information has yet to reach the public of the U.S.— and such is the purpose of this book, and my *"Confessions"* trilogy, to follow.

It is also why I decided to include, below, the answers given by Zanardi to the Italian journalist Ferruccio Sansa of *Il Fatto Quotidiano*. For further confirmation and clarification, I contacted him personally. Zanardi seems to be the one who has revealed the existence of a mysterious witness, with proof and serious evidence in his hands, that could expose what is really happening within the walls or the Vatican.

The man who contacted him is a high level manager, and he did so at the beginning of what is now known as "The Vatileaks Scandal." Confessing to Zanardi that he was disgusted by the system of corruption and sex in the Vatican, he confided in him and gave him the confidential report. Zanardi had the opportunity to record this special witness during his testimony, which seems so shocking and is at times *unbelievable*. Because of the number of crimes

Zanardi detected in the witness report committed by these high prelates in the Vatican, and after listening to these stories in detail, he rightly decided to address the Italian authorities about such crimes. Denouncing the whole thing to the public prosecutor of Savona, to whom he later entrusted all of the material he gathered from the witnesses. I believe his is an act of great courage from a man who could risk his own life by doing so. The words he stated at the end of this interview seem to confirm how dangerous this situation is for him. Below you will find excerpts, including the last segment in question:

The man spoke of orgies with minors, inside the Vatican. The involvement of top prelates, one referred to as a papal candidate at the last conclave. Besides this he referred to cases of corruption, with public money and the Church. I have recorded everything. I spent months studying the case, but it was too delicate, because it involved the lives of young boys. So in the end I decided not to make a public complaint, and to act with the utmost discretion, to entrust the material I gathered to the Prosecutor of Savona, who has faced with courage in the past, cases of child molestation by priests. I want them to understand if it was a case of blackmail or not. But the truth has to be established.

Francesco Zanardi, you have been fighting against sexual violence committed by priests through your "network for exposing abuse." How does this story begin?

Those were the days of the Crow, of poison in the Vatican. I've been contacted by a man who claimed to be the manager of a multinational company. Claimed to have been involved in a round of partying and prostitution, including child abuse inside the Vatican. He wanted to get the information out. Stories to sicken me. He wants justice, even to return to his life. He says he fears for his own safety.

It could be blackmail. He could be a braggart, a slanderer ...

I'm perfectly aware of the allegations that are being made. We are not here to spread a falsehood. I tested this man and he actually turned out to be a manager, also from public documents. The location of his mobile satellite confirmed frequent inputs to the Vatican.

That's it?

No. The man has provided precise tales, detailed and never contradictory. Phone numbers, for example, a well-known manager of the public near the Vatican, which we found to be true. So we decided to investigate to see if he's telling the truth.

What did he tell you?

He said he had access to a computer at work to the archives of the Vatican and prelates. From here he derived information and data. What's more, he had won the confidence of a well-known manager who had introduced him to an environment of gay sexual encounters also organized inside the Holy See, involving men in show business, but also children.

And a high prelate ...

Yes. The man told us of feasts that took place when the prelate was in Rome. A specific day of the week, a fixture. A dinner experience, with six or seven boys who were put in a circle. They took turns having sex with the Cardinal. Everything would have gone smoothly, until a couple of young males would take pictures with their phones. The pictures, claimed our contact, had become an object of exchange, perhaps blackmail and had ended in his possession. Threatening to have them handed over to two notaries, one in Rome, the other in Lugano. He feared for his safety. He promised us several times a confession, but then disappeared for a few months.

Could be libelous or a crazy braggart. Has he given evidence?

I was talking on the phone with one of the young people who was involved. He is, as stated on his Facebook page, a street kid. A valet who attended the Roman homosexual prostitution rings.

An element that prompted us to investigate. He then gave us phone numbers of other alleged participants in the orgies. No one has agreed to speak to us. The framework given by our source was disconcerting: feasts, meetings in gay saunas frequented by dozens of priests visiting Rome, recruitment of children via the internet. Children pursued even at night, from one end of the city to the other, to satisfy the sexual tastes of the high prelates. A system, he said, that was out of hand and exposed senior figures of the Vatican.

Does it seem credible?

I do not know. Again, the man certainly had contacts with Roman male prostitution. He was a manager for a company that invoiced the Vatican, which added reason for caution. He had access to the Vatican. Some of the contacts that he had given us ... we were able to verify him. Could he be a braggart or a blackmailer? A desperate man trying to change his life? We have been working for months, because if this story IS true, the lives of defenseless children could be at risk.

Are you not afraid for yourself?

Three days ago there was a hangman drawn on my door. The tires of my car were cut, and it was broken into. It happens all the time since the beginning of my battle, I'm getting used to it, but it's hard.

There is more that confirms certain homosexual tendencies in the Vatican. In March 2013, in an article by Carlo Bonini, the newspaper *La Repubblica* spoke about a strange story that concerns a palace and a Cardinal who purchased it. The price doubled in one day. The building could then be resold to Propaganda Fide, which is the Vatican's infamous real estate company, to make a huge profit. There was a particular embarrassment in the Vatican regarding this big business deal due to the "oddities" on the final price, obviously the result of someone's speculation. Also located on the same premises is the most popular gay sauna in Italy. The "purchase" was strongly desired by the then Secretary of State, Cardinal Tarcisio Bertone, who many rumor is one of the leaders of the Vatican gay lobby, and who will be portrayed during the course of my work as the main villain. This is a building that encloses and unites the worst of the contemporary Church, namely, those who participate in orgies and fraudulent business deals. The noble palace, located at number 2 on Via Carducci, in the heart of the city of Rome, is a hundred yards from the Italian Ministry of Economy. An elegant atrium enclosed by large windows, that holds, between the same walls, the Congregation for the "Evangelization of Peoples," is also known as Propaganda Fide, the largest gay sauna in Italy.[3] This fact has been underlined by a TV report conducted by the author and journalist Gianluigi Nuzzi for the Italian television network, *LA 7*, which was broadcast in mid-June of 2013, and is to be considered very serious.[4]

In this broadcast, Nuzzi uncovered direct evidence of *attendance at the sauna by many priests*. They would use the sauna as a meeting place, along with meeting in the philosophy and religion section of a well-known library near the Spanish Steps. These locations, it seems, guarantee them a certain amount of discretion. They would then move to a nearby sauna located in the handsome building called the Europe *Multi* Club, that has a very revealing website (http://www.europamulticlub.com/). A veritable den of Christian iniquity, the site bluntly claims to be "the number one gay sauna in Italy." They don't seem to care about the discretion of its customers and priests, who assiduously frequent these ambiguous places where you can make homosexual acquaintances involving gay priests. Priests who occupy positions of prestige and responsibility in the offices of the Roman Curia. It is a dedicated website with the catchy name of *"Venerabilis,"*[5] that is promoted by authoritative homosexual members of the Roman Catholic priests fraternity. Check it out and you will better understand the hypocrisy in which many priests that publicly condemn sex in all its forms, and homosexuality in particular, live and practice the exact opposite, in private.

This is what I personally cannot stand. While I believe that there is nothing wrong in being gay, as long as *pedophilia is not involved,* and as long as people

3   http://www.repubblica.it/cronaca/2013/03/11/news/lo_strano_affare_del_palazzo_del_cardinale_che_in_un_giorno_raddoppi_il_suo_prezzo-54291988/?ref=HREC1-4 ‡ Archived from the internet June 25, 2013.

4   http://www.la7.tv/richplayer/?assetid=50344445 ‡ Archived from the internet July 4, 2013.

5   http://venerabilis-fraternity-chat.blogspot.de/2013/06/blog-post.html ‡ Archived from the internet June 26, 2013.

Pope Francis: The Last Pope?

are honest about their sexual identity, something most priests are not.

We can only hope that *il Papa,* as he is referred to by Italians, goes from words to deeds—so that the Church of the Pope Francis era can bring a real Christian Church back to life. A Church that is not merely an illusory and hypocritical institution. There are growing doubts that Pope Francis will bring a truly transformative change regarding such matters. Some Vatican experts have criticized the highly publicized arrest of the now ex-Archbishop Jozef Wesolowski in Vatican territory for pedophilia, in September 2014, as just another charade to protect him from an embarrassing arrest. If Wesolowski opened up to non-Vatican authorities, it could bring further scandals to the public arena, something that has happened before in the recent history of the Church. Earlier on, in fact, a scandal broke out in the aftermath of another revealing TV documentary produced by the Italian network *LA 7,* broadcasted on June 25, 2013. This broadcast revealed new evidence of child prostitution. Even so, most media outlets remained silent about these new allegations against the Vatican.

These allegations included the abuse of Romanian children, collected on a regular basis, by an ex-policeman who turned out to be a member of the Carabinieri, the national military police of Italy. The children were picked up in *via Giolitti,* in a pub discotheque called *"Twins,"* near the Termini Train Station in Rome, to later prostitute them inside the Vatican walls. These disturbing claims find further evidence in a giant police operation by Europol called *Archimedes.* Conducted at the end of September 2014, it was described as the biggest crime crackdown in Europe to date, with 1,027 arrests. Reportedly, the police rescued 30 Romanian children during this operation. These child victims had been used in child prostitution rings, including one involving the Vatican, and some even say Satanic black masses. On June 27, 2013, driven by some kind of sudden pressure, the same television station that had broadcast the investigation a couple of days earlier was forced to clarify and retract some of the allegations they had previously made. In their retraction, they proclaimed that there was no real evidence against Mauro Parmeggiani, the Bishop of Tivoli. Yet, Parmeggiani was arrested in this pedophile scandal along with other high-ranking characters, including Monsignor Francis Camaldo, vice master of ceremonies in the Papal States. The TV reporter instead accused the accuser himself, Don Patrizio Poggi, who was blamed for wrongly pointing the finger against the Bishop of Tivoli, for reasons of revenge. Father Poggi was arrested one day later, on the 28th of June, by the Carabinieri, and charged with slander. For the same reasons, two other priests faced disciplinary sanctions by the Vatican: Don Marco Valentini and Monsignor Luca Lorusso, a high-level member of Vatican diplomacy, who was also Poggi's lawyer. All three would later be condemned publicly by Pope Francis in March 2014, who apologized to the priests involved in the scandal, and thus displayed the strength of the infamous Vatican *"Gay Lobby."* In short, this became another pathetic scene of contemporary journalism, and of the police force bowing to service the powers that

Leo Lyon Zagami

be, including, obviously, the Vatican. Nevertheless, before disappearing forever into the Italian prison system, Don Patrizio Foggi made one more shocking revelation, stating that the ex-policeman involved in this child trafficking ring was also involved in selling holy wafers to Satanic sects. I anticipate that after such astounding claims, we will never hear from Poggi again.

Personally, I have to admit to a certain degree of satisfaction stemming from the initial attempt by *LA 7* to investigate and name an untouchable like Monsignor Francis Camaldo. Suspected for years to be at the top of all the Vatican-based pedophile rings, Camaldo is faithful to Archbishop Mauro Parmeggiani, who is a hypocrite, as well as the clergy who should be ashamed of their leader. This is why I attacked them, verbally, during a Mass celebrated in the Christmas period of 2013. It created quite a stir among his ranks of followers when I deliberately substituted baby Jesus in the presepe, or Holy Nativity (a typical Italian Christmas tradition), with a small Lucifer. I did this to show the public who is the god that these pedophile priests of Satan really worship. In fact, in November 2012, one week after the presentation of the third volume of my trilogy in Italy (that I presented at the Brancaccio Castle of Roviano in the province of Rome), Bishop Monsignor Mauro Parmeggiani himself suddenly visited the town of my presentation. He spent a week, something he had never done before, with his faithful *Rovianesi*, the inhabitants of the municipality of Roviano. Likely, this was to help them recover from the "shock" of my public disclosures, and amplified by the presence of local media. Included in my disclosures was an in-depth revelation about his friend, Monsignor Camaldo. Of course it will be difficult, if not impossible, to have them arrested, since "Jessica," the CIA code name for Monsignor Camaldo, is a highly influential character that belongs to Vatican Freemasonry, and has links to the mysterious Loggia Monte Carlo, which I was also a member for a time. Camaldo is a key figure in the American intelligence community in the Vatican, and is well-protected by the U.S. State Department (with whom he collaborated actively in the 1980's). For this reason, and because of his frequent homosexual connections, it does appear that his unusual background even attracted the attention of the prestigious gay website, Gay TV, that reported Camaldo's story. Camaldo, it was reported, often used blackmail, as was published in the famous Wikileaks files of Julian Assange.[6]

It is said that once Pope Francis makes a decision, he doesn't go back on it. In at least one case, however, Bergoglio's actions backfired, and again demonstrated a weakness towards figures like Camaldo, and not in line with what people would expect from a representative of the Church of Pope Francis. Sandro Magister of EspressOnline.it wrote it this way: *"After a thirty-year career as papal master of ceremonies, Monsignor Francesco Camaldo has been appointed in recent months,*

6   http://www.gay.tv/news/attualita/wikileaks-jessica-alias-di-un-prelato-vaticano/
‡ Archived from the internet June 28, 2013.

Pope Francis: The Last Pope?

Canon of the Archbasilica of St. John Lateran. But when the designation was to become operational the decision was counter-banned. Instead, he was awarded by Pope Francis, the most prestigious and well-paid position of Canonico of St. Peter's in the Vatican."[7]

As you can see, time and time again, it all ends well for Mons. Camaldo. He can continue undisturbed with his reprehensible deeds in the heart of the Holy See, even during the pontificate of Pope Francis. I am hoping that sooner or later the competent authorities will have the courage to truly investigate the tragedy of pedophilia and child prostitution occurring in the heart of the Vatican, but I have my doubts. Most of the time, the Holy See cares only about its own image, and not its essence or sins. In September 2011, a group of associations for victims of pedophile priests, called SNAP (Survivors Network of those Abused by Priests), and the Center for Constitutional Rights, deposited evidence at the International Criminal Court in The Hague that accused Pope Benedict XVI, the then Secretary of State Cardinal Tarcisio Bertone, his predecessor Cardinal Angelo Sodano, and the former Prefect of the Congregation for the Doctrine of the Faith, Cardinal William Levada, of crimes against humanity for allegedly covering the many crimes committed by priests against children.

One year before the resignation of Ratzinger, in February of 2012, and following a notification by the same attorney Jeff Anderson, who blamed Benedict XVI, Cardinal Bertone, Sodano and Levada, the charge was withdrawn. The lawyer for the Holy See, Jeffrey S. Lena, explained that the notification had resulted in *"the immediate filing of the case, without the need for a judgment on the subject issued by the court."* The reason for this sudden choice is explained by Lena: *"They all withdrew because they knew that they would lose if they continued to pursue the case. They did not want a negative decision by the court, in fact, if it had continued, the acquittal would make judicial history."*[8]

Can we be sure this was the reason, or has someone from the Vatican put pressure on the clients of Jeff Anderson? If carried forward, this case would have opened the classic Pandora's Box. Perhaps it is no coincidence, that after two years, the main protagonists of the scandal, Ratzinger and Bertone, have both left their positions. It is clear that the investigations into both the Vatican's sex and financial scandals have not been allowed to continue. The successor to Cardinal Tarcisio Bertone is now a confidante of Pope Francis, as well as another Jesuit named Pietro Parolin, who is an ex-apostolic *nuncio* to Venezuela. Since taking this new position, and despite Parolin's young age, health problems have already surfaced for him. Poor Pietro Parolin, I hope that he can resist the strong poison of the Vatican, but I doubt it.

7   http://chiesa.espresso.repubblica.it/articolo/1350607 ‡ Archived from the internet on the 28th of June 2013.

8   http://it.wikipedia.org/wiki/Tarcisio_Bertone ‡ Archived from the internet June 28, 2014.

Chapter: I
HABEUS JORGE

THE GREAT REFUSAL FROM CELESTINE V AND RATZINGER

"I, Pope Celestine V, urged on by legitimate reasons, by humility and weakness of my body and the malice of the people, in order to recover with consolation the life beforehand, the lost quiet, I leave freely and spontaneously the Papacy and expressly renounce the throne, to the dignity, to the burden and to the honor that it involves. I give in this moment, The Sacred College of Cardinals, the ability to choose and provide, according to Canon law, a shepherd of the Universal Church"
–Celestine V, Papal Bull, Naples, December 13, 1294

This is the text of the previously best-known papal abdication in the history of the Church, issued by Celestine V, born Pietro Angelerio da Morrone, who died a prisoner to his successor the Cardinal Benedetto Caetani, who then ascended to the Papal throne as Boniface VIII in the castle of Fumone. After only four months of his coronation, and despite numerous attempts by Carlo d'Angiò to dissuade him, on December 13, 1294, during consistory, Celestine V began reading the abdication, risking the creation of a schism. With this gesture, Celestine V was the sixth historical Pontiff after San Clement I, Pontian, Silverio, Benedict IX and Gregory VI, to abdicate in church history.

Seven centuries later, Benedict XVI decided to follow in Celestine V's footsteps. Only history will tell us what judgment posterity will ascribe to the

Pope Francis: The Last Pope?

shocking choice made by Joseph Ratzinger to abandon the Petrine ministry. The historiography portrays an uncertain picture on the abdication by Celestine V, who, until the pontificate, had been described as being unanimously devoted to contemplation and the search of God. Very few cardinals have had judgments as controversial regarding Celestine V as the condemnation by Dante Alighieri, who stated that he made the great abdication because of cowardice. In fact, provoked by his abdication, Dante would challenge the Pope's act, and the ascension to the throne of Boniface VIII as the White Guelph, as an interference into politics, and deeply disapproved of. (From Wikipedia: The Guelphs and Ghibellines are factions supporting the Pope and the Holy Roman Emperor, respectively, in central and northern Italy.) For this reason the Florentine poet immortalized the Pontiff in the third Canto of *"The Divine Comedy,"* and placed him in the anti-hell, a place where you would find the souls of resignation, namely those that were profoundly mediocre. In this place, you would find those who have not committed anything egregious in life, but nothing grand either. They are excluded from hell, but at the same time are denied justice and access to paradise.

Yet Dante didn't reveal the name of *"the shadow of the man who resigned in cowardice."* It was the first commentaries on the *Comedy* that attempted to uncover the identity of the soul placed by Dante in the anti-hell. With the exception of the poet's son, Jacopo Alighieri, the great majority agreed to identify him as Pietro da Morrone, also known as Celestine V. In 1324, Graziolo Bambaglioli identified the indolent with *"Brother Peter de Morono, who so cowardly resigned the pontificate."* A more in-depth comment was made by Jacopo Della Lana when he suggested that Pietro da Morrone was a hermit of great faith and penance, who despised the *"intrigue and duplicity of the court"* and this was the motive that has put him on a collision course with the papal court. The Cardinals, unable to convince him with arguments that *"worldly wealth acquired was misused and appropriated,"* devised a deception of voices at night in his bedroom, pretending to be angels sent by God, and urging him to give up the papacy. Upon hearing this for several nights, "Celestine" convinced himself, believing them to be *"insufficient and bad, and to refuse, and so he did."*

Around this time, Guido da Pisa became convinced that Dante referred to Celestine, but pointed out that no one that had renounced the papacy for *"indolence of heart,"* but instead to *"save his soul by humility."* Among his contemporaries, Celestine's gesture was welcomed in sharply contrasting ways. Prompting some praise, as with Francesco Petrarca, who called the Pontiff's choice a gesture *"by a great and free spirit, who knew no limitations, a truly divine spirit,"* yet from others, a condemnation. In line with the thought of poet Petrarca, while on a visit to Abruzzo, the land in which Celestine lived and was ordained, in his Homily given at Sulmona on July 4, 2010, Joseph Ratzinger exalted Celestine for his inner strength in his search for God, assisted by that internal silence one obtains when, *"perceiving the voice of God, capable of guiding his life."*

Leo Lyon Zagami

Ratzinger thus insinuates this as a way to consider Celestine's entire life and an understanding of his abdication as a gesture "inspired" by God's grace: *"Pietro Angelerio since his youth was a 'searcher of God,' a man who was consumed with searching and finding the answers to the grand questions of our existence. Who am I? Where do I come from? Why do I live? For whom do I live? And there he embarked in the search for truth and happiness. He embarks in the search for God and to hear the voice decides to separate himself from the world and live the life of a hermit. The silence thus becomes the element that characterizes his daily life. And it is in this exterior silence, but more than that, in this internal silence that he perceives the voice of God, capable of giving orientation to his life. Here is the important aspect for us: We live in a society in which each space, each moment seems as if it must be 'filled' by our initiative, from our activity, our thoughts and dreams: it seems thus, that there is not the time to listen, nor to communicate with God. Dear brothers and sisters! We should not fear the creation of silence within us and outside of us if we want to be capable of perceiving the voice of God, but also the voice near us, the voice of others. But it is important to delineate a second element: The discovery that Pietro Angelerio makes is not the result of an exertion, but rather, it was through the grace of God, that he perceives it. Thus all he had, all he was, came from within: It was given to him through grace, it was thus also a responsibility before God and before others. Whilst our lives are very different, even for us the same rule applies; everything that is essential for our existence was donated without our contribution. The fact that I live doesn't depend on me; the fact that there were people who introduced me to life, that taught me what it is to love and be loved, who have transmitted to me faith and opened my eyes to God: everything thus is grace and is not 'done by me.' By ourselves we could do nothing without it being donated to us: God always anticipates in every single life the good and the bad so that we can easily recognize His grace, with a ray of light he reveals his goodness. This is why we must pay attention, always paying attention to our 'internal eyes,' those within our heart. And if we begin to recognize God in his infinite goodness, then we will be able to see, with stupor, in our own lives—like the Saints—the signs that God, who is always near us, who is always good to us, who says to us: 'Have faith in me!' In this internal silence, in the perception of his presence, Pietro del Marrone matured, and further, experienced the beauty of creation, done through the hands of God: He knew how to perceive the profound sense, respected the signs and the rhythms, he used it for what is essential in life. [...] Finally, one last element: Saint Peter Celestine, in conducting the life of a hermit, he wasn't 'closed within himself,' but was possessed with a passion to bring the good news of the gospel to his brothers. It is the secret of his pastoral fruitfulness that he wanted to 'remain' with God, in prayer, as it is remembered in contemporary Gospel songs: The first imperative is always to pray to the Lord of the harvest (cfr LC10,2). It is only after this calling that Jesus defines certain obligation to his disciples: The serene announcement, clear and courageous of the message of the Gospel—Even in moments of persecution—without surrendering to the fashions of the times, nor to the violence or imposition of the times; the detachment brought about by our preoccupation with things—such as money or clothing—confiding in the providence of the Father; the attention and cure for the sick in body and in spirit (cfr Lc 10,5-9). These*

Pope Francis: The Last Pope?

were the characteristics of the brief and agonized pontificate of Celestine V, and these are the characteristics of the missionary activity of the Church in each epoch."[1]

Benedict XVI closed the homily by asking *"the example and intercession"* of Celestine V, which would accompany himself, and all the faithful in their path. A plea which was made evident just three years later, with his abdication. But the similarities between Celestine V and Pope Benedict XVI go well beyond the choice of abandoning the Petrine ministry. Both are, in fact, proven to be driven more to asceticism, contemplation and solitude, than that of the leadership of the Christian flock. Both Benedict XVI and Celestine V were willing to abandon the clerical life to devote themselves to ascetic vocation.

Fate had something different in mind with a very different responsibility, namely the papacy. The Monaco hermit and the cardinal theologian were "forced" to give up their plans for an ascetic life of peace, solitude and research to ascend to the papal throne, bringing upon them the hopes and expectations of the faithful. Pietro da Morrone was emotionally overwhelmed by the investiture, initially choosing to decline the engagement. Ratzinger told the biographer Peter Seewald in the summer of 2010, in the last of what has been defined as the "longest interviews in Church history," and at the root of the various bestsellers written by Seewald before and after Ratzinger became Pope. In a veiled way, he revealed that on the eve of his seventy-eighth birthday, he was now confident he could abandon the ecclesiastical career to retire to private life: "I hope to finally find peace and tranquility."[2] While he was already looking forward with his employees to early retirement, in a matter of days he found himself to be invested as head of the Universal Church which has 1.2 billion faithful. A real "shock" to Ratzinger, after many grueling years,[3] he was certain that God would, "allow him a bit of peace and tranquility."[4] Evidently God's will was working in another direction. Assuming the position that God had decided for him, Ratzinger, however, was immediately aware of the immense responsibility that the induction involved. In particular, in his years of papacy, he has never made any secret of being aware of the *"filth,"* or the *"threats,"* and the *"wolves"* that lurk in the Vatican, even though he was certainly not a lamb himself. Only after he ascended to the Papal throne as Benedict XVI, however, did he realize, like Celestine V a long time before him, the severity of the crisis of the Church fueled by the pedophilia scandal, the Williamson case connected to the schismatic Lefebvrians, homosexuality in the

1   Benedict XVI, Homily in Sulmona, July 4th, 2010 at Piazza Garibaldi.

2   Peter Seewald, Luce del mondo. Il Papa, la Chiesa e i segni dei tempi Una conversazione con Peter Seewald, (Milan: Oscar Mondadori, 2010), p. 13.

3   *Ibid.*

4   *Ibid.*

Leo Lyon Zagami

Vatican, and the crisis of vocations. This worried him because of *appearances, not because of the substance*. To begin with, the vicissitudes of Vatican finances were left totally in the hands of its employee, the "Godfather" of the Vatican, Cardinal Bertone. Pior to the "Vatileaks" scandal, which detailed even more disturbing scandals, and referring to the sexual abuse cases, Ratzinger told Seewald in 2010: *"It was shocking for all of us. Suddenly so much filth. It was almost like the crater of a volcano, out of which suddenly came a tremendous cloud of dirt, darkening and soiling everything, so that above all the priesthood suddenly seemed to be a place of shame and every priest was suspected of being 'one of them.'"*[5]

More superficial than with Celestine eight hundred years prior, Benedict decided to fight against the "abyss" of dirt and intrigue that is today "disfiguring" the Church. He felt it was his duty to not give the faithful the wrong impression of what should be a Holy Institution. Constantly aware of this, Ratzinger said, *"If the Church depended only on men it would have sunk a long time ago."*[6] In his eyes, that is proof that divine providence and grace sustained the community of the faithful beyond the errors and evil that lurk in the Church as a humane institution. Both Popes, the only to willfully resign in Church history, were crushed by the weight of Vatican bureaucracy. The power struggle and the poison of the Vatican hierarchy eventually forced them to desist. Celestine died in the prison of Fumone, a victim of his arch-enemy Caetani, who would take his place on the throne of Peter, as Pope Boniface VIII.

Benedict XVI chose to initially retreat to Castel Gandolfo by helicopter, *"climbing the mountain"* dressed in white, as in the vision of the Third Secret of Fátima. In a state of isolation, he went from the heart of the Vatican State to one of his dependencies in the outskirts of Rome. He was only to return a few months later and retire in a monastery built for him inside the Vatican walls, now officially known as *"Pope Emeritus."*

"It is a mistake to think that the prophetic mission of Fátima is over," remarked Ratzinger himself during a visit to Fátima, Portugal, and indirectly, with this message, airing something well beyond the official interpretation given by the Catholic Church. In the year 2000, thanks to his and Bertone's possible censorship of the Third Secret of Fátima, it seems he wanted to communicate to the faithful, those that comprehend this "coded" language, the real truth about the message that the Virgin Mary our Lady of Fátima had given to her young shepherds. A message that was not fulfilled with the terrorist attack of Ali Agca in St. Peter's Square that badly wounded Wojtyla in 1981.

Is the vision described by Sister Lucia, a vision shown by the Lady of Fátima to the three shepherds, of a bishop dressed in white going up the

5   *Ibid.*, p. 32.

6   *Ibid.*, p. 46.

mountain of the city and killed by his own soldiers, not, in fact, John Paul II, but Ratzinger himself, or even Pope Francis, perhaps, suggesting a fulfillment to the vision that is yet to come? We need speculate more on this possibility.

THE DRAMATIC CHOICE OF BENEDICT XVI

"Dear Brothers, I have called this Consistory, not only for the three Canonizations, but also to communicate a decision of great importance for the life of the Church. After repeatedly examining my conscience before God, I came to the certainty that my strength, advanced age, are no longer appropriate to exercise properly the Petrine ministry. I am well aware that this ministry, its spiritual essence, must not only be accomplished with works and words, but with suffering and praying, no less. However, in today's world, subject to rapid change and agitated by issues of great importance for the life of faith, to steer the boat of St. Peter and proclaim the Gospel, you must also have the force of the body and of the soul. A force which, in recent months, has diminished in such a way as to acknowledge my inability to properly administer the ministry entrusted to me. For this, I am well aware of the seriousness of this act, with full freedom, hereby renounce the ministry of the Bishop of Rome, the Successor of St. Peter, entrusted to me by the hand of Cardinals April 19, 2005, so that, from February 28, 2013, at 20.00, the See of Rome, the seat of St. Peter, will be vacant and shall be convened by those who have this task, the Conclave for the Election of the Supreme Pontiff ..." It is with these words spoken in Latin, on February 11, 2013, that, at the feast of the Blessed Virgin of Lourdes, the world heard the lapidary statement of his resignation. Most were shocked by the petrified manner in which it was announced, by Pope Benedict XVI, who had given his "resignation" from the Throne of the Vicar of Christ for no apparent reason, other than a "lack of strength of mind and body" due to his advanced age. There is an overshadowing feeling and recognition of failure by this person, now well-advanced in years, as his inability to cope with the duties of his office finally surfaced.

"It was a painful decision," said Father Federico Lombardi, the Vatican spokesman, who ensured at the same time that Ratzinger was in good health for his age. So why did Benedict XVI make the decision to "come down" from the Cross, thus abandoning the role of pastor that he had been awarded nearly eight years before? Many have wondered why. Ratzinger used the Consistory like Celestino did 700 years before, officially, on that day, calling for the canonization of 800 martyrs of Otranto. He communicated such shocking news in Latin to a rapidly changing world immersed in technology, and in a manner that was truly of another era, to say the least. He felt he did not have the physical force and the fortitude to continue with his work. The Pontiff gave up his high throne for retirement like any other human being would do.

This gesture propels us towards a Church in full secularization. An institution more and more materialistic and secular, and much less Holy. Beyond the confusion of the faithful there have been signals in the preceding years that foreshadowed the forthcoming decision, signals that provided some Vaticanists with a more probable reason for the abdication of the Pontiff. As will be demonstrated here, the fate of Benedict XVI can be comprehended by his own words, his repeated appeals to the faithful to support him before the *"wolves"* he lashed out against, those who sullied the Church. In addition, in 2010, Ratzinger himself spoke of *"resignation"* when inquired on the subject by biographer Peter Seewald, who asked if, in the wake of the scandals that afflicted the Church, he even thought of resigning.[7] Ratzinger replied:

"When the danger is great, you can not escape. That is why this is definitely not the time to resign. It is precisely at times like these, that we must resist and overcome the difficult situation. This is my thought. One can resign at a time of peace, or when you simply can not do it anymore. But you can not just run away in times of danger and say, let another deal with it."[8] Seewald asked if it was deemed appropriate for a pope to resign? Benedict XVI meets this inquiry with disarming clarity: *"Yes. When a pope arrives at a clear awareness of not being able to physically, psychologically and mentally carry out the task entrusted to him, then he has the right and in some circumstances, even the duty, to resign."[9]*

It is clear that Ratzinger had reached an "awareness" to resign when talking with Seewald two and a half years prior to such a decision becoming public. However, it is not the only question behind the real motives that would drive the Pope to this drastic decision. More so, a question of whether the timing behind the decision to resign was really the right one. It is not possible to define this moment in history serenely. Not for the Church, not for the world.

To make matters worse, the Middle East crisis had become increasingly more serious. This was due to the mercenaries of the NWO, unleashed by the CIA and the Mossad, to destabilize the area in search of bringing an end of times scenario to fruition. To add to this, we also have the outbreaks of violent protests in Europe, namely Ukraine and Greece. Along with Italy, these regions are currently *hot,* and this is even though the crisis in the so-called *"Bel Paese"* (Italy) hasn't yet come to full fruition.

In Italy, the implications would become even worse than expected, as the Vatican was eventually implicated in the corruption of the Italian political class. The only story that can be said to be officially *"closed,"* is the Vatileaks case … although the shadows on the "Crow," aka Paul Gabriel, remain.

As it emerged during the trial, Gabriel, the butler, began making copies of secret documents at the beginning of his tenure in the papal apartment, in 2006. The idea that the actions of a "romantic" but disappointed man, of whom the Pope would not have been aware of, collapsed. Gabriel left more the impression of a real secret agent, seemingly for the Jesuits, sent in to

---

7   I remind you that the interview was published in 2010.

8   Ratzinger, Seewald, *op. cit.,* p. 38.

9   *Ibid.*

Pope Francis: The Last Pope?

destabilize the vertices of the Vatican. Once again, the Holy See silenced the hornet's nest that was rising around the Corvo.

Who, or what, had prompted "Paoletto" to make the Vatican documents public? A war between Cardinals, corruption, homosexuality within the walls of the palace, or suspicious maneuvers around the Vatican bank? Vatileaks shocked and disgusted the Catholic world. So who stands to gain from all this? The Romans would have said, *"Cui prodest?"*

I will try to answer these and other questions during the course of this work. The statements by the Crow, who described himself as an *"infiltrator of the Holy Spirit"* and who by *"seeing evil and corruption everywhere in the Church,"* decided to put things back on track by shocking the media and the public, in my investigation, has not been deemed credible. As I mentioned above, the depositions show that Paolo Gabriel, the infamous "Crow," began gathering information right from the start of his tenure. [10]

This suggests that the Vatican had been "infiltrated" by someone, to spy on, *ad hoc* (or blackmail) the pope up close. The reason stated by the Vatican did not make sense. Rather, they made sure that the truth did not emerge. The theme of blackmail and pressures, internal and external, are in fact an issue that we will face in the course of my work. I will demonstrate how Ratzinger suffered pressures and guidelines both from the Vatican's hierarchy, and also from exterior forces: the so-called ecclesiastical Freemasonry.

This was all contradictory to what the Holy Father had embarked on since his election. It was a split path between the intention to reform the Church in a more traditional way, and the pressures of Ecclesiastical Masonry which is in league with the architects of the New World Order. This inevitably lead to confrontation, and eventually it collided with scandals of pedophilia and homosexuality in the Vatican, the plots within the IOR, the Gotti Tedeschi affair, and generally, more Vatileaks. Many have wondered what might have actually occurred in Ratzinger's mind prior to making such a decision? What pressure was put on this German Pope, seemingly unshakable and previously known as the "Rottweiler of faith," to leave his office? Why did he resign in 2013? To facilitate the closure of the Vatileaks scandal, as some propose? But why not at least wait for the celebration of Easter? Who and what was he referring to in these harsh accusations? Accusations made on February the 13th, 2013, two days after the announcement of his abdication, and during the Wednesday homily against *"the religious hypocrisy"* which disfigures the Church? Rather than stay on the cross until the end, to suffer and cure the ills of the Church, Ratzinger chose to abdicate, returning to embrace the old

---

10   In the official Vatican hearing of October 2, 2012 regarding the involvement of the Pope's butler Paolo Gabriele in the Vatileaks affair, Monsignor Georg Gänswein told the court he had noticed there were among the material seized, documents dating from the same year in which Gabriele started working for Benedict XVI.

27

dream that the papacy seemed to have broken, toward a lonely and isolated old age of writing and prayer.

Following in the footsteps of Celestine V, Ratzinger chose a gesture that expressed weakness, or, more accurately, a gesture of *discontinuity* to demonstrate to the faithful the sad situation in which the Church finds itself today. A gesture that seems, paradoxically, the subject of the 2011 film, *Habemus Papam,* by Italian director Nanni Moretti, a well-known intellectual who has always been close to and politically involved with the pro-Bilderberg Italian left wing Democratic Party.

The movie begins with a newly elected Pope in the midst of a panic attack—and literally running away after his election. In the general confusion this action creates, the ceremony is interrupted before his name is publicly announced. At this point, the Vatican is called in to sort out the matter with a psychoanalyst. In real life, things went differently, of course, but this film is proof that the crisis of Ratiznger's papacy did not go, as I said, unnoticed by some interested observers.

What about the concerns ventilated in the upper echelons of the Vatican? What about the huge hole in the finances of the SMOM, the notorious Knights of Malta? They are the ones who presided over the ***Institute for the Works of Religion*** (known by the acronym ***IOR***) for 900 years, with an anniversary celebration stretching from February 15th 2013, through July 2014, thanks to the treasurer and manager of the German branch of the Order, Ernest Von Freyberg. This was a sudden twist manifesting at the end of Ratzinger's pontificate, and far from the parallel that had been improperly drawn with Papa Luciani, who was a staunch opponent of Marcinkus and the atrocities of the Vatican bank, who died under mysterious circumstances.

The nomination of Von Freyberg was the definite end of the Gotti Tedeschi presidency, and the bank was then left entirely in the hands of his Knights. The new President Ernest von Freyberg was, at least officially, there to implement a new compliance strategy with the goal to make the structures and regulations of the IOR more transparent, to clarify and, if necessary, to put an end to unlawful practices. It seems that von Freyberg, the controversial "God's banker" and merchant of death who is still active in the weapons industry, has not been successful, given that he was sent away by Papa Francesco in the summer of 2014, and quickly replaced with an illustrious unknown Frenchman Jean-Baptiste de Franssu. At this point, the Holy See informed the media that *"over the next three years,"* the Statutes of the IOR *"will be revised, and activities will be redrawn according to three strategic priorities: to strengthen the business of the IOR, to gradually move the asset management to a new and central Vatican Asset Management (VAM) in order to overcome the duplication of efforts in this field between the institutions of the Vatican, and concentrate on the activities of the IOR financial advice and payment Services for clergy, congregations,*

Pope Francis: The Last Pope?

dioceses and lay employees of the Vatican."[11]

Throughout all this, the predecessor, Ernst von Freyberg, would remain for an initial period of transition and *"has agreed to participate during a transition period to ensure a proper handover."* This was announced by the Vatican [12] after its sudden and mysterious decision. Let us not forget that the IOR has, at its side, the Sovereign Military Order of Malta, a Roman Catholic lay religious order traditionally found near the top levels of the Vatican institution, and charged to defend the interests of the Houses Rulers and the Aristocracy of the European Union. We also should count the presence of another key figure, Carl A. Anderson, Supreme Knight Grand Master of the Knights of Columbus. Along with the Knights of Malta, the Knights of Columbus Order is among the most powerful in the USA, and, more than any other, represents the pro-Israel lobby of the Church of Rome. Then, there is also the long reach of the Bush family, that I predict will make another attempt at the White House, in 2016, with Jeb Bush. Jeb is not only a loyal knight to the Pope, but also a point of contact with the most occult and evil side of the Illuminati, the *Skull and Bones* Lodge, that has its headquarters at Yale University, and where both his brother, *George H.W. Bush,* and his father, *George Walker Bush,* attended. In the initiation to the infamous Skull and Bones, aka "The Order," we find the figure of *Don Quixote,* who was made famous by the Jesuit student Miguel de Cervantes (1547-1616) in what was probably the first international bestseller. According to many Jesuits, the Quixote character was based on the founder of the Jesuits: Ignatius of Loyola.

THE WHITE SMOKE SIGN

At 19:06, on the 13th of March 2013, under pouring rain, the white smoke from the chimney of the Sistine Chapel announced to the crowd gathered in St. Peter's Square, and to all the faithful and the curious worldwide, that there was a newly elected Pope. The cheers and screams of joy were suddenly pierced by the sound of bells. After an hour the clouds gave break to the faithful gathered in the square, and from the *lodge* of the basilica, Cardinal Jean Louis Tauran faced the crowd from the balcony to reveal the identity of the new pontiff. Many in Italy believed that the choice would fall on Angelo Scola, Marc Ouellet or Timothy Dolan. Instead, the new Bishop of Rome took everyone by surprise. On the fifth ballot, in what was a sharp and ahead-of-schedule decision, in fact, a strong signal by the College of Cardinals, that despite the recent scandals that had rocked the Catholic Church, they moved quickly to elect a successor to Pope Benedict XVI.

---

11   http://www.quotidiano.net/ior-franssu-presidente-1.33116 ‡ Archived from the internet April 4, 2014.

12   http://vaticaninsider.lastampa.it/inchieste-ed-interviste/dettaglio- articolo/articolo/america-latina-latin-america-america-latina-12945/ ‡ Archived from the internet April 3, 2014.

He is now the one chosen to "reform" a Church in crisis, and since that day, two billion followers have opened their hearts in hope toward the new selection. In his white robe, appearing at the window of St. Peter's Square to bless the faithful, the Jesuit Cardinal of Argentina, Jorge Mario Bergoglio, had become Pope Francis. He is the first pope from Latin America, the continent where Catholicism has hundreds of millions of faithful, but from which only 19 cardinals have entered the actual conclave to participate in the elections. He is the first Pope in history to be a Jesuit, and the only Jesuit Cardinal present in the Conclave after Archbishop Emeritus of Jakarta. The Jesuit Julius Riyadi Darmaatmadja had to quit for health reasons. Perhaps, however, this could signal the appearance of the Last Pope, at least of the Church as we know it.

FIG. 1. Former Florida Governor Jeb Bush, and the Knights of Columbus' Jim Bob McGivern, Bill Stoye, Dave Busch, Dean Bunton and George Englemark, all present at the 0170 meeting, and all participants in the traditional "Red Mass" in Tallahassee.

THE FIRST JESUIT POPE IN HISTORY

In 2005, Bergoglio made headlines for being a contender for the job that Joseph Ratzinger would eventually gain during the conclave. Denying that there was anything constructed, Bergoglio then took the position Ratzinger previously held. The successor of Benedict XVI is, paradoxically, his antagonist. Who, according to rumors insistently spread during that period, was preferred over the German Cardinal in 2005. Some even say that Bergoglio was even elected as Pope back then, but that he apparently preferred to decline, and cast his own votes to Ratzinger. Bergoglio, due to his vast experi-

Pope Francis: The Last Pope?

ence in the Third World and his reputation as a "simple" man of recognized "humility," had, in fact, managed to collect the support of both conservatives and moderates. Yet, as I will explain shortly, the decision of the 2005 conclave might have been influenced by the possibility of a scandal investigated by the Argentinian journalist Horacio Verbistky. He accused Pope Francis of collusion with the dictatorship in Argentina, and involvement in the kidnapping of two of his own Jesuit priests who were disliked by the dictatorship in place at that time. An accusation that, despite the anger and the denial of the Cardinal himself, could hardly go unnoticed, and probably weighed on the final result of the 2005 Conclave, that decided instead for Pope Ratzinger. Bergoglio was 77 years old at the time of his election, and the Cardinals may have preferred him to a younger Pope. The Cardinals, perhaps, thought it better to put an experienced man of the Church in this position of responsibility. Someone estimated by both conservatives and liberals to not make secret the risks of careerism within the Roman Curia, *"the Cardinals are not the agents of an NGO, but are servants of the Lord,"* Pope Francis once said, condemning harshly the excesses of capitalism and imperialism.

Vaticanists portray him on a daily basis as determined to reform the Roman affairs and the Vatican business. But in what way? Will he instead sink the Church to its final decline?

This is how he expressed himself in an interview with journalist Andrea Tornielli of the website "Vatican Insider," when he spoke about the role of the evangelization of the Church:

> *We must go out ourselves, go to the suburbs. We should avoid the spiritual illness of Church that talks only about itself: when this happens, the Church becomes ill. It is true that going out on the street, as it could happen with any man or women, accidents happen. Or there is the old way, the church is closed in on itself, self-referential. Between a Church in difficulty coming out on the street, and a self-referential Church, I have no doubt in preferring the first.* [13]

He is, as I stated earlier, the first pope belonging to the Jesuit Order. Vatican spokesman Federico Lombardi, in an evening briefing to the press after the papal election sought, with a hint of emotion, to emphasize the continent and history of origin behind the name chosen by Father Bergoglio. Saint Francis of Assisi, the patron saint of Italy, is where the family of Bergoglio originally comes from. But Pope Francis is a Jesuit, just as is Ladara Luis Francisco Ferrer, the Spanish Archbishop appointed by Ratzinger in 2008 to be Secretary of the Congregation for the Doctrine of the Faith, formerly the Holy Office, or the infamous Inquisition. Now Ferrer will become

---

13   http://vaticaninsider.lastampa.it/inchieste-ed-interviste/dettaglio- articolo/articolo/america-latina-latin-america-america-latina-12945/ ‡ Archived from the internet April 3, 2014.

Leo Lyon Zagami

the "Ratzinger of Pope Bergoglio," as was communicated from the Vatican Secretary of State after the election of the Argentinian Pope, a loyalist of the Order founded by Saint Ignatius, The Society of Jesus, the most militarized amongst the Catholic religious orders, and who appreciates being surrounded by members of its own order, the Jesuits.

Bergoglio became Provincial of the Society of Jesus in Argentina during its raging dictatorship, and for problems that I will discuss later in detail, he was deposed by the Provincial authority of the Jesuits. Since then, Bergoglio had disappeared in the shadows until he was appointed auxiliary Bishop by Archbishop Antonio Quarracino in 1992. From that point on, he began his ascent to the throne of Saint Peter. In the autumn of 2001, the Vatican called on him to lead a major department. *"For heaven's sake, in the curia I die,"* implored Bergoglio, reluctant to expose himself to public scrutiny and traveling. In 2005, they "graced him," but this time was different, and he was forced by circumstances to become Pope of the Catholic Church.

FIG. 2. Pope Ratzinger with the then Cardinal Jorge Mario Bergoglio.

A BRIEF BIOGRAPHY OF THE NEW POPE

Pope Francis was born in Buenos Aires on December 17, 1936, by Italian immigrant parents from a rural area near Turin. He embarked on a strange course of study, graduating as a chemical engineer, and then chose the

Pope Francis: The Last Pope?

priesthood, entering the seminary in Villa Devoto. On March the 11th, 1958, he began his novitiate to the Society of Jesus. He took on humanistic studies in Chile, and in 1963, when returning to Buenos Aires, he graduated in philosophy from the Colegio Máximo de San José in San Miguel, of the Buenos Aires Province. Between 1964 and 1965, he was a professor of literature and psychology in the Colegio de la Inmaculada Concepción, a high school in Santa Fe, and in 1966 taught the same subjects at the Colegio del Salvador in Buenos Aires. On the 13th of December 1969, after finishing his theological studies two years prior, he was ordained a priest. He then became the master of novices at Villa Barilari, San Miguel (1972-1973), professor at the Faculty of Theology, and Consultant of the Province. He took the final fourth vow (obedience to the pope) in the Society of Jesus on the 22nd of April, 1973, which added to the previous three, and on the 31st July, 1973, he was elected Provincial of Argentina, a leading position in the Jesuit Order of Argentina, which he exerted for six long years. In the 1980's, he became the Rector of the College of San Miguel for the faculties of Theology and Philosophy, and he continued his mission for the Jesuits as spiritual adviser in the city of Córdoba. During this period, he did everything possible to oppose Liberation Theology. According to the *Catholic Herald*, Pope Francis was all too familiar with liberation theology when he was the Jesuit provincial in Argentina, and opposed it, *"even when this stand left him isolated among the Jesuits."* Liberation theology, which was very popular in the 1970's, had its ideology heavily influenced by Marxism and Communism. It is something the Jesuits were the first to promulgate as a way of life during their establishment of settlements known as the "Jesuit Reductions," created for indigenous people in South America during the 17th and 18th centuries.

At the time, Bergoglio's apparent fascistic position diverged from the majority of Jesuits and was more in line with the fascist and traditionalist ideology of the infamous P2 Masonic Lodge. The P2 lodge was very powerful in Argentina in the 1970's and early 80's, until the end of the Argentinian dictatorship that followed the Falklands war in 1983. The P2, which stands for Propaganda 2, was a key player for the CIA and the Vatican, not only in Europe but in the whole of South America, and used Bergoglio on more than one occasion. During this time, the Argentinian dictator Videla sheltered many Nazi fugitives, along with Juan Perón before him. Some P2 Freemasons say this was one of the reasons that later pushed the future Pope to study in Germany in the 80's, and why, for no apparent reason, he spent several months at the Sankt Georgen Graduate School of Philosophy and Theology in Frankfurt. Officially, he was there considering a possible dissertation topic for a thesis in theology that was apparently never presented. So what was he really doing at the end of the "Cold War" in West Germany? Fighting Communism?

While in Germany, he saw the painting of Mary Untier of Knots in Augsburg, and brought a copy back to Argentina where it has since become an important part of Marian devotion in his country.

Leo Lyon Zagami

After all his missions and his "strange behavior" during the Argentinian dictatorship, Bergoglio was rewarded by the Vatican hierarchy. On May 20th,1992, Pope John Paul II appointed him Titular Bishop of Auca and Auxiliary Bishop of Buenos Aires. On the 27th of June, that same year, in the cathedral of Buenos Aires, he received his Episcopal Ordination from the hands of Cardinal Antonio Quarracino, the Apostolic Nuncio, Archbishop Ubaldo Calabresi, and the Bishop of Mercedes-Luján, Monsignor Emilio Ogñénovich. On June 3rd, 1997, he was appointed Coadjutor Archbishop of Buenos Aires with the right for automatic succession as Archbishop of Buenos Aires following the death of Cardinal Quarracino, a position he took on the 28th of February, 1998. From November 2005 through November 2011, he was the President of the Episcopal Conference of Argentina. He was finally ready for Pope stardom after he was proclaimed Cardinal by John Paul II in the consistory on the 21st of February, 2001, the year the world would have their biggest shake up to date.

THEY TOOK A POPE
"ALMOST AT THE END OF THE WORLD"

Francesco's election changes the paradigm behind the election of the bishop of Rome, and the first to bear witness of this is Bergoglio himself. From the *lodge* of the Basilica, on the evening of his election, he joked about his appointment before his flock cheering: *"I have been taken almost at the end of the world."* Notice how he specified that he has been taken *"at the end,"* and not *"in the end"*—it seems that his wording refers to a temporal dimension, not a spatial one. In fact, there is a sort of cheating on bad Italian pronunciation on Bergoglio's side, who as a good Jesuit, knows very well his every word must be calibrated to perfection, even within so-called mistakes. In this case, the "end of the world" to which he refers seems very close. He seems to inherit what is regarded as the thoughts and ideology of what was considered the *"standard-bearer of the progressive Catholic"*—the Jesuit Cardinal Carlo Maria Martini.

Martini, a friend and supporter of Bergoglio, was a Freemason (something also said of Bergoglio), and was, until his death in August 2012, considered an antagonist of Catholic traditionalism, as carried out by Ratzinger. It evoked an opening of the Church toward a One World Religion scenario, a mission he actively endorsed by working on the One World Bible project, a subject analyzed in depth by David W. Daniels in the recent book, *Why They Changed The Bible: One World Bible For One World Religion* (Chick Publications, 2014). Martini's work shows that it was possible to embrace the doctrine of Liberation Theology, so disliked by Benedict XVI and much of the Vatican, and its most loyal agents, including Bergoglio in the 1970's and 80's. At present, but perhaps not, it would seem to contradict the current project of the New World Order.

Pope Francis: The Last Pope?

But when does the "dialogue" end, and the NWO project effectively kick in, and begin emptying the doctrine of Catholicism with the opening of themes completely "modern" and liberal, which is incompatible with Catholic doctrine? Cardinal Martini, a loyal pro-Israelitè until his death, and even wanting to be buried there, was a Jesuit as well, and initiated into Freemasonry as I mentioned earlier—at least according to the Grand Master of the Grande Oriente Democratico and known author Gioele Magaldi. Upon his death, in fact, on the site of his Masonic obedience was dedicated a "touching" greeting to the Jesuit Cardinal that ends as follows:

> *Carlo Maria Martini wanted to be initiated a Freemason. But this fact—and the way in which the event took place—you're likely to find in a few illustrated traces of the book by Brother* **Gioele Magaldi, MASSONI.** *Società a responsabilità illimitata,* **Chiarelettere Publisher (Italy),** *originally for release in November 2012. As far as we are concerned, however, with great simplicity and emotion, with great affection and esteem infinite, we want to greet Brother Carlo Maria Martini in his journey to the ETERNAL ORIENT.*
>
> *Signed by THE BROTHERS OF THE GRANDE ORIENTE DEMO-CRATICO [Article 12-14 September 2012][14]*

The problem is, despite numerous announcements made by Magaldi and his publisher over the last several years, at the time of this writing, Magaldi's book has yet to be published. Recently, even while many were wondering if the content was deemed too revealing, and perhaps had led to a total suspension of this book project, it was finally announced that the book will be published on the 20th of November, 2014.

I know Magaldi very well. He is a well-known Freemason, author, and former Worshipful Master of the Grand Orient of Italy (*Grande Oriente d'Italia,* known by the acronym GOI). A couple of years ago, he abandoned the main Italian Masonic Communion and replaced it with a new Masonic reality: Grande Oriente Democratico. The Grand Orient of Italy has accused him of being an agent of the Jesuits (even if not officially announced). This explains the attitude of its pro-Jesuit site, and its alleged Masonic Obedience, whose acronym "GOD" says it all. Magaldi also confessed openly to the author his sympathies to the Jesuit and Zionist causes. You see, even if we are opposed to each other, we maintain an ongoing open dialogue. It is a custom that follows Masonic tradition.

But let's get back to Pope Francis. In the homily of his pontificate, the newly elected Pope promised to ferry the community of the faithful along "*a path of brotherhood, of love, of trust between us,*" asking the crowd gathered in St. Peter's Square to pray for God's blessing on him: "*Let us pray also for us:*

---

14   http://www.grandeoriente-democratico.com/Adesso_che_le_celebrazioni_retoriche_Martini.html ‡ Archived from internet April 4, 2014.

one for the other. Let us pray for the whole world, because there is a great brotherhood. I hope that this journey of the Church, which began today and which I will do with the help of my cardinal vicar, here present, to be fruitful for the evangelization of this beautiful city! And now I would like to give the blessing, but I would like first, to ask you a favor: before the Bishop blesses the people, I ask that you pray to the Lord to bless me: the people's prayer asking for the blessing of his bishop. We make this prayer in the silence of you on me." Suddenly he wants his faithful to pray for him and not the other way around, breaking the tradition and, with this unusual act, demonstrating the weakness of the Church.

Yet there is something more beyond this sober and "clean" image with which he greeted the faithful, this "Bishop of Rome," as he likes to call himself. He shows the shadows of progressivism: having been accused in 2005 of collusion with the dictatorship in Argentina in the extermination of nine thousand people. It is a shocking accusation, launched by the Argentine journalist Horacio Verbitsky, who has studied and investigated the most tragic period in the South American country, and who has worked on the reconstruction of events through careful and serious research. As I mentioned earlier, if brought forward, his accusations might have stopped Bergoglio from becoming Pope in 2005.

Chapter: II
THE MANY SECRETS OF POPE FRANCIS

FRANCIS XAVIER ... OR FRANCIS OF ASSISI?

Before doing further research into Argentine journalist Horacio Verbistky's groundbreaking work, let's quickly analyze the choice of his papal name and the papal logo. Why did Bergoglio chose the name "Francis"? The Jesuit order never did really get along with the order of the Franciscans, although in reality, the founder of Ignatius Loyola was inspired by St. Francis as to the very constitution of his order, while following purposes and acting in a very divergent way. In the book, *Divina seduzione. Storie di conversione: Paolo, Pacomio, Agostino, Ignazio* written by E. Ronchi, the author illustrates how Ignatius Loyola confronted the great figures that preceded him in the story of the Church. In particular, the founder of the Franciscan Order, St. Francis, and also St. Dominic, founder of the Dominicans, to this day are linked to the Jesuits. As proof, here are the words of the founder of the Society of Jesus: *"And what if I also did what St. Francis or St. Dominic did?"* In this way, Ignatius reviewed his predecessors many initiatives, and chose what he found fitting for his growing new order, The Society of Jesus. By doing this, he proposed an increasingly more difficult task. Yet, as he took inspiration from the raw models of the past, he seemed, within himself, to find the strength to carry about this new project with ease. Ronchi writes: *"All his talk was a repeat to himself, 'Dominic did this,*

Leo Lyon Zagami

I do it too; St. Francis did that I have to also do that.'"[1]

Was Bergoglio's intent to do the same, or is it just an act of propaganda designed by the manipulative mind of a Jesuit? Since the election, the interpretation regarding the choice of Bergoglio's papal name by the majority of journalists, more than likely set in motion by the agents of Vatican propaganda, immediately determined that he was referring to St. Francis of Assisi. The American Cardinal, Sean Patrick O 'Malley, also confirmed that the choice was based on St. Francis. Finally, Bergoglio himself explained the reasons for his extraordinary choice: *"I'd like a poor Church for the poor, that's why I chose the name Francis, as Francis of Assisi."* He further explains that the Saint of Assisi was a *"man of peace"* and represents *"the man who loves and preserves the Creator, and today we don't have such a good relationship with Creation."* Bergoglio continued by saying that, even during the votation of the Conclave, *"When I was at a quorum of two-thirds, and I took the applause for it, Claudio Hummes, the Archbishop of Sao Paulo hugged me and told me: 'Do not forget the poor.' Then I thought about poverty. The wars and St. Francis of Assisi. I decided to name myself after him. Meanwhile, the counting continued."* What if things happened in a different and much more calculated way from Bergoglio's explanation? Or at least not entirely like he prefers to describe it. Sometimes in situations such as these there are various levels of interpretation. One for the initiated, and the other for the profane. Something that has been studied in which they conceal from the masses a deeper meaning than that understood by the public. What is certain, is that the name chosen by the predecessor, Pope Benedict XVI, outlines publicly a more sober choice.

In reality Saint Benedict *was* the history of the Church, the creator of the monastic tradition that later inspired Saint Francis. Benedict XVI took the name of the illustrious Saint who gave birth to Western monasticism and its Benedictine order. For his last public speech as Cardinal, Ratzinger chose the monastery of St. Scholastica in Subiaco. Let us not forget that St. Francis of Assisi was especially devoted towards St. Benedict, so much so that the only portrait of the Saint of Assisi was done while he was still alive. Painted during one of his visits to the Subiaco monasteries, it is located in the so called "Sacro Speco," and is within walking distance of the more well known St. Scholastica, also known as Subiaco Abbey. It is located in the very cave where Benedict began his spiritual journey of revenge against a decadent Rome, and a church that was already corrupt, perhaps as it has always been, since its foundation. Surprisingly, the Italian researcher Marcello Pamio of *disinformazione.it* has published another equally plausible hypothesis about the name decision from his website, a thesis that leads us to a different way to interpret the choice made by Bergoglio: *"It is much more likely that Jorge*

---

1   E. Ronchi, Divina seduzione. Storie di conversione: Paolo, Pacomio, Agostino, Ignazio, (Milan: saggistica Paoline, 2004), p. 84.

Pope Francis: The Last Pope?

Mario Bergoglio chose the name Francis, not to remember the Saint of Assisi, but to honor Francisco de Jasso y Azpilcueta Atondo Aznares de Javier," also known as St. Francis Xavier, co-founder of the Jesuit Order, who led the first missionary in Asia. A confirmation comes from the Jesuit Giovanni La Manna, president of the Center Astalli of Rome who, in an interview, states literally: *"I immediately thought this reference was to our Francis Xavier, who is a saint critical to the Jesuits... Xavier spent a lifetime in his mission of evangelization... Francis Xavier was a Spanish Jesuit missionary in 1500 and one of the first witnesses of the Society of Jesus as well as one of the founders. Papa Gregory XV, on the same day of March 12, 1622, canonized Francis Xavier along with the historical and recognized founder of the Jesuits: Ignatius of Loyola!"* [2] Pamio was referencing an interview on March 14, 2013, to Father La Manna made by the *Huffington Post,* in which, following the election of Bergoglio, he answered the following questions:

And what does this name mean? Do you think that he has chosen it in reference to St. Francis and to his vow of poverty? "His Holiness, having a history as a Jesuit, I believe, he has chosen this name having in mind St. Francis Xavier, one of the early missionaries that tried to evangelize new lands. I believe that the choice of the name belongs to the history of His Holiness and therefore has its roots in the history of the Jesuits. Thinking and living as a Jesuit, I immediately thought this reference was to our Francis Xavier, who is a Saint critical to the Jesuits, one of the first witnesses of the holy Society of Jesus who spent a lifetime in his mission of evangelization. I am sure that this name resonates in the soul of His Holiness."

What kind of Pope is Pope Francis? A Pope who is breaking free, or resuming with the past? "Definitely he will take into account the line followed by his predecessors. But in his own way he will have certain priorities, and identifying these priorities will weigh the fact of being a Jesuit. Taking into account the name he chose, he will certainly be a busy man in the new evangelization in the Year of the Faith." (Note by the author: "Year of Faith" ran from Oct. 11, 2012 until Nov. 24, 2013*). "He will lead the Church with the attention to those who look at the world from another point of view, which in his case is Argentina. Doing so he will bring a breath of fresh air to help the Universal Church revise its priorities. This will only bring new energy and enthusiasm to the Church. From his first speech as Pope he asked the faithful to bless him, he has started a dialogue, a new relationship, a two-way one. It is not a one-way speech: it means being part of a single reality."* [3]

In this curious choice of name, is there value being interpretative in comparison to the meaning made public by the Pope himself? The message sent out from the Vatican is narrow and offers no other interpretations. During the

2   http :// / www.disinformazione.it / papa_ francesco.htm ‡ Archived from the internet June 3, 2014.

3   http://www.huffingtonpost.it/2013/03/13/papa-gesuita-intervista-padre-giovanni-la-manna_n_2870717.html Interview with Julia Belardelli Father Giovanni La Manna, March 14, 2013 ‡ Archived from the internet June 3, 2014.

pontificate of Bergoglio, in the name of Francis, the Church will embark on a new path. But which one? Becoming very poor and for the poor, as was done in the time of St. Francis of Assisi—or to evangelize and win the confidence of rulers and distant peoples in the name of the Society of Jesus, as did St. Francis Xavier? As a Pope, he must tend to the defense of the faith. But as a Jesuit, he must defend the papacy at all costs!

The name he chose should foretell what will happen, as is already happening, for example, with Pope Francis going to Korea in the summer of 2014, and again returning to Asia in January of 2015. This looked like a typical St. Francis Xavier kind of move, not that of St. Francis of Assisi. Many would have preferred that he return to the Middle East in these difficult times, and open a dialogue on peace, than to dine with Korean pop stars. And so, what will become of the Church? As he stated from the beginning, he was chosen *"… almost at the end of the world."*

For now, beyond the proclamations of peace and poverty, we can clearly glimpse a step backwards compared to the attempts toward "restoration" of the old doctrinal and liturgical ways put in place by his much more traditional predecessor. It would appear to be a step towards a more secular—and more *Masonized*—kind of Church. An opening to modernity, which is likely to drag the community of the faithful towards the extreme dissolution of Catholic tradition into the New World Order and a One World Religion. Once it begins, in fact, modernity can lead only to the degradation and depletion of the traditional doctrine in view of something else. The future of the Church will weigh upon the membership of the Pope to the Society of Jesus, a "training" that you can neither forget nor deny. To emphasize this point, Father La Manna stated:

> The new Pope is a person who has received a Jesuit education. And he **who was a Jesuit for years can not erase his origins.** His training has influenced the way in which he acted as Archbishop of Buenos Aires: what forges a man is not easily forgotten. The fact of his being a Jesuit will show in the way he will serve the Church.

In this case, remember that for some researchers, including the historian Jean-Charles Pichon and others, that I will discuss in another publication, the Jesuits are not only a Catholic order, but a secret society dedicated to magic and deception. In the book by François Dumas Ribadeau *Secret Dossier of Witchcraft and Black Magic* (Ed.Mediterrannee, Rome, page 259) he writes:

> In the Monita Secreta Societati, a Jesuit named Zanorowski Jerome, whose revelations made scandal, gave the impression that the Society of Jesus has the appearance of being an inhumane sect, with terrible secrets, commanded by a 'black pope' omnipotent. He ensures that the society uses evil powers and performs executions. One point is certain: the Jesuits have always given great attention to magic.

Pope Francis: The Last Pope?

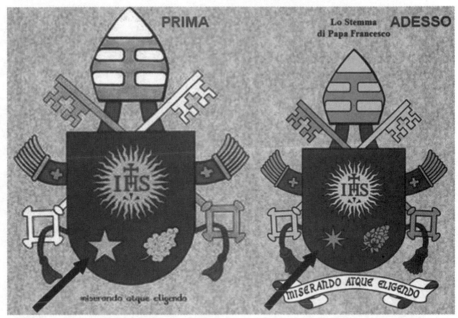

FIG. 3. The two versions of the episcopal coat of arms compared before and after the change. Pic from: http://giacintobutindaro.org/2013/03/27/clamoroso-il-papa-francesco-ha-fatto-sostituire-il-simbolo-massonico-sul-suo-stemma-con-un-altro-simbolo-massonico/ ‡ Archived from the internet July 6, 2014.

In short, even if the information concerning the Jesuits circulating on the internet, and in the field of conspiracy literature, can be considered 100% genuine, such as their alleged oath, considered by many historians to be a total fake, it is certainly not with innocence, with his choice of the name Francis, that we should be fooled by a Jesuit. We need to judge him by the facts, that for the moment, seem to be few, at least compared to the many promises made. My inside sources in the Vatican seem to confirm a general disappointment with the so-called "Francis Mania," that we could simply call *"Keeping up Appearances,"* like the title of that famous BBC television sitcom of the 90's. In regards to the previous work of Pope Francis, it has been quoted, *"doing a little, is better than doing nothing."* In July 2014, he suddenly decided to meet a small group of Church victims of pedophilia, reflecting and praying with them in his residence. Six people came all the way from Germany, Great Britain and Ireland, accompanied by Cardinal Sean Patrick O'Malley of Boston—a staunch fighter of the phenomenon of child abuse in his diocese, and the coordinator of the Commission for the protection of minors ordered by Pope Bergoglio. They attended a Mass together, celebrated with the Pontiff at Casa Santa Marta, his actual residence, and then met in what seemed little more than a symbolic gesture, given the presence of six real people, and not 600 or 6,000 in St. Peter's Square. In regards to the never ending pedophilia scandal, this would suggest a real revolution concerning the *modus operandi* within the Vatican. The Pope that promises "zero tolerance" should have the courage to let the many police forces from around the world into the Vatican, which over the years, have often found themselves forced to give up their investigations when they concerned certain men in the Vatican who were at the top of the pedophile rings. This is still the case today, as I will demonstrate, in depth, in the next chapter.

FIG. 4. Father Federico Lombardi at a press conference on March 18ᵗʰ, 2013, who demonstrates clearly the first version of the episcopal coat of arms chosen by Francis, which has a five pointed star. From: http://gianmicheletinnirello.org/category/gesuiti/
‡ *Archived from the internet July 6, 2014.*

THE PAPAL MASONIC EMBLEM

If the name Francis has raised some doubts on the direction behind his intentions, the mystery becomes even more dense and full of intrigue when we consider the papal coat of arms. In fact, the first version, officially presented by Father Lombardi on March 18ᵗʰ 2013, a few days after Bergoglio's election, had been quickly changed, for no apparent reason, after just a few days. So what happened?

As far as I am concerned, at the bottom left, the first version (as pictured) clearly shows a stave, which is a Masonic pentagram! The five-pointed star was then promptly changed for an alternative version containing eight rays. The image of the original coat of arms, however, had time to go around the globe on websites and social networks all over the internet, and was noticed by those with eyes to see. It appears that Bergoglio decided to keep the essential traits included in his old Cardinal's coat of arms.

The episcopal coat of arms features a light blue background topped by the symbols of papal dignity (a miter placed between crossed keys of gold and silver, bound by a red cord). This is identical to aspects desired by his predecessor, Benedict XVI. In Bergoglio's version, the top is then adorned with the emblem of the Society of Jesus, a radiant and flaming sun with the letters IHS in red, and the monogram of Christ. The letter H is surmounted by a cross; and at the tip, three nails in black. Below, you will find the star (now a eight pointed version) and the flower of nard. According to the ancient heraldic tradition, the star symbolizes the Virgin Mary, mother of Christ, and the Church (Stella Maris/Star of the Sea); while the flower of nard represents St. Joseph, the patron of the Universal Church. In iconographic tradition, Hispanic tradition, in fact, St. Joseph is depicted with a branch of nard in his hand. By placing these images on his shield, the Pope, apparently, wanted to express his own particular devotion to the Blessed Virgin and to St. Joseph.[4]

In truth, behind this loyalty to his faith, there is a well-crafted pagan symbolism of nature, inspired by the Hermetic tradition of the Society of Jesus, originally inspired by the Jesuit Athanasius Kircher (Geisa May 12, 1602 – November 28, 1680 in Rome). These symbols relate to the female deities, specifically Isis from the Egyptian tradition, and the Assyrian Babylonian Ishtar. Both are represented by an eight-pointed star, and mostly, in particular, Ishtar, whose cult was associated with the planet Venus and sacred prostitution, a practice that appears to have a strong following in today's Vatican. Among other things, Ishtar[5] has, as its counterpart, the deity *Astarte* in Phoenician tradition.[6]

In particular, we have the work of Madame Blavatsky's *Isis Unveiled* that *emphasize* not only the female regenerative role in nature of the goddess, but also their underworld (infernal) side. The role of Blavatsky, the founder of the Theosophical Society, is considered to be the origin of what we now define as "New Age." Its acts of Luciferian subversion of the classical interpretation of the sacred texts is certainly of primary importance in the globalist context. During a course of time, and thanks to Freemasonry, the Theosophical Society has assumed more and more relevance in the One World Religion project. Around the same time, inspired figures such as the English black magician Aleister Crowley also reached prominence. He who boasted of being born in

4   http://attualita.vatican.va/sala-stampa/bollettino/2013/03/18/news/30649.html
    ‡ Archived from the internet June 3, 2014.

5   Hugo Gressmann, Julian Obermann,The Tower of Babel (New York: Jewish Institute of Religion Press, 1928), p. 81.

6   Carl G. Liungman. Symbols: Encyclopedia of Western Signs and Ideograms. (Lidingö, Sweden: HME Publishing, 2004), p. 228.

the year of the founding of the Theosophical Society, to which many original *Ordo Templi Orientis* members belonged.

Even Crowley, in fact, was devoted to the goddess Ishtar, who will assume a key role in the pantheon of his perverse cult of "Thelema," so dear to the Illuminati, as a figure present in the key passage of the Apocalypse of St. John, called *"Babylon the Great, the mother of harlots and abominations of the earth."* This is from the King James Version, the New International Version, which uses "prostitutes" instead of "harlots."

For some non-Catholic Christians, it appears that Vatican City is at the end of times, and who can really blame them for such an interpretation? While it is true that the star with eight rays represents the "star of Bethlehem" in the Judeo-Christian tradition, it is also true that this ancient pagan symbol has taken on an increasingly important role that is far more nefarious in the NWO scenario. In the New Age tradition, the eight-pointed star is linked to mental manipulation, and to what we define as counter initiation. This is the opposite of *true* initiation, a practice conducted by the many sects operating within the New World Order.

Not surprising to informed observers, during the halftime musical break at the 2004 Super Bowl sporting event, the actor/singer Justin Timberlake shocked viewers at the stadium, and the American CBS television audience, by tearing a piece of the leather from the jacket worn by Michael Jackson's sister, Janet Jackson. This exposed the world to the symbol of the goddess Ishtar, an eight-pointed star, that was attached to the nipple of the singer.[7] As confirmed by the images, that same star that is now inextricably linked to Pope Bergoglio, and, more generally, to the Italian Jesuits, who use it as a logo on their new website.[8] Recently I wrote a book defining and explaining the many connections between; *THE ILLUMINATI AND THE MUSIC OF HOLLYWOOD* (Ed.Harmakis, Montevarchi, Arezzo. Italy, November 2014).

On March 18, 2013, the papal coat of arms was officially unveiled at a press conference by Father Federico Lombardi, also a Jesuit, and the master propagandist of the Vatican. He made a brief explanation about what was contained in the symbols, and spoke of the motto that is taken from the Homilies of St. Beda the Venerable (Om. 21, CCL 122, 149-151). A priest, who, commenting on the Gospel story of the Calling of Saint Matthew, writes: *"Vidit ergo Iesus publicanum et quia miserable atque eligendo vidit, ait illi Sequere me,"* which means, literally: "Jesus saw a tax collector and as he looked at him with feelings of love, he chose him, and told him: Follow me." This homily is a tribute to God's mercy, and is reproduced in the Liturgy of the Hours of the feast of St. Matthew. It

---

7   http://mindcontrolblackassassins.com/tag/star-of-ishtar/ ‡ Archived from the internet June 3, 2014.

8   http://gesuiti.it/ ‡ Archived from the internet June 3, 2014.

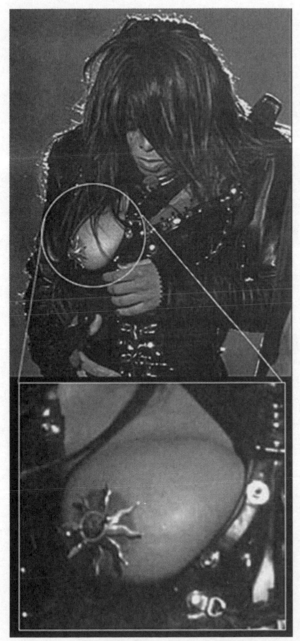

apparently plays a particular meaning in the life and in the spiritual path of the Pope. On the feast of St. Matthew, in the year of our Lord, 1953, the young Jorge Mario Bergoglio, at the age of 17, experienced the vocation to enter the Society of Jesus, founded by "the magician" Ignatius Loyola.

FIG. 5. During the episode that shocked the Super Bowl audience in 2004, the singer Janet Jackson exposes the eight-pointed star that covers her nipple. The original clip is viewable on: http://www.youtube.com/watch?v=nnR2K8JQEX4/ ‡ Archived from the internet July 15, 2014.

Loyola was a controversial figure, as described by Francois Dumas Ribadeau in the previously mentioned *Secret Dossiers of Witchcraft and Black Magic,*[9] where he is described as a person who was arrested by the Inquisition five times before finally being accepted by the Pope. He Founded the Jesuits, and among other propositions, Loyola

9   Francois Ribadeau Dumas, DOSSIER SEGRETI di STREGONERIA e di MAGIA NERA (Translation by Maddalena Casalis), (Rome: Edizioni Mediterranee, Roma, Giugno, 2005), pp. 260-261.

Leo Lyon Zagami

"dedicated himself to reunions for the evocation of spirits, where he would bring students and young girls who could be hypnotized, putting them on their knees, with their arms crossed, their face wet with tears; where they confessed aloud their sins and received salvivic visions. He prepared them for ecstasy. But the Inquisition" (Note from the author: it was not yet in the hands of the Jesuits, but the Dominicans at that time) *"saw in these facts a ceremony that put into play satanic forces."*[10] I want to emphasize, that just as with Ignatius Loyola before him, Pope Bergoglio *"was illuminated by the example of St. Francis,"* and, with the help of Pope Paul IV, *"who protected him for some mysterious reason,"*[11] eventually succeeded in founding his Jesuit Order.

Joël Labruyère, a contemporary French researcher, in his book *Kali Yuga* (published only in France and Italy) helps us to understand the true spirit of elite Jesuit members like Bergoglio: *"The Society of Jesus is the secret society more structured and probably more (active than any other) on earth. In any case it is the only organization that has really focused and who has effective occult powers, a fact that is entirely unknown to most people."*

A few lines later, Labruyère is more specific: *"we are not talking about the ordinary Jesuit, very nice, with whom you would have met in school, in a social organization or in an educational center. We refer to the initiated, who profess to have issued the fourth vow, and among the latter who are recruited on the basis of the luciferian court, the real Illuminati."*[12]

This is exactly what we need to keep in mind when examining the figure of Pope Francis. Returning to the original coat of arms presented by Padre Lombardi, let's further discuss the controversial five-pointed star present in the first version, and still available in articles in and around the internet, and in video presentations available on YouTube.[13]

The star in question is most commonly associated with Christ as the bright morning star. But as we know, every symbol can have multiple meanings. In the *Apocalypse* of John (22, 16), it indicates Christ. In the heraldry of the Virgin, it is known to be an emblem of magic. At the same time, it is one of the "icons of Freemasonry," where it is known among the initiated to represent "the Flaming Star"— revealed to the candidate in the second degree of Freemasonry. In pagan times, it was a prominent symbol favored by the ancient Pythagoreans, who were the first to take up mathematics.

For certain, the five-pointed star weighs heavily in magical traditions. With

---

10   *Ibid.*

11   *Ibid.*

12   Joël Labruyère, Kali Yuga, Lumi sulla civiltà dell'Era Nera (Trad. di Angelo Bianchetti) (Argelès-Gazost, FR: Editions l'ile Blanche, 2012), pp. 115,116.

13   http://www.youtube.com/watch ? kBkcQFH6O3M v = ‡ Archived from the internet July 4, 2014.

its point up, it shows the positive side of magic, but when pointed downwards, it is a key symbol in the world of black magic. The blazing five-pointed star is a symbol important to magic and Freemasonry, where it alludes to celestial geometry, and to God—or gnosis—for the initiated. In the Catholic Church, it represents the spiritual light that "enlightens" the world.

In the past, a star with five rays has only appeared on the coat of arms of Pope John Paul I, whose mysterious death I write about in detail in the third volume of *Confessions*. This is a sad episode linked to Vatican Freemasonry. John Paul I was sacrificed on the 33rd day of his brief pontificate, due to his genuine will to reform the Vatican Bank.

Confirming that the five-pointed star was previously only used by Papa Luciani, Giorgio Aldrighetti of Chioggia, a famous heraldic expert and papal dignitary, writes: *"Mary is the star of the morning, but the design has surprised me: a five-ray star had only been seen in the coat of arms of Pope Luciani. Usually, in ecclesiastical heraldry, the stellar rays are eight, as the beatitudes. Or at least six."*

As I have already explained, and what is really "strange" to the experts in the field, the five-pointed star is an icon typically associated with Freemasonry. Aldrighetti said that he wrote to the Vatican Secretary of State to warn them of the anomaly that could cause *suspicion* after the Bergoglio coat of arms was presented on March 18th, 2013. If this heraldic expert and papal dignitary confirms all this, I have to agree. The coat of arms containing the pentagram was quickly changed. How is it possible that the Vatican was not aware that the use of the five-pointed star would have aroused such discontent? Perhaps they were well-aware, and the symbol was briefly displayed publicly to communicate the presence, or proximity, of the new pontiff to Freemasonry?

In light of this data, I may venture the following interpretation. Firstly, the presence of the staff would address the close connection Bergoglio had to Vatican Freemasonry, the mysterious Lodge Ecclesia, that had, since the 1970's, helped him in his slow but steady ascent to the Papal Throne. Secondly, the flower of nard indicates the Universal Church. According to sources inside the Vatican, the Universal Church is now conspiring to overtake the Catholic Church, with itself to become the cult of "state" behind the impending global government as construed by the New World Order. This move is led by a certain type of Freemasonry, which specifically relates to the Luciferian thoughts of Madame Blavatsky, and is expressed via the symbols present on the coat of arms. They represent the mondialist program behind the reign of Pope Francis, and are fueled with *ecumenism*, secularisation, and a sort of *Masonic* doctrine. With its consequent shift to a Universal Church, and in step with modernity; open to inter-religious dialogue and globalist thought, it is a Church increasingly distant from tradition, and closer to what is defined as *New Age*. It is a Church that seeks to swallow up and hold all the future citizens of the New World Order in their long-anticipated One World Religion.

Leo Lyon Zagami

THE RING OF THE FISHERMAN

The Ring of the Fisherman is the main symbol of the Petrine ministry. The second symbol, in fact, is the pallium, but it is shared with the metropolitan Bishops. The word Metropolitan, used without any qualification, means the Bishop of the Metropolitan See, usually a styled Archbishop, and among those who share with the pope the ministry of oversight over the Bishops. The ring, instead, is a unique symbol of the pope's office, and it was formerly used to seal papal correspondence. Upon the death of a pope, it was traditionally destroyed to prevent the production of false documents, and more simply, to symbolize the end of the pontificate. Although the papal ring hasn't been used as a seal for almost two centuries, even the ring belonging to Pope Benedict XVI, at the end of his papacy, was obliterated with two cross-cuts.

Pope Francis chose, for his papal ring, between sketches drawn for his predecessor, Paul VI, by the artist Enrico Manfrini, a known Freemason. This is where we find the symbol of Peter with the keys. This represents the power to administer the divine mercy. Francis' ring is made of gold coated silver, and not just gold. This is to appear more in line with his mission—sobering up the present decadence of the Church. Upon his choice, he was immediately praised for his apparent simplicity.[14]

The Pope only wears the Fisherman's Ring during papal celebrations. On other occasions, such as the Angelus, or the Hearings, he wears his bishop's ring, made of sterling silver. In the newspaper "Varese Report," it was described: *"The ring that has been chosen by Pope Francis is the work of Italian artist Enrico Manfrini, a sculptor very close to Paul VI and his secretary, Monsignor Pasquale Macchi from Varese. The model chosen by the new pope had been given by Manfrini to Monsignor Macchi. It was proposed to the pontiff by the master of the Pontifical Liturgical Celebrations, Monsignor Guido Marini, together with two other models. The Pope chose Manfrini's work. The artist from Romagna died at age 87, in 2004, in Milan, he was also known as 'the sculptor of the popes.'"*[15]

You can read the following news of Manfrini's membership to Freemasonry on the website of Evangelic Minister Giacinto Butindaro (giacintobutindaro. org/) *"Both Enrico Manfrini and **Pasquale Macchi** turn out to be Masons, they are present in fact in the Masonic list presented in the Catholic website 'Non possumus' where we read the following about such list: Below is a list of Masons reprinted with some updates from the Bulletin de l' Occident Chrétien NR.12, July, 1976, (Director Pierre Fautrad to Fye - 72490 Bourg Le Roi-France.) All the men on this list, if in fact they are Masons, are excommunicated by Canon Law number 2338. Every man's name*

---

14   http://www.linkiesta.it/stemma-anello-francesco-bergoglio ‡ Archived from the internet June 3, 2014.

15   http://www.varesereport.it/2013/03/18/lanello-del-varesino-monsignor-macchi-al-dito-di-papa-francesco/ ‡ Archived from the internet on June 20, 2014.

Pope Francis: The Last Pope?

present on the list is followed by his position, the date on which he was initiated into Masonry, his code number, and his code name, if known."

Macchi, Pasquale. *Cardinal. Pope Paul's Prelate of Honour and Private Secretary until he was excommunicated for heresy by Pope Paul VI and was reinstated by Secretary of State Jean Villot and made a Cardinal* (Author's Note: A former bodyguard of the Most Reverend Marcel-François Lefebvre C.S.Sp., who served from November 29, 1905 until March 25, 1991, recently confirmed that, in the 70's, Villot was a Freemason on the infamous Masonic list of Vatican Freemasons published by the magazine *OP*). *4-23-58; # 5463-2. "MAPA."*

Manfrini, Enrico. Lay Consultor of Pontifical Commission of Sacred Art *(laico consultore della Pontificia Commissione per l'arte sacra). 2-21-68; # 968-c. "MANE"*[16]

The news that Manfrini, the creator of the new papal ring, was a Freemason, has gone unreported by the majority of the media, who are, of course, controlled by the Vatican. The faithful would probably be disappointed to learn that their Pope is wearing a ring designed by a Freemason—somebody who has been personally linked to the second Freemason in the history of the Papacy, Pope Montini. Pope Roncalli (Pope John XXIII) is considered to be the first Freemason to ascend to the throne of Peter. Pope Francis seems to appreciate this Masonic connection, or at least, he doesn't mind it. After all, he is a Jesuit, and Jesuits have always worked secretly, and hand-in-hand, with certain branches of Freemasonry—especially and specifically the Ancient and Accepted Scottish Rite.

BLACK SHOES VS. RED SHOES

To further support the well-crafted image of "humble Pope Francis" by Vatican manipulators, the absence of red vestments in his wardrobe also needs to be addressed. Francis and Benedict XVI could not be more different in their fashion choices. Francis is seemingly simple and innovative, while Benedict XVI was a traditionalist, and regal in every detail. In the eight years of his pontificate, Benedict XVI had, from the papal closet, dusted off certain items of clothing that had fallen into disuse. In fact, some of Benedict XVI's papal robes and vestments were last used by his distant predecessor, Pius IX, the last Pope-king of the Papal States. In 2007, the U.S. magazine *Esquire*, which mainly deals with men's fashion, devoted a long article on the clothing and accessories worn by Benedict XVI, in particular, the famous red shoes that were initially said to be designed by Prada, but in reality, were

---

16   http://giacintobutindaro.org/2013/03/19/lanello-del-pescatore-del-nuovo-papa-francesco-e-stato-fatto-da-un-massone/ ‡ Archived from the internet June 20, 2014.

Leo Lyon Zagami

hand-crafted in Novara by the hands of the artisan Adriano Stefanelli.[17]

Francis, however, has instead been praised for his simplicity in wearing a white dress and black shoes. Unlike Benedict XVI, he never wears the papal red shoes, and has specifically requested that his shoemaker in Argentina continue to provide him with the old model of black shoes he usually wears. Why is that? Is it a stylistic choice, or is there something more to it?

Many have seen this choice as a gesture of poverty, and adherence to the Franciscan model. Beyond the quality craftsmanship, the red shoes—as well as the red cardinal's robe or sash—has a specific meaning that alludes to the blood of Christ. The pope wears the color red as a sign of royalty, and because red recalls the blood that should be required as the ultimate sacrifice for the Church.

Pope Benedict XVI has also restored the traditional use of three forms of the papal mozzetta. Only the red satin summer mozzetta was used by Pope John Paul II, for example. Benedict XVI made use of the winter papal mozzetta, and the paschal mozzetta, both of which were last worn by Pope Paul VI in the mid-20th century. The winter papal mozzetta is red velvet and trimmed with white ermine, and worn from December 8th, on the Pentecost, until Easter. The paschal mozzetta is made of white damask silk, trimmed with white ermine, and worn only during the Eastertide.[18]

After Ratzinger reintroduced the ancient traditions, and its use of fur, the Italian Association, The Defense of Animals and the Environment, began an online petition, signed by 1,900 people, asking him to stop wearing ermine on his hats and robes. Nevertheless, he continued to do so, shamelessly, until the end of his papacy, thereby ignoring such animal cruelty requests.

Even after the announcement of his election, not even when on the balcony overlooking the central loggia of St. Peter's Basilica, Pope Francis has not worn such vestments. Contrary to what has been practiced by all of his predecessors, he prefers to wear white on such glorious occasions.

To justify the choice to not wear the traditional vestments, Vatican Radio spread the rumor that Bergoglio replied angrily to the master of ceremonies, who wanted him to wear the skullcap, the gold cross, and so on, "*you put them on, I will not wear them.*" Such a statement suggests an effort to separate himself from orthodoxy. A desire to create a different image, one that is both simple and humble. Not only does Francis not wear anything red, he usually refers to himself not as "Pope," but as the *"Bishop of Rome."* Some might conclude that he is merely denying his own "kingship"—a sacrifice that every pope should

17   http://www.ilfattoquotidiano.it/2013/02/28/benedetto-xvi-il-guardaroba-papale-scarpe-rosse-e-abiti-di-altri- tempi/516036/#foto-papa-con-camauro-2 ‡ Archived from the internet June 20, 2014.

18   http://en.wikipedia.org/wiki/Ceremonial_of_Benedict_XVI ‡ Archived from the internet June 20, 2014.

Pope Francis: The Last Pope?

be ready to do for the community of the faithful. These facts could also suggest that Francis is only a temporal ruler of the Petrine throne. As long as Benedict XVI is alive, for many, Pope Francis will be *only* the Bishop of Rome.

Even though this book is dedicated to Bergoglio, presumably the "Last Pope," Ratzinger still needs to be considered a central figure. As a "Shadow Pope," and from behind the scenes, consider Ratzinger the true occult manipulator of the Holy See. On May 1st, 2013, Ratzinger moved into his new apartment within the Vatican. This is another symbolic date, as on May the 1st, 1776, The Order of the *Illuminati of Bavaria* was founded. Ratzinger lives on the first floor of the monastery *Mater Ecclesiae*, behind the Basilica of St. Peter, and where the Pope Emeritus Benedict XVI can view the wonderful Vatican gardens. Every day he likes to walk among the trees, flowers and fountains, amidst what can be described as one of the most amazing gardens in the world. Usually with him on these daily walks, we find what many Vatican insiders report to be his lover, the always faithful (and good-looking) Monsignor Georg Gänswein, his secretary and prefect of the Pontifical Household, and officially at his side since 2003.

Bishop Gänswein, who has been seen on many official occasions next to Pope Francis, seems to have the key role of a trusted messenger between Ratzinger and Bergoglio, the "twin" Popes. For all intent and purposes, he lives with, and appears to be, Ratzinger's companion.

The *Pope Emeritus*, now a "Simple Pilgrim," lives in a strange reality. While professing an ascetic and monastic intent, at times, especially when he plays with his dogs or plays the piano, he will show his feminine side. Ratzinger's piano-playing has been likened to the late George Liberace, who was born near Milwaukee, on May 16, 1919, and died of AIDS in Palm Springs, on February 4, 1987. Both are musicians and alleged homosexuals, and Liberace, like Ratzinger, never confessed his real sexual tendency. The stakes are much higher for the *Pope Emeritus*, because in doing so, Ratzinger could put an end to 2,000 years of hypocrisy.

The monastery where Ratzinger and Gänswein live, built under the direction of John Paul II, is not located far from Santa Marta, the residence where Bergoglio has chosen to live "in poverty," instead of the Apostolic Palace, traditionally the residence of the pope. Thus, the two popes are conveniently close to each other. This would confirm, once again, the important role of Ratzinger, who, for many, remains not only the true Pope, but also the one who holds the secret keys to the financial side of the Vatican. The German weekly, *Der Spiegel*, spoke openly of money laundering by the infamous Vatican Bank (the IOR), and operations inside the IOR related to gangs and corporations. This is an issue that I will be discussing further in this book, issues that have never worried JP Morgan, nor its subsidiary in Frankfurt, Germany, who remain the main ally of Ratzinger.

In the last years of his pontificate, Ratzinger would have moved all the gold assets related to his person to this bank, and numerous secret accounts of the IOR, belonging to "all the usual suspects." This was prior to his giving the all-clear for external inspections, as has been required several times in recent years by the international anti-money laundering authorities. Despite this, from a court in Rome, the Italian judiciary has begun an investigation on the subject, with an international rogatory letter, seeking knowledge regarding the movement of these assets from the Holy See to the homeland of Pope Ratzinger. The account in question at JP Morgan, in Frankfurt, has been put under the magnifying glass. In my humble opinion, because of the ostracism of the German authorities, who appear to be in league with their beloved Ratzinger, the success of this investigation has been only partial. Meanwhile, in March of 2014, the prosecutor of Rome sued the former director general of the IOR, Paolo Cipriani, and his deputy Massimo Tulli, for violating two articles of the Decree of 2007, on money laundering. Of course Ratzinger was not implicated in any way. In 2010, this investigation began with the seizure of 23 million euros. Euros that, upon input of the then leadership of the Institute for Works of Religion, were to be transferred... 20 million from a branch of the Italian bank, Credito Artigiano, to JP Morgan, Frankfurt, and 3 million to the Bank of Fucino, all in violation of the money laundering legislation. This episode initially led to an investigation of the then president of the IOR, Gotti Tedeschi, who is a dear friend to Ratzinger. Yet, in 2014, the newly established Cardinal commission, desired by Pope Francis, cleared Gotti Tedeschi of these accusations. Meanwhile, the mysteries involving the fate of the Vatican Bank continue.

FIG. 6. Detail of black shoes worn by Pope Francis. Pic from: http://vaticaninsider.lastampa.it/nel-mondo/dettaglio-articolo/articolo/francesco-francis-francisco-24079 ‡ Archived from the internet June 20, 2014

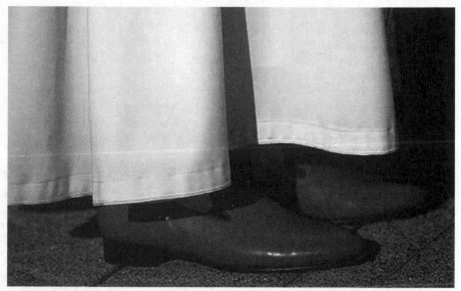

FIG. 7. The Red Shoes of Benedict XVI, made by the artisan Adriano Stefanelli. from: http://www.ilfattoquotidiano.it/2013/02/28/benedetto-xvi-il-guardaroba-papale-scarpe-rosse-e-abiti-di-altri-tempi/516036/#foto-papa-con-scarpe-rosse ‡ Archived from the internet June 20, 2014

THE "SANITARY CORDON" OF THE JESUITS

Bergoglio, as a Jesuit, and by virtue of the fourth vow of his Order, must give total obedience to the Pope, who may remain Benedict XVI. This might be the main reason Francis chose not to live in the papal apartments, even if, as rumored within the Vatican, that the choice has not been made for this reason alone. The choice could also depend on the fact that his own personal safety would be put into question by the numerous enemies, such as those who would have preferred someone like Cardinal Scola on the throne of Peter, who are present in those sacred halls. Within the walls of the Vatican, the so-called Leonine Walls, the Pope would, in fact, be more vulnerable than at his current residence at the Casa Santa Marta, a place where he is well-protected by what the Vatican correspondent of the newspaper, *La Republica,* Marco Ansaldo, called a few days after his election, the creation of a "sanitary cordon" issued by the Jesuits to protect Pope Bergoglio. Ansaldo wrote, *"The danger is alerted to such an extent that the Jesuits, the order to which Jorge Mario belongs, are thinking about issuing a sort of 'sanitary cordon' to support the Pope, until he makes his final choice. 'These key strategic decisions must be done for him,' said a senior member of the Society of Jesus."*[19]

19   http://www.repubblica.it/esteri/2013/03/18/news/governo_papa-54795283/
       ‡ Archived from the internet June 20, 2014.

*FIG. 8. Benedict XVI with red satin robes and a skullcap. Taken from: http://
it.wikipedia.org/wiki/Casi_di_pedofilia_all 'interno_della_Chiesa_cattolica/ ‡ Archived
from the internet July 28, 2014*

This choice to stay in Santa Marta would, therefore, seem not to be tied
to issues connected to his "Franciscan" style—a style that distinguish him

Pope Francis: The Last Pope?

from his predecessors—but is, instead, a decision taken by his loyalists, and linked to a factor of safety, and not that of a supposed vow of poverty in line with the original Saint Francis. This discretion is also confirmed by a senior member of the Knights of the Holy Sepulchre, an order traditionally close to the Jesuits, who have their headquarters across from the Headquarters of the Company of Jesus, on Borgo Santo Spirito in Rome.

Cav. Luciano Sciandra, who is also a member of the Pontifical Equestrian Order of St. Sylvester Pope, has, on two separate occasions, personally told me that every time the Pope eats, there are three Jesuits present who intermittently play the role of trustworthy "food taster" to the Holy Father, who ensure that there isn't an "unpleasant surprise" in his meal. This tradition, if revived by Pope Francis, would carry us back to the dark ages, when the rulers had to protect themselves against everyone and everything.

Long ago, there was the job of "food taster," the person who enjoyed the fantastic food of the rulers, to the delight of his palate, but who could run into the errors of a careless cook, or even worse, consume dishes spiked with deadly poison. That, according to many historians, may have killed more than one pontiff. Such historical footnotes would not be lost on Pope Francis. There are also recent revelations, as this made by a magistrate, who seems to worry, at least in appearance, about a hypothetical revenge of the 'Ndrangheta (the Calabrian Mafia) against Pope Francis, "*The Pope wants to clean up the scene, but this is not liked by the 'Ndrangheta.*"

Perhaps such a move is not agreed upon by his colleague Ratzinger, who has always had good relations with the leaders of power in Calabria, where the secret, and at times irregular, Lodges of Freemasonry are prevalent. They rule the scene when connected to people like the previously mentioned Mons. Camaldo, who was also mentioned in the press for his Masonic links in the area. Perhaps Ratzinger, resulting from the full-scale Jesuit/Papal investigation into his past actions, found himself in a difficult situation, and ordered his friends down to Calabria. Perhaps this was a way to send a strong gesture to his neighbor, Pope Bergoglio, in true mafioso style.

Could Pope Francis be targeted by gangs? It is a most credible hypothesis, at least according to Nicola Gratteri, the deputy prosecutor of Reggio Calabria, interviewed by the *Fatto Quotidiano*, who warns:

> '*He who has been feeding the power of the Church is nervous. If the bosses could, they would stop him: he is a danger for them.*' According to the magistrate, Bergoglio is in danger because he is dismantling centers of economic power in the Holy See the bosses relied on. Before they kill in the 'Ndrangheta, their members go to pray. The priests will continually go to the bosses house to drink coffee. I did not find one of their bunkers where there is not present, an image of the Holy Mary or of Saint Michael the Archangel, said Gratteri,

88% of the mafioso declare to be religious. They turn to the Virgin Mary for protection. They think to be righteous. The point is that Pope Francis, Gratteri said, is working against luxury. He aims to make a total cleaning. The Mafia might not like that. The financial side is worried by this behavior, continued the magistrate, those who feed from the power and wealth that come directly from the Church, are nervous, agitated.

In short, according to Gratteri, the author of a book recently released with the symbolic title of *Acqua Santissima*, or "Holy Water," [20] he states *"The danger for the Pope could be concrete."*

Gratteri concludes: *"I do not know if organized crime is in a position to do something like this, but there is certainly reflection on it. It could be dangerous."* [21]

I believe, therefore, that Bergoglio has no intention in the near future to live at his official residence, at least unless his enemies were eliminated in a single night. This seems rather unlikely in the age of transparency, where the physical elimination of a number of high senior members of the Vatican hierarchy would definitely set off a thousand speculations in the media. There also remains the fact that Ratzinger, as long as he remains alive, still exerts that "royal" power that Pope Francis will not receive in its fullness until the death of his predecessor. In conclusion, red shoes, ancient skullcaps, the official apostolic apartment, and other "gifts" could be used by Francis only after the passing of Ratzinger. This may never be for Pope Francis and his Jesuits, who, in the best tradition of St. Ignatius, believe identity and true power are much more important than appearance. Jesuits want to be the ultimate spiritual controllers of the New World Order, and leave temporal power in the hands of groups like the Zionist, or China, to whom the Jesuits have a particular connection that goes back to the very early stages of their order, through people like Father Matteo Ricci SJ (1552-1661). After almost 500 years, the Jesuits have finally reached the top of the power pyramid in the Vatican. With the help of Judaism and Freemasonry, now more corrupted by greed and materialism then ever before, this is an opportunity to finally implement their globalist plan. This can be the only real goal that interests Pope Jorge Mario Bergoglio. The White Pope, who is always in line with the Black Pope, who is the Superior General of the Society of Jesus, Adolfo Nicolas Pachon, reportedly until 2016. (Villamuriel de Cerrato, April 29, 1936).

Let us recall that the Society of Jesus was banned in Europe seventy times. The order was even suppressed in the Vatican, on July 21st, 1773, by Pope Clement XIV, with the brief *Dominus ac Redemptor,* for its scandals, freedoms,

---

20   See. Nicola Gratteri, Antonio Nicaso, Acqua santissima. La Chiesa e la 'ndrangheta: storia di potere, silenzi e assoluzioni (Milan: Mondadori, 2013).

21   http://www.affaritaliani.it/cronache/la-ndrangheta-vuole-uccidere-papa-francesco131113.html?refresh_c/ ‡ Archived from the internet June 6, 2014.

heresies, disturbing compromises, political intrigue, and finally, theories and practices that belong to people of witchcraft, and not of the Church. The profane crowds are ignorant of such misdeeds carried out during the existence of the Church. They are still willing to gather in huge crowds to applaud Pope Francis wherever he goes. I will, instead, follow Bergoglio's advice, as given on several occasions in public speeches, *to go against the current.*[22] That, for me, means criticizing this dangerous Jesuit theater of compromise, evil and falsehood—*whatever the cost!*

These are not simply the words of an author, but from someone who knows, very well, the Jesuit Order... who still, from time to time, try to have a dialogue with me. They have offered me positions of responsibility in their elite circles on more than one occasion in the past. They admire me, at least to a certain extent, for my mission in search of purity. Even in the Vatican, an institution that seems long lost, there remain good people of true spiritual faith and understanding.

"THE ISLAND OF SILENCE" AND THE SECRETS OF POPE BERGOGLIO

Beginning on March 24th, 1976, and lasting until the beginning of the 1980's, within the Catholic hierarchy, in what became Argentina's infamous military dictatorship, there is evidence of an unusual role played by Bergoglio. The book *The Island of Silence: The Church's role in the Argentine dictatorship,*[23] originally published in Argentina in 2005, and followed in Italy in March 2006, a year after the conclave that chose Ratzinger over Bergoglio by only a few votes, implicates Bergoglio in the CIA supported coup. According to Verbitsky's investigation, in the early 1970s, at age of 36, Bergoglio became the youngest Provincial Superior of the Society of Jesus in Argentina. In becoming the head of the Congregation, he inherited a lot of influence and a lot of power. During that time, the religious institution played an important role in overseeing all ecclesiastically-based communities active within the slums of Buenos Aires. All Jesuit priests who worked in the area were under its dependencies. So, it was in February of 1976, a month before the coup, that Bergoglio asked two of his Jesuits who were working in the communities to leave immediately, and to abandon their work in the slums. Their names were Orlando Yorio and Francisco Jalics, and they refused his order. They did not desire to leave all of the poor people who relied so much on them. Verbitsky wrote about how, after the refusal of his two priests, Bergoglio reacted with two immediate steps. First, without even informing them, he excluded

22   http://www.famigliacristiana.it/articolo/papa_1941.aspx ‡ Archived from the internet June 2, 2014

23   See. Horacio Verbitsky L'isola del silenzio. Il ruolo della Chiesa nella dittatura Argentina. (Rome: Fandango Libri, 2006. Original title: El Silencio, 2005).

them from the Society of Jesus. Then, he lobbied the Archbishop of Buenos Aires to deprive them permission to deliver Mass. A few days after the coup that installed the dictatorship, the two were kidnapped.

The two priests suggested that Bergoglio's revocation and subsequent acts were a signal to the military... a green light to act against them. Meaning, specifically, that the protection of the Church had ceased to exist for them. This hypothesis, which is confirmed by a number of documents found by Verbitsky, places the blame on Bergoglio, who is accused to have reported the two priests as subversive to the dictatorship. In those years in Argentina, the meaning of "subversive" referred, in fact, to people of all levels: university professors, supporters of Peronism, those who sang songs of protest, women who dared to wear skirts, those traveling around armed to the teeth, and those involved in bringing awareness of their rights and freedoms to the poor and uneducated. After six months of torture at the notorious *Navy School of Mechanics* (in Spanish, *Escuela de Mecánica de la Armada,* commonly referred to by the acronym *ESMA* for *Escuela Superior de Mecánica de la Armad*), thanks to pressure from the Vatican, the two men were released. According to the reconstruction by Verbitsky, it was only the involvement of the Vatican, and not Bergoglio, that allowed the release of the two priest-prisoners.

Verbistky writes:

> *Orlando Yorio never fully recovered. He worked in the Vicariate of Quilmes, but feeling threatened, he settled in Uruguay, where he died in 2000. Sometime after the kidnapping he recalls his relationship with Bergoglio with these words. 'I don't have any reason to think he did anything for our freedom, but rather the contrary.' The two priests were released thanks to the intervention of Emilio Mignone, and the intercession of the Vatican and not for the conduct of Bergoglio. On the contrary, 'he was the one who delivered them there,' maintains Angelica Sosa de Mignone.*

In 1990, during one of his return visits to Argentina, Jalics had a meeting at the institute "Faith & Prayer," Via Oro 2760, with the above mentioned Emilio Fermín Mignone and his wife, Angélica Sosa. He told them that *"Bergoglio opposed the fact that once he was free he could stay in Argentina, and talked to all the Bishops so they would not accept him in their churches."*[24]

As of this writing, the Hungarian Jalics lives in a house of prayer in Germany. Responding to a request for a telephone interview, he said, *"It's been a quarter of a century, I feel very distant from all this. Why reawaken memories that are so painful, when responding to a request by telephone."*[25]

---

24   http://www.controlacrisi.org/notizia/Politica/2013/3/17/32006-verbitsky-ber-goglio-sempre-il-doppio-gioco-lammissione/ ‡ Archived from the internet June 6, 2014.

25   *Ibid.*, p. 60.

Pope Francis: The Last Pope?

Yet, a few years earlier, Jalics had confessed to the same journalist that Bergoglio had spread the rumor that the two priests were on the side of the guerrillas, thus voluntarily exposing them to the kidnapping. Yorio added: *"I don't have any evidence to think that Bergoglio wanted to free us, quite the contrary. He informed my brothers that I had been shot, so they could psychologically prepare my mother."* According to Yorio's testimony, Bergoglio would have *"washed his hands"* of their abduction, and even was present during a meeting with the prisoners at the Navy headquarters.[26] Bergoglio, however, has always denied such accusations: *"I never had a way to label them as guerrillas or communists, among other things because I never believed that they were."* [27]

Among the documents in the archives of Ministry of Foreign Affairs collected by Verbitsky, we find one that refers to a specific episode. In 1979, after that terrible episode, Father Francisco Jalics fled to Germany, and then asked that his passport be renewed in order to avoid going back to Argentina. Bergoglio offered to act as an intermediary, pretending to plead the cause of his priest, but the application was (of course) rejected. A note appended to the documentation by the Director of the Office of Catholic Worship, then a body within the Argentinian Ministry of Foreign Affairs, states: *"This priest is a subversive."* Another document, a classified document addressing the direction of the cult, present in wallet 9, B2B file, in the archives of the Archbishop of Buenos Aires, would show even more clearly the role of Bergoglio: *"Despite the good will of Father Bergoglio, the Argentinian Company"* (Author's note: of the Jesuits) *"did not cleanse inside. The smart Jesuit for some time remained on the sidelines, but now with great support from the outside coming from some Third World bishops they have begun a new phase."* What follows is the epilogue within the Italian edition of the *Island of Silence*, written by Verbitsky one year after the election of Benedict XVI, when it seemed that Bergoglio could no longer reach the Throne of Peter:

> *The first edition of this book (The Island of Silence), to which I have worked for over fifteen years, went to press in Buenos Aires in February 2005, when Pope John Paul II, who then died on the 2nd of April, was hospitalized in Rome. According to Italian newspapers, the Argentine Cardinal Jorge Bergoglio was the only serious opponent of the German Joseph Ratzinger, who was elected on April 19 and took the name of Benedict XVI. In those days, the military bishop of Buenos Aires said that the Minister of Health of Argentina deserved to be thrown into the sea with a millstone around his neck for handing out condoms and having expressed himself in favor of the decriminalization of abortion. ... When the bishop Baseotto tied the sentence with a biblical millstone around the ministerial neck, President Néstor Kirchner urged the Vatican to appoint a new holder of the Military Bishop-*

---

26   *Ibid.*, p. 63.
27   *Ibid.*, p. 61.

ric of Argentina" (Author's Note: in Spanish Obispado Castrense de Argentina). "When the Apostolic Nuncio was informed that there was no reason for doing so, the government revoked the consent lent to the appointment of Baseotto and deprived him of his salary for having claimed methods of dictatorship. The Vatican ignored both 'the interpretation that they wanted to give to the gospel citation' and the presidential authority to revoke the appointment of the military bishop.

Reasons to doubt that Baseotto naively chose a biblical quote about people thrown into the sea, are plenty. His first act was to visit the Deputy to the Supreme Court of Justice, to argue the need to close the court processes related to the Dirty War of the military against the Argentinean society. Its secretary-general in the Military Bishopric (the same post that in 1976 was in the hands of Emilio Grasselli) is the priest Alberto Zanchetta Angel, who was chaplain of Esma during the years of dictatorship and who has demonstrated detailed knowledge of what was happening there. ... After turning on the public controversy with his words, Baseotto referred to the events that took place, it is said, during the famous military dictatorship. No member of the Episcopate must complain about the provocative phrase, because the whole Church in Argentina continues to entrench itself in an island of silence.

Bergoglio replied to the book through its official spokesman, Father Guillermo Marco. He said he had saved the life of priests Orlando Yorio and Francisco Jalics, and that any assertion to the contrary was a disgrace. ... to discredit my investigation. He said that Yorio could not refute the claims made in the book because he was dead, that my source on Jalics was anonymous and that there was a picture of a friendly meeting with the Hungarian priest and Bergoglio during a visit of Jalics to Buenos Aires. ... Neither Bergoglio nor his close friends have said a word about the irrefutable evidence of the duplicity of which Yorio and Jalics accuse him of. Yorio was still alive when I published the first interview in which he accused Bergoglio, in 1999. He sent me a few lines entitled, 'Thanks,' and we kept in touch until his death. ... The son of a landowner and Hungarian army officer, Jalics states in his book, Ejercicios de Contemplacion that his father was poisoned at the headquarters of the communist political police, and that his mother taught him not to hate, so 'I learned what reconciliation means.' In speaking of his abduction he says: 'Many people who had extreme right-wing political beliefs do not take kindly to our presence in the slums. Interpreting the fact that we lived there as a support for the guerrillas, and proposing to denounce us as terrorists. We knew the origin and the slander of those responsible. I went to talk to the person in question and explained that he was playing with our lives. He promised me that he would tell the military we were not terrorists. From statements made subsequently by an officer and thirty documents to which I was able to access later on, we were able to determine beyond a shadow of a doubt that the man had not kept his promise and that, on the contrary, had

Pope Francis: The Last Pope?

filed a false complaint to the military.' During the five months of the seizure, his anger was directed more to 'the man who had made that false complaint against him,' then to his captors.

That man was Bergoglio. His identity is revealed in a letter Yorio wrote from Rome on November 24, 1977, to the assistant general of the Society of Jesus, Father Moura. The brothers and nephews of Yorio gave me a copy, in a sign of gratitude, for the publication of the book.

Given the continuing rumors about my participation in the guerrilla war, Jalics addressed again the issue with father Bergoglio. Father Bergoglio recognized the seriousness of the offense and has pledged to put a stop the malicious talk in the order and urged him to talk to people of the Armed Forces to prove his innocence. 'Since the Provincial did nothing to defend us, we began to doubt his honesty.' ... In our correspondence, Yorio gave me a description of the duplicity of his former Provincial, which coincides with the one that emerges from the documents that years later I discovered in the archive of the Ministry of Foreign Affairs of Argentina. In the climate of fear and denunciation established within the Church and society, the priests who worked with the poor 'were demonized, viewed with suspicion within their own institutions and accused of subverting the social order.' In that context, 'they could give us permission secretly to celebrate Mass in private, but does not set us free from the prohibition and public infamy of not being able to exercise the priesthood publicly, thus giving the forces of repression a pretext for making us disappear.'

After his release, Jalic traveled to the United States and then to Germany. Despite the distance, 'lies, slander and unjust actions did not cease.' ... Many people linked to the Church and the Society of Jesus gave me additional and confirmatory data regarding this. One of them is the Irish priest Patrick Rice, who in 1976 was at the top the community of the small monks at the Gospel in Argentina. Kidnapped at the end of that year in Buenos Aires, they questioned him without truce, they burned his face and hands with cigarettes and made him swallow high pressure water up to the limit of his endurance. Other priests of his brotherhood disappeared, but Rice was able to escape with the help of the Irish Government and traveled around the world to denounce the situation in Argentina.

In 1979 he learned that Massera,[28] who resigned from the Navy and was involved in political activity, was participating in a workshop held at Georgetown University in Washington conducted by two academics who later played a leading role in the future U.S. government of Ronald Reagan: Jeane Kirkpatrick and Eliot Abramas. While Massera made his speech, Rice and an American priest interrupted him with questions about the repression of bish-

---

28 Massera was one of the key people involved in the CIA coup of 1976 in Argentina.

ops, nuns, priests and lay Christians. Massera could not continue and left the room in anger. Even Georgetown University belongs to the Jesuits. Patrick Rice argues that 'given the structure of the Church, it is unthinkable that this invitation could be left without the initiative or at least the consent of the Provincial Argentine Society of Jesus.' Also in this case, the Jesuit Provincial was the then priest Jorge Mario Bergoglio. [29]

In his first press conference following the election of Bergoglio, his spokesman Father Federico Lombardi, discarded old slanders of the anti-clerical critics, and dismissed the allegations concerning the actions of Bergoglio as the former provincial head of the Society of Jesus during the Argentine dictatorship, and especially the claim that he played a role in the disappearance of his two priests. In a public statement made on the 15th of March, 2013, following the election of his former superior, the old Jesuit priest clearly inferred that Jalics had reconciled with Bergoglio. He described how, years after the kidnapping, they met up and co-celebrated Mass together: *"I have been reconciled to the events and from my side consider them closed."* Basically, he was forced by his own order to retract his previous position. Reconciliation is, for Catholics, a sacrament. What resonates from the words of the elderly priest elude to his being at peace in his heart regarding the past, and that he will not go back now that Bergoglio is Pope. He does not, however, deny the facts, as is narrated in his book of meditation exercises called *Ejercicios de Contemplacion* (published in 1994), material that has been widely cited in Verbitsky's own book.

One thing is for certain, and that is that both Jalics and Orlando Yori left the Jesuit Order in 1976. When later offered to be reinstalled, only the still obedient Jalics accepted the proposal. Yorio did not, and only Jalics is alive today. Most likely because of his choice to stay a Jesuit, a loyal servant of the papacy, no matter any judgement he might personally have against Bergoglio.

Following a press conference by Vatican spokesman, Father Lombardi SJ, regarding Bergoglio's infamous involvement in the Argentinian dictatorship, Verbitsky replied to the Argentinian newspaper, *Página 12*, and, among other things, pointed out Bergoglio's involvement in the notorious militancy of the *Guardia de Hierro* (Spanish for "Iron Guard"), the Argentinian right wing group active in the early 1970s, whose findings reveal:

In these pages we analyze in depth, the case four years before Kirchnerism came into government. The first article, published in April 1999, 'Con el mazo dando,' said that the new Archbishop of Buenos Aires, depending on the source you consult, is the most generous and intelligent man who has ever said Mass in Argentina. Or is he a Machiavellian villain who betrayed his brothers for an insatiable desire for power? Perhaps the explanation lies in the fact that

Pope Francis: The Last Pope?

Bergoglio brings together things that do not always go together: extreme conservativeness in matters of dogma which manifest a clear social unrest. In either respect it resembles the person who placed him at the head of the country's main diocese, Pope Karol Wojtyla. [30]

Verbitsky concluded:

During the investigation, I found by chance in the archives of the Foreign Ministry, a folder with documents, in my opinion, that put an end to the discussion on the role of Bergoglio in the relation to Yorio and Jalics. I tried to find a notary who would certify the placement in the archive, whose director at the time, Minister Carlos Dellepiane, kept in his safe to prevent them from being stolen or destroyed. The story told in that folder sounds familiar. Released from prison in November 1976, Jalics went to Germany. In 1979, his passport had expired and Bergoglio asked the Clerk that it be renewed without him returning to his homeland. The Director of the Catholic Cult of the Chancellery, Anselmo Orcoyen, recommended to refuse the request 'because of the background of the applicant,' which was provided by the same father Bergoglio, who signed the note, with a special recommendation that this request not be accepted. He said that Jalics had conflicts of obedience and a dissolving activity in female religious congregations, and was 'imprisoned' in ESMA together with Yorio, 'suspected of being a contact of the guerrillas.'

That is to say that the same charges that have been expressed by both Yorio and Jalics (and confirmed by many priests and lay people that I interviewed) show that Bergoglio, while pretending to help, was accusing them behind their backs. It is logical that this fact from 1979 is not sufficient for a legal conviction for the kidnapping of 1976. The document signed by Orcoyen and was not even included in the practice, but indicates Bergoglio's course of action. Adding the Director of Worship in a conspiracy against the Catholic Church would be too much. For this reason, Bergoglio and his spokesman are silent on these documents and prefer to discredit those who found, preserved and published them. [31]

In the end, the attempted legal conviction mentioned by Verbitsky began on the 15th of April, 2005, when a human rights lawyer filed a criminal complaint against Jorge Mario Bergoglio, the then Archbishop of Buenos Aires, and who would become Pope Francis in 2013. As a superior in the Society of Jesus of Argentina, he accused him of involvement related to the kidnapping. [32]

30   http://www.pagina12.com.ar/diario/elpais/1-215961-2013-03-17.html ‡ Archived from the internet on June 6, 2014.

31   *Ibid.*

32   http://articles.latimes.com/2005/apr/17/world/fg-cardinal17 ‡ Archived from the internet on August 14, 2014

In 2011, Ms. De la Cuadra, daughter of Ms. Alicia Zubasnabar De la Cuadra, the first president of the "Abuelas de Plaza de Mayo," due to the kidnapping of many members of the De la Cuadra family in the late 1970s, asked *Tribunal 6* in Argentina for a declaration from Jorge Bergoglio, inquiring why he delivered a false testimony to another tribunal (in the trials regarding the priests Jalic and Dorio one year earlier), when stating that he knew nothing about the kidnapping of children in the late 1990s. *"The De la Cuadra family search led the brothers exiled in Italy to ask for assistance from Pedro Arrupe,"[33] who was the twenty-eighth Superior General (from 1965 to 1983). "Arrupe handed the task to Jorge Bergoglio. Finally, a La Plata suffragan bishop named Mario Picchi took the matter to the intelligence services. 'The girl is with a good family,' was Picchi's message. He would later be revealed to be a collaborator."[34]*

According to some commentators, due to Ms. De la Cuadra legal claim, Jorge Bergoglio will not make further visits to Argentina as Pope Francis. This is also being reported by Kevin Annett, field secretary of the International Tribunal into Crimes of Church and State (ITCCS.Org). Annett's investigation on behalf of the ITCCS revealed that a former Argentine government official is scheduled to testify against Pope Bergoglio regarding his role in child trafficking during the Junta government and the Dirty War in Argentina.[35]

Of course I cannot vouch for these claims, but it sure looks like Bergoglio's Argentinean past may have included more than one skeleton in his closet. And it is for this reason that Father Jalics was invited to the Vatican October 5th, 2013, to meet again with Bergoglio, his ex-Father Superior in the Jesuit Order. The Pope hoped to close this dark episode from his past, and give the media a completely different spin on the whole affair. A week later the Vatican media wrote how nice it was for the Pope to hug and meet Jalics, the old Jesuit who they said, *"Took some time to recognize publicly the good intentions of his Jesuit Superior at the time."* As a loyal Jesuit, Jalics released a further statement saying that, *"Orlando Iorio and he had not been denounced to the authorities by Bergoglio."* The Vatican media offensive was up and running, and *Avvenire,* the Vatican newspaper, gladly announced a new book by Nello Scavo, in which Pope Francis was suddenly addressed as a person who saved the lives of many during the Argentinian dictatorship. The book that was published by *Editrice Missionaria Italiana,* which of course belongs to the Catholic Church, is subtitled: *"La lista di Bergoglio. I salvati da Francesco durante la dittatura. La storia mai raccontata,"* and translates as: *"The list of Bergoglio. The ones that were saved by Bergoglio during the dictatorship."*

---

33   http://www.buenosairesherald.com/article/166728/a-grandmother-licha-and-her-granddaughter-ana-libertad ‡ Archived from the internet on August 16, 2014.

34   *Ibid.*

35   http://itccs.org/tag/pope-francis-the-first/ ‡ Archived from the internet on August 16, 2014.

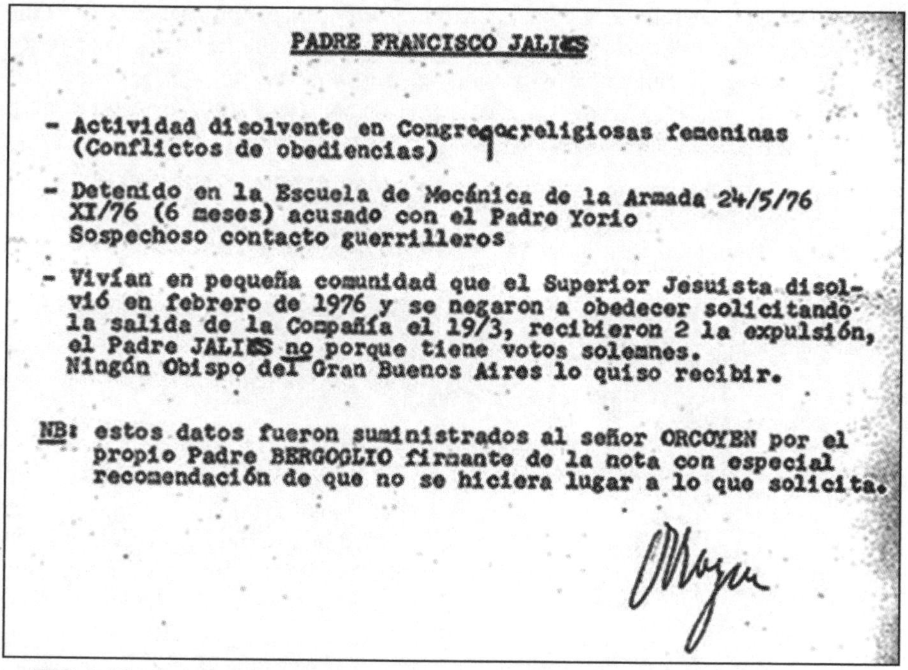

PADRE FRANCISCO JALICS

- Actividad disolvente en Congregacreligiosas femeninas (Conflictos de obediencias)

- Detenido en la Escuela de Mecánica de la Armada 24/5/76 XI/76 (6 meses) acusado con el Padre Yorio Sospechoso contacto guerrilleros

- Vivían en pequeña comunidad que el Superior Jesuista disolvió en febrero de 1976 y se negaron a obedecer solicitando la salida de la Compañía el 19/3, recibieron 2 la expulsión, el Padre JALICS no porque tiene votos solemnes. Ningún Obispo del Gran Buenos Aires lo quiso recibir.

NB: estos datos fueron suministrados al señor ORCOYEN por el propio Padre BERGOGLIO firmante de la nota con especial recomendación de que no se hiciera lugar a lo que solicita.

FIG. 9. The document found and published by journalist Horacio Verbitsky shows how Bergoglio had two priests accused of contacts with guerrillas. Source: http://www.pagina12.com.ar/diario/elpais/1-215961-2013-03-17.html ‡ Archived from the internet 15, July 2014.

The book includes a detailed account of the 3-hour, 50-minute interrogation of the then Archbishop Bergoglio of Buenos Aires, as given to the Argentinian Police in 2010, regarding the human rights violations during the dictatorship. There is also testimony by the Jesuit Juan Carlos Scannone, a very good friend of Bergoglio, who stated to the author that Bergoglio was responsible for creating a clandestine network during the dictatorship to save the persecuted.[36]

The majority of people in Argentina were not aware, but Father Scannone SJ cleverly stated that *in those days* it was very important that no one know what Bergoglio was doing to forward the success of such an operation. Adolfo Maria Perez Esquivel, who won the Argentinian Nobel Peace Prize in 1980, the day after the election of Pope Francis, stated that Bergoglio could not be considered in any way close to the dictatorship, and had nothing to do with the Yorio-Jalics case.[37] In the preface to Nello Salvo's book, Esquivel conve-

---

36   http://www.avvenire.it/chiesa/pagine/papa-incontra-padre-jalics-dittatura-videla. aspx ‡ Archived from the internet on August 16, 2014.

37   http://www.treccani.it/enciclopedia/francesco_(Enciclopedia_dei_Papi)/ ‡ Archived from the internet on August 16, 2014.

niently claimed that Bergoglio had helped a hundred people to escape from the dictatorship.[38] Unfortunately, the names of these people are not known (but I am sure the Vatican will find them soon). History is written by the winners, so let's hope, at least, that my work will provide a trace of truth for my readers.

In his book *The Island of Silence,* Horacio Verbitsky picked up the term *"Silence"* from the inscription on a sign placed at the arrival of a brainwashing facility built to hold the rebels of the Argentinian regime. The facility was *conveniently* based inside the "ex" mansion and resting place of a Cardinal, and was located on an island in the Paraná delta near the town of Tiger in Argentina. On the island, detainees were forced into a mysterious program of *"disintoxication and re-education."*

A SHORT BIO OF HORACIO VERBITSKY
Excerpted from Wikipedia

Born in 1942, Horacio Verbitsky is an Argentine left-wing investigative journalist and author with a past history as a leftist guerrilla (i.e. the Montoneros).[39] In the early 1990s, he reported on a series of corruption scandals in the administration of President Carlos Menem, which eventually led to the resignations or firings of many of Menem's ministers. In 1994, he reported on the confessions of naval officer Adolfo Scilingo, documenting torture and executions by the Argentine military during the 1976–83 Dirty War. His books on both the Menem administration and the Scilingo confessions became national bestsellers. He writes for the Argentine newspaper *Página/12* and heads the Center for Legal and Social Studies (CELS), an Argentine human-rights organization.

Early Life

Verbitsky was born in Buenos Aires, Argentina. Since 1960, he has earned national acclaim for his writings and political columns, focusing primarily in the unmasking of political corruption and the promotion of a free press, denouncing any government policies that may affect the constitutional rights of free speech to journalists and citizens. He has also become known under the nickname *el perro* or "the dog," for his determination in uncovering stories.

During the 1970s he was a member of Montoneros, a Peronist guerrilla organization that was engaged in terrorist activities in Argentina.

---

38   Eric Frattini, LA CIA IN VATICANO, (Milan: Sperling and Kupfer, 2014), p. 27 Original title: La Cia en el Vaticano), 2014.

39   http://en.wikipedia.org/wiki/Horacio_Verbitsky ‡ Archived from the internet on October 14, 2014.

Pope Francis: The Last Pope?

"Swiftgate" and "Milkgate"

In 1991, Verbitsky came to national attention when he reported in *Página/12* that U.S. Ambassador Terence Todman had complained to the Argentine government that Emir Yoma, a brother-in-law and advisor of president Carlos Menem, had asked for a bribe from the U.S. corporation **Swift Armour meatpacking.** The story soon became a national scandal known as "Swiftgate."

Verbitsky later played a role in reporting "Milkgate," a scandal in which Menem's private secretary Miguel Angel Vicco was linked to the sale of spoiled milk to a government agency, forcing his resignation. In 1992, Verbitsky published a compilation of the Menem administration's scandals titled *I Steal for the Crown*, a quip reportedly from Interior Minister Jose Luis Manzano. The book became a national bestseller. Menem was eventually forced to change half his cabinet in an attempt to regain the lost political credibility.

Verbitsky was approached on the subway in November 1994, by naval officer Adolfo Scilingo, who offered to discuss human rights abuses by the Argentine military during the 1976-83 Dirty War. During that time, Scilingo was stationed at the Navy Petty-Officers School of Mechanics (ESMA), the site of some of the worst violations. He met with Verbitsky for several taped sessions telling him *"We did terrible things there, worse than the Nazis."* Most notably, Scilingo admitted that the military had disposed of unwanted prisoners by throwing them naked, drugged, but still alive, from airplanes into the Atlantic Ocean.

Verbisky has written for the newspapers *El País* (Spain); *The Wall Street Journal* and *The New York Times* (USA). In 2004, his colleague Julio Nudler accused Verbitsky of defending the government after Verbitsky played down that *Página/12* refused to publish Nudler's corruption allegations against Alberto Fernández who was the chief of the cabinet of Néstor Kirchner.

He made news in March 2013, due to his critical book about Pope Francis' involvement with two priests who were tortured during the Dirty War. Others have denied this claim.

Because Verbitsky had the former president Carlos Menem impeached with corruption allegations, Verbitsky was criticized for judging similar allegations against the governments of Néstor Kirchner and Cristina Fernández de Kirchner, but not with the same critical attitude. Verbitsky admitted that he does not have the same critical attitude towards the Kirchner governments because he agrees largely with their politics.

Chapter: III
NWO AND THE ISLAMIC CRISIS OF THE VATICAN

THE TRANSFORMATION OF RATZINGER

A *brilliant mind can also change brilliantly,"* [1] declared Wolfgang Beinert, a former student and colleague of Joseph Ratzinger, and his successor to the Chairs of Dogmatic Theology and History of Dogma at Regensburg University. With this ironic statement, Beinert greeted the arrival of Pope Benedict XVI, a known advocate of globalist ideology, and, in turn, foreshadowed his decision to abdicate later, which explains fluctuating reports regarding the Pope's up and down relations with Ecclesiastical Freemasonry. A "brilliant mind" is an interesting choice of words, as Benedict XVI has proven to be a fragile navigator of the Church, and more sensitive to theology then to the organization of the "flock." He always appeared more comfortable among his books and his studies than being among the faithful. He always seemed fragile, which begs the question ... has his fragility made him a target for blackmail?

During the course of Ratzinger's pontificate, he completely changed his position on various matters, including the delicate issue of globalization and the New World Order, as I would now like to demonstrate. Writing, back in the year 2000, in the Italian newspaper *Avvenire*, Cardinal Joseph Ratzinger slammed the UN's proposals for a *"New World Order."* He targeted with spe-

1   Marco Politi, Joseph Ratzinger. Crisis of a Papacy (Rome: Laterza, Rome, 2013), p. 308.

cial criticism the UN's goal of depopulation. The Cardinal, Prefect of the Congregation for the Doctrine of the Faith, noted that the philosophy coming from the UN conferences and the Millennium Summit in those years was deplorable. Cardinal Ratzinger stated: *"proposals (and) strategies to reduce the number of guests at the table of humanity, so that the presumed happiness (we) have attained will not be affected.*" He criticized this philosophy specifically for *"not being concerned with the care of those who are no longer productive or who can no longer hope for a determined quality of life."* Cardinal Ratzinger also noted on that occasion, *"at the base of this New World Order,"* is the ideology of *"women's empowerment,"* which he erroneously sees as, *"the principal obstacles to (a woman's) fulfillment of family and maternity."* The cardinal advised that, *"At this stage of the development of the new image of the new world, Christians—and not just them, but they, even more than others—have the duty to protest."* [2] It seems the only thing he will not comprise are his views on faith, that remain similar to those he had when he was head of the Congregation for the Doctrine of the Faith. During the seven and a half years of his pontificate, Ratzinger never compromised his theology, navigating against the rocks of his Church that, in the aftermath of his abdication, he called *"spoiled."* Ratzinger, the cardinal who apparently did not want to become pope, became a Pope who repeatedly expressed his desire to withdraw, and who preferred to pray and oversee the power of the Church from behind the curtains. In the end, he did exactly what he wanted to do from the start: resign. He failed in his rendezvous with history. And, by lacking the skills of public leadership, he instead wound up involved in one crisis after another. He was seemingly incapable of leading the congregation throughout these difficult times, where there existed a dramatic economic situation complicated by a set of international equilibriums arranged by the New World Order.

On the geopolitical front, and contrary to the performance of John Paul II, Ratzinger exposed the limits of his ability. In his previous position during the pontificate of John Paul II, as even the BBC remarked after his election, he earned unflattering nicknames such as "The Pope's Enforcer" and "God's Rottweiler."[3] Before his ascension to the Papal throne, Ratzinger remained on the margins of public scrutiny, but was described by Michael Baigent (1948-2013), a well-known author of Freemasonry, as *"in effect the Vatican's 'Theologian in Chief,' and as such, responsible for much of the Church's policy. As one might expect from a high-ranking prelate and former theology professor Ratzinger is extremely clever, if not particularly imaginative. He is articulate, frequently even eloquent. His arguments are pointed, focused, lucid, consistent and within their own circumscribed frame of reference—ostensibly persuasive, even if*

---

2   http://www.ewtn.com/vnews/getstory.asp?number=7135 ‡ Archived from the internet August 15, 2014.

3   http://news.bbc.co.uk/2/hi/europe/4463397.stm ‡ Archived from the internet August 15, 2014.

Leo Lyon Zagami

they do involve elements of sophistry." [4]

Pushed by public criticism, Ratzinger attempted to make a transparent move to reshuffle IOR finances. Subsequently, he was blocked by Tarcisio Bertone, his own Secretary of State, and as a result, lost his *supposed* reform momentum. Why did Benedict XVI, usually so careful to measure out words and actions, consistent when condemning the excesses of capitalism, nihilism, and materialism, abandon his own friend, Ettore Gotti Tedeschi, who at the time was president of the Vatican bank? Was he actually working towards a more ethical and transparent IOR? Or, did he fall into the deception of the IOR's infamous board of directors?

What made Ratzinger change his opinion on such a heated topic like the New World Order? In the homily carried out during Christmas 2005, a few months after his election to the papal throne, Ratzinger suddenly gave an open invitation to embrace the *New World Order,* whose underlying ideology was born and developed in Protestant circles, and is blatantly anti-Christian. What happened to Ratzinger after his election to the See of Peter? Who or what caused him to radically change his ideas and push him to eventually "come down" from the Cross, and thus abandon the Christian model of total sacrifice generally required in his position as pope? To leave the Petrine ministry means, in fact, to *escape* from the example of Jesus, who has made the divine self-sacrifice, by offering his blood for the salvation of mankind.

As discussed in the chapter THE TRANSFORMATION OF RATZINGER, in the introduction to *New World Disorder,* by Michel Schooyans,[5] and released in Italy in the year 2000, the year of the Catholic Jubileum, Ratzinger's use of the term "globalist ideology" gives us a very different image of Ratzinger's views on the New World Order prior to his Pontificate, as did his statement against the UN that same year.

According to this interpretation, Benedict XVI's final acts could be viewed as cowardly. In the words of the Middle Age poet Dante, a *"great refusal"* was used by his predecessor Celestine V. This position is completely incompatible with the role of Vicar of Christ on Earth. We read in the Gospel of Mark (Mark 10: *42-45*):

> *42: But Jesus called them to Himself and said to them, 'You know that those who are considered rulers over the Gentiles rule over them, and the great ones exercise authority over them.' 43: Yet it shall not be so among you; but whoever desires to become great among you shall be your servant. 44: And whoever of you desires to be first shall be slave of all. 45: For even the Son of Man did*

---

4   Michael Baigent and Richard Leigh, THE INQUISITION, (London: Penguin Books. 2000). p. 248.

5   See. Schooyans Michel, Nuovo disordine mondiale, (Cinisello Balsamo, Milan: Edizioni San Paolo), 2000.

Pope Francis: The Last Pope?

not come to be served, but to serve, and to give His life, a ransom for many.[6]

Jesus established that his throne was a cross, and his crown was made of thorns. His Vicar should follow His example even at the cost of martyrdom. Arrogating to themselves a power against evil, and not just that of another temporal ruler. As we are reminded by the renowned Italian Catholic writer, Antonio Socci,[7] a *servus servorum Dei,*[8] the Pope should not be a "king 'or' chief." During his pontificate, Benedict XVI had many times repeated that the ministry of Peter is itself mysteriously linked to the sacrifice, and yet he decided to step down from that throne, *seemingly,* in a hurry.

The esteemed Catholic intellectual Enrico Maria Radaelli, a Professor of Philosophy and Director at the Department of Æsthetic Philosophy of International Science and Commonsense Association, who has always opposed the resignation of Ratzinger, wrote after Ratzinger's decision: "IT IS NOT YET TIME FOR A NEW POPE BECAUSE HE WILL BE AN ANTIPOPE," explaining that:

> The office held by a Pope is charged by which the sacrifice is his indestructible nature and absolute condition prior to all other considerations. ... The cross is the status of every Christian: Christ, is the crossroad between God and man, the Imago Dei,[9] from heaven, to represent God for men, and for men to represent God on earth; he is the exemplary model to all of his followers. There is not a follower of Christ, there is no "Christian" to which the cross can be lightened, nor removed: St. Paul for example, pleaded with the Lord three times to lift him from the torments, and Christ said, 'You my grace, are sufficient. My power is made perfect in (your) weakness.' (2 Cor 12, 9)

In addition, Radaelli brings an interesting insight into the fact that even in his day St. Peter tried to give up his position of responsibility. As you know, Peter is considered the first Pope:

> On the Appia Antica" (Author's Note: one of the main roads in Rome since antiquity), "at approximately the intersection with Via Ardeatina, at the time of the first persecution of Nero, the Acts of Peter, though apocryphal, tell us of a fugitive Peter. Frightened and terrified by the ferocity of Nero, who was unleashing his fire against the new sect of the Christians, fearing to lose his life, flees to Brindisi. From there he would embark to Israel so he then could go

6   https://www.biblegateway.com/verse/en/Mark ‡ Archived from the internet August 15, 2014.

7   http://www.antoniosocci.com/2013/03/wojtyla-e-ratzinger- consigliano-ai-cardinali-in-conclave-guardate-mi chelangelo/ ‡ Archived from the internet August 15, 2014.

8   *Servus servorum Dei* is Latin for "Servant of the servants of God" term used also by Pope John Paul I to describe what will be his brief papacy.

9   *Imago Dei* is Latin for "The Image of God."

to Jerusalem; he runs into Jesus walking in the opposite direction, towards the Urbe: 'Quo vadis, Domine?' 'Where are you going, Lord?' To his amazement Jesus says to him: 'I'll die in your place, Simon.'" (Note: he says Simon, not Peter.) "The fugitive is no longer worthy to bear the name he received from Christ. Cephas, Stone, Rock, 'the infallible certainty of the highest Truth.'[10]

The timid and very selfish human Simon certainly would have received a more complete understanding by the liberals around the world today inside and outside of the Church, as this act would be perceived as, 'for the good of the Church.' A gesture of great freedom and ardent courage, 'a prophetic gesture,' as even the most motivated secularists, now cry arrogantly. Simon himself, with this act, found himself naked with his ancient name. The fisherman, good for nothing, a man detached from the Cross at that point. You may wonder if the man has been untied, in some way, even by the Providence from above. This is what happens when a Pope (as well as any bishop), a cleric amongst many others, (the last of the faithful) flees from the place where Christ placed him to suffer, perhaps die. Yet, yes it happens that Christ must suffer too, perhaps even die, in his place. The fact is someone must go through that suffering. Someone must suffer so they can offer such suffering. Evil cannot be lost: evil, every evil, should be redeemed. It must be redeemed, not only, it must be collected and turned into the well it originally was, as with the advent of Christ. It should be elevated to the fullness of divine good, and divine good needs to be fueled. The evil of the world, as the Psalm says: 'The insults of those who insult you have fallen on me' (Ps 69, 10): Evil, the insult of the demons of hell—to the wonder of creation. The accomplished work of God the Father, the Son on the cross has taken everything on him, so that He has collected all the evil of the world and nailed it to himself. All Christ's faithful are left imbued with desire for love of dedication to participate in the crucifying fullness of his sacrifice. Even with the simple everyday life gestures. Trivial acts such as standing on an overcrowded public transport or standing in the cold and frost, to do something more than their duty. Not answering to an unjust attachment. Setting the table with love, even when at the end of the day, you are struggling with fatigue. Ready to rise instead, in the total offering of yourself with more and more heroic acts—being public or silent— always the most generous offer of yourself. Extreme obedience to the laws of God and his will. Crucifying yourself in every way as He, pierced by the nails of the same demonic insults, at any moment, and winning. Here we are not wondering about what might be the reasons for his withdrawal, and what and why of the reasons given—'I came to the certainty that my strength, advanced age, are no longer appropriate to exercise adequately the Petrine ministry.' Or, you can open the door to a more imaginative speculation. This leaves us to a fundamental point: Does this resignation constitute or does it

---

10   *Cephas* is Aramaic for "rock" and Peter stand for *Pietra*, meaning stone or rock.

Pope Francis: The Last Pope?

not constitute, an asset for the Church. That is, is it a morally weak point, or is it the only road to take for the remainder of the journey to evangelization and sanctification for the world. [11]

The questions raised by Radaelli are legitimate, and I am sure many Catholics will have the same reservations. Currently, author Antonio Socci's new book *"Non è Francesco" (It's Not Francis)*, published by Mondadori Editore in Italy in November 2014, is causing a real controversy as it brings into question the validity of Pope Francis' election. This is supported by the careful analysis of another book recently written by the Argentinian Pope's biographer, Elisabetta Piqué, entitled *"Francis Life and Revolution."* (On pages 39 and 40) Socci writes of Piqué's book, noting a small anecdote that reveals the violation of article 76 of the *Universi Dominici Gregis*, the Apostolic Constitution of the Catholic Church, promulgated by John Paul II in February, 1996.

Apparently, a cardinal deposited two votes instead of one, thus making the 5th attempt to elect Ratzinger's successor invalid. Finally, at the sixth Conclave of the elections, Pope Francis was elected, but a more in-depth investigation of the rules of the Apostolic Constitution, as noted by Socci, shows that they should have simply disregarded the vote from the cardinal, and not invalidate the whole election. Additionally, the *Universi Dominici Gregis* does not permit more than four election attempts in one day; two in the morning, and two in the afternoon (Article 63). So why did they attempt a fifth vote that day, thereby violating the rules of their own Constitution?

The answer was simple for Socci, as it is for me. They didn't really elect a new Pope, only an acting one, who is without the legitimacy of their own Constitution. Beyond any reasonable speculation, the real Pope is still Ratzinger. He is the only Pope elected *in a regular way* after the creation of the *Universi Dominici Gregis*. Such statements might come as a surprise to some, but they are carefully documented in Socci's book, a book that has been banned from all Catholic libraries in Italy. This is something they did earlier with my own books. It shows how afraid many powers inside the Vatican are of the truth, the truth that the *transformation of Ratzinger* is just another charade.

THE CRISIS

After only four years into his papacy, Ratzinger had experienced *"... the failure of the decisions he imagined profitable. Touching with his own hand with ineffectiveness, those in the Curia who should have supported him. Assisting helplessly to a revolt that was propagated thanks to the media. And most bitter of all, he had to open his eyes on the radical breaking point emerging in the Catholic world in respect to is own linear thought,"* writes Marco Politi in *Joseph Ratzinger: Crisis of a*

---

11   http://www.unavox.it/ArtDiversi/DIV422_EMR_Ritirare_dimissioni.html
      ‡ Archived from the internet August 15, 2014.

Papacy. [12] Yet, the pedophilia scandal had not yet erupted in its fullness, and the Vatileaks case was just beginning. It was the beginning of an irreversible crisis that led him to realize how dramatic the situation really was, as he was becoming the scapegoat for the more twisted fringe of the clergy. In fact, instead of being protected by the Curia, Benedict XVI found himself in the paradoxical position of repeatedly exposing himself to defend his own prelates. The then Secretary of State, Tarcisio Bertone, was accused by many for his inability to manage the "curial machine," because of his "traditional" and non-public spirit, being firm and uncompromising in matters of doctrine, and too cultured for the mass of believers. He appeared far too distant for the average Catholic believer. He was called *"A professor with his head in the clouds,"* by the Italian journalist, and CIA long-time collaborator, Giuliano Ferrara. [13] The image of Ratzinger had been repeatedly exploited and attacked from all sides, relegating him to the role of lonely and misunderstood. The dead end Ratzinger found himself in before resigning is partly due to having naively believed, at the beginning of his pontificate, that he would be able to preserve within himself the mission to theologically, and lead and inspire the faithful. He delegated instead to Bertone and his collaborators from the "Gay Lobby," plus those aligned to Ecclesiastical Freemasonry, the bureaucratic arm of the Church.

Ideally, the community of the faithful should have a strong leader. A leader open to modernity, without betraying the Christian message, or the one proposed by the NWO. He should be sensitive to the changes going on in society, without betraying Catholic morality. Most times Ratzinger found himself in the eye of the storm, displeasing everyone from Muslims, to the Jewish community, to the Catholic world, and including the development and negotiations with the pre-conciliar Lefebvrians. The world was shocked by the excommunication removal of the Holocaust-denying bishop Richard Williamson. Scientists were disappointed by his statements on the condom while traveling in Africa. The faithful became frustrated by the never ending pedophilia scandal. Ratzinger has, in fact, handed over to his successor Pope Francis, a Church-victim of immobilism and disorder. A Church that is *"tired,"* as the former Archbishop of Milan, the already cited Jesuit Carlo Maria Martini, a dear friend and some say even a mentor to Bergoglio, stated a few days before Martini's death. Martini asked the Church publicly, in what would become his last interview, to change their position that, in his eyes, was *"200 years behind."* This sort of spiritual testament made by Cardinal Martini was put together by the Jesuit Father George Sporschill and Federica Radice, and was read and approved by the Cardinal who approved it for public distribution. When during the interview they asked Martini, *What tools are recommended against the fatigue of the Church?* He replied:

12   *Ibid.*

13   http://it.wikipedia.org/wiki/Giuliano_Ferrara ‡ Archived from the internet March 6, 2014.

Pope Francis: The Last Pope?

I strongly recommend three. The first is conversion: the Church must recognize their mistakes and must follow a path of radical change, starting with the Pope and the bishops. The scandals of pedophilia push us to embark on a journey of conversion. The questions on sexuality and all issues involving the body are one example. These are important for everyone and sometimes maybe they are too important. We must ask ourselves if people still listen to the advice of the Church on sexual matters. Is the Church still an authority in this field of reference, or is it only a caricature in the media? The second is the Word of God. The Second Vatican Council returning to the Bible of the Catholics.

Only those who feel in his heart that Word, may be part of those who help the renewal of the Church and will answer personal questions with a right choice. The Word of God is simple and is your hearts companion. ... Neither the clergy nor the right Church can replace the interiority of amen. All external rules, laws, dogmas, there is no data to clarify the inner voice and the discernment of spirits. What are the sacraments? These are the third instruments of healing. The sacraments are not one tool for discipline, but an aid to men in the moments of the journey and weaknesses of life. Do we bring the sacraments to the people that need renewed power? I think of all the divorced and remarried couples, families enlarged. These need special protection. The Church supports the indissolubility of marriage. It is grace when a marriage and a family go well. The attitude we take toward extended families will determine the approach of the Church to a generation of children. A woman was abandoned by her husband and finds a new partner that takes care of her and her three children. The second love fails. If this family is discriminated, is cut off not only the mother but also her children. If parents feel outside the Church or do not feel the support, the Church will lose the next generation. Before Communion we pray: 'Lord I am not worthy.' We know we are not worthy. ... Love is grace. Love is a gift. The question of whether the divorced can go to Communion should be reversed. How can the Church help, with the power of the sacraments, those who have complex family situations?[14]

The already cited Marco Politi, who often appears in the media, especially on Christiane Amanpour's CNN show, and is one of the most established Vatican experts, foreseeing the possibility of papal abdication, wrote in 2012: *"The result today (that worries the world of Italian Catholicism and those loyal to the institution around the world), is the image of chaos that the Vatican is spreading with this absence of leadership. While the Pope gradually and systematically withdrew from direct contact with the papal legates and bishops (because of his fatigue he sees them only collectively), the Secretary of State was becoming increasingly centralized and intolerant of positions that differ from his own. So far as to demand that the Cardinals have to go through him if they want to talk to the pontiff."*

---

14   http://www.wir-sind-kirche.de ‡ Archived from the internet August 16, 2014.

Leo Lyon Zagami

Marco Politi concluded:

> The key of the underground conflicts deflagrated in the dissemination of secret documents. He finds himself in the intertwining of money and power. Always to reappear, the figure of Cardinal Bertone in a clash with Cardinal Tettamanzi for the presidency of the Toniolo Institute. For the ousting of Msgr. Viganò. In the conflicts with Cardinal Nicora for the transparency of the IOR. In the secretive clash with Gotti Tedeschi for the adventurous maneuvers around the San Raffaele. [15]

From all these scandals emerges an image of a disfigured Church from Ratzinger's era. A victim of different personalities, and a cradle of apostasy, as Ratzinger himself finally had to admit with his resignation in February 2013, thereby raising the curtain on a bleak landscape made of intrigue, betrayal, and poison. It is as if the leadership of Ratzinger had reached a dead end no longer being able to continue with his ministry. On the one hand the intention to "clean up" the Church from within, on the other the inability to implement his plan due to internal clashes and terrible compromises. In the case of Vatileaks, among other sources, the bureaucratic mess and external pressures revealed the fragility of man and his limits. Ratzinger was more inclined to dominate in the realms of theology and internal politics, than those of public leadership and geopolitics. We may also assume, from the statements he made during his pontificate, that he gradually fell into wicked compromise with various powerful groups. Mainly Ecclesiastical Freemasonry, British Freemasonry, Zionism, and the malevolent proponents of the New World Order, active in the Church since the 1950's, that gave birth to the Second Vatican Council.

Yet it appears that Ratzinger was well aware of what was waiting for him when he became Pope, and he never made a secret about it. Consider the invocation addressed to the faithful with whom he began his pontificate: *"Do not leave me alone, pray for me, that I may not flee for fear of being before the wolves."* An unusual plea that resonates today as an eerie foreshadowing, especially related to an event without precedence in modern history, such as the abdication of the Pope. On the first anniversary of his pontificate, in a reiterated exhortation to the faithful, Benedict XVI, between-the-lines, seems to indicate that the dangers he had alluded to a year earlier may threaten to materialize: *"I ask everyone to continue to support me, praying to God to grant me to be a gentle and firm Pastor of His Church."* If we also read the previous statements of Benedict XVI, when he was still *"The Grand Inquisitor"* of the Holy Office, we will notice how he has

15   The *San Raffaele Hospital* mentioned at the end of Marco Politi's article taken from site: http://www.nicodemo.net/NN/giornali_pop. asp? ID = 1763 ‡ Archived from the internet June 6, 2014, *is one the most famous catholic hospitals in Italy and is based in Milan and has been involved in a colossal money scandal in the last few years.*

never hidden his concern for the health of the Church and its destiny. In the Via Crucis of 2005, a few days before the death of John Paul II, the then Cardinal Ratzinger had strongly denounced, live on TV, the *"filth in the Church."*

This was neither the first nor the last speech he gave against the profound crisis in the Institution of the Church that he was trying to save from total disgrace. On March 19, 2010, in the middle of the pedophilia scandal, we find one of the bravest documents of his papacy. It is an open letter to the Catholics of Ireland. Benedict XVI confesses the serious sins that have for decades consumed the Irish Catholic community. He assumed full responsibility for the crimes committed by his clergy: *"In the name (of the Church) I express shame and remorse."* Ratzinger had already recognized and blamed his pedophile priests in 2008, confessing to journalists present during his flight to the United States his utmost contempt. *"I am ashamed,"* he said. With his open letter to the Irish Catholics his *mea culpa* was symbolically routed to all Catholics, and all those who have been victim to the horrors of the clergy, not just the faithful in Ireland. Of course, this was not enough to stop his inevitable decline and shocking choice of escape from his own responsibilities. Especially when such responsibilities were not only moral, or strictly religious, but also criminal, as in the pedophilia cases, as many victims are gradually moving towards the idea of refusing any compromise, and instead legally challenging the monsters who ruined their lives. In the long run Ratzinger, as well as Bertone, may have been referring to key people in the Vatican responsible for the many criminal acts against poor innocents, which continued for so many years.

Tolerated and covered-up by Church officials such as Ratzinger, who, in his previous role, should have been a true *"Grand Inquisitor,"* so as to send them all to the stake (or at least to jail), as the Holy Office did in the old days. Instead Ratzinger, who some say was blackmailed over his own gay sex secrets, continued tolerating the many satanists who practice pedophilia in the clergy, until it was too late, even for him, and he was forced to leave.

The link between satanism and pedophilia has been confirmed by the studies of Dr. Tonino Cantelmi, a well-known Italian psychiatrist who is also the president of the highly influential Association of Italian Catholic Psychologists and Psychiatrists, known by the acronym AIPPC, which is of course endorsed by the Vatican. Such studies were made public in a book he co-wrote with Dr. Cristina Cacace, a clinical psychologist, called *Il Libro Nero del Aatanismo,* or "The Black Book on Satanism," published in 2007 by the main Vatican publisher *Edizioni San Paolo.* In this book the two academics write: *"The relation between satanism and pedophilia has been proven again and again. Various journalist investigations and centers for the protection of the infancy, have launched the message that more often then we like to believe, the prostitution of minors and pedophilia are managed by Satanic sects."* The two authors dedicate a whole

Leo Lyon Zagami

chapter to the subject.[16] The link has also been proven on a scientific level in the Catholic world, and I will, in other publications, provide proof that there are Satanic sects operating in the Vatican. It is clear that the Church is partially controlled by a bunch of Satanists. This is not a religious statement, but a clinical and factual one.

THE VATICAN AND THE INVASIVE PRESENCE OF ISLAM

Considering the evidence I have shown on Ratzinger's pontificate failures, it is natural to wonder what then happened to the intransigent *"Guardian of the Faith,"* who initially, after his arrival on the Throne of St. Peter, began a traditionalist battle in defense of Christianity. That which brought him numerous attacks by the press around the world, beginning with the Islamic protest of September 2006, after he was apparently misunderstood during his now famous address at the University of Regensburg. In that key moment in history, Benedict quoted Manuel II Palaeologus (1350-1425), soldier, statesman, and Byzantine emperor:

> *In the seventh conversation edited by Professor Khoury, the emperor touches on the theme of the holy war. The emperor must have known that sura 2, 256 reads: 'There is no compulsion in religion.' According to the experts, this is one of the suras of the early period, when Mohammed was still powerless and under threat. But naturally the emperor also knew the instructions, developed later and recorded in the Qur'an, concerning holy war. Without descending to details, such as the difference in treatment accorded to those who have the 'Book' and the 'infidels,' he addresses his interlocutor with a startling brusqueness, a brusqueness that we find unacceptable, on the central question about the relationship between religion and violence in general, saying: 'Show me just what Mohammed brought that was new, and there you will find things only evil and inhuman, such as his command to spread by the sword the faith he preached.' The emperor, after having expressed himself so forcefully, goes on to explain in detail the reasons why spreading the faith through violence is something unreasonable. Violence is incompatible with the nature of God and the nature of the soul. 'God,' he says, 'is not pleased by blood—and not acting reasonably is contrary to God's nature. Faith is born of the soul, not the body. Whoever would lead someone to faith needs the ability to speak well and to reason properly, without violence and threats.' ... To convince a reasonable soul, one does not need a strong arm, or weapons of any kind, or any other means of threatening a person with death.*

The contested phrase, quoted by Benedict XVI on the occasion, was specifically this: *"Show me just what Mohammed brought that was new, and there you will find things only evil and inhuman, such as his command to spread by the*

---

16   Tonino Cantelmi, Cristina Cacace, Il libro nero del Satanismo, (Cinisello Balsamo, Milan: Edizioni San Paolo, 2007), pp. 146-155.

sword the faith he preached."[17]

After Ratzinger became *Pope Emeritus,* my friend Alberto Roccatanno wrote the following for the Italian edition of *Nexus* magazine: *"Is his renunciation to the office of Bishop of Rome indicating a severe problem existing in the high ranks of the church on the relationship between Islam and Christianity?"*[18] Previously, in November 2010, Alberto wrote a short essay in *Nexus* entitled *"But what is this crisis?"*[19] He provides a very detailed analysis on the crisis and the improbable connivance of the Catholic world with Islam. He spoke of the influential role of the Jesuit Father Thomas Michel, who was Secretary of the Federation of Asian Bishops' Conferences from 1981-1994, and the disbelief of the findings by Magdi Allam, who is a well-known journalist and political figure. Allam was shocked when he learned that on the site *www.islam-online.net* that belongs to the firebrand Islamic preacher Youssef Qaradawi, Father Thomas Michel SJ had himself replied directly to the visitors of the website. Michel, known as one of the most influential contributors to the inter-religious dialogue conducted by John Paul II, according to the predetermined plan of the New World Order, had set a policy of reconciliation and openness with the Islamic faith. In 2008, after retiring as Secretary of Interreligious Affairs for the Jesuits, this led him to move to Ankara, Turkey, where some say he lives as a full-time Muslim. Here are some of the words written in the article of Magdi Allam cited by Roccatano:

> *I was stunned to discover that on the site www.islam-online.net, linked to the Islamic hate preacher Youssef Qaradawi, was the reply, on Tuesday evening, directly to visitors of the Jesuit Father Thomas Michel. He was for thirteen years head of the Islamic Office for Interreligious Dialogue in the Vatican.*

The shock was reading his total condemnation of Pope Benedict XVI: *"We Christians must apologize to Muslims."* Magdi Allamm could not understand how such a statement from a key man of the Jesuits and the Vatican could be making such remarks. He replied with anger in the article, *"What does a Catholic priest of this stature have to do with someone like Qaradawi, who preaches the defeat and annihilation of Christianity and Western civilization, the destruction of Israel and the eternal punishment of the Jews, praising as legitimate Palestinian suicide terrorism and attacks against Westerners in Iraq and Afghanistan? Yet from the responses by Father Michel filters the anxiety to please the disciples of Qaradawi."* [20]

---

17   http://en.wikipedia.org/wiki/Regensburg_lecture ‡ Archived from the internet June 6, 2014.

18   http://www.nexusedizioni.it/attualita/caro-papa-non-dimetterti/ ‡ Archived from the internet June 6, 2014.

19   http://old.nexusedizioni.it/apri/Argomenti/Riflessioni/Ma-cos- and-this-Crisis -- Alberto-of-Roccatano/ ‡ Archived from the internet June 6, 2014.

20   http://www.corriere.it/Primo_Piano/Editoriali/2006/09_Settembre/28/occidente.shtml/ ‡ Archived from internet August 15, 2014.

Leo Lyon Zagami

FIG. 10. *Magdi Allam photographed on the night of his high profile conversion to Roman Catholicism from Islam that took place during the Easter Vigil on March 22, 2008 in a service presided over by Pope Benedict XVI. Photo taken from the website of the newspaper: IL GIORNALE: http://www.ilgiornale.it/news/interni/bersani-ora-basta-899699.html/ ‡ Archived from the internet September 2, 2014.*

MAGDI ALLAM THE CATHOLIC REPENT

In 2013, five years after having received a high-profile baptism in St. Peter's Cathedral directly by Benedict XVI, Magdi Allam decided, now in the era of Pope Francis, to leave the Catholic Church. A curious change of heart, considering it was Magdi Allam himself who hyped-up his conversion from Islam to Catholicism, as he is a well-known public figure in Italy. In his eyes, they seemed too weak against Islam, or maybe, like the Jesuit Thomas Michel, they had secretly become Muslim. What he wrote this time from the pages of Berlusconi's newspaper *Il Giornale* is what has become a well-known article in certain circles due to its heavy condemnation of the Church. I have decided to insert the most controversial part in order to help Americans understand what's really going on with the Islamic agenda in Vatican:

> *The Papal idolatry that has inflamed the euphoria for Pope Francis and has quickly archived Pope Benedict XVI, was just the straw that broke the camel's back of an overall framework of uncertainties and doubts about the Church, which I have already described correctly and frankly in my 'Thank you Jesus' in 2008 and 'Free Christian Europe' in 2009. It was Benedict XVI who denounced 'the dictatorship of relativism' and who attracted and fascinated me. The truth is that the Church is physiologically relativist, being at the same time a universal magisterium and secular state. It has meant that the Church has always welcomed in her bosom a multitude of communities, congregations, ideologies and material interests that result in putting together everything and the opposite of everything. The Church is physiologically globalist relying on the communion of Catholics around the world, as is clear from the Conclave. This means that the Church takes positions ideologically contrary to the nation as an identity and to preserve civilization, preaching in fact the overcoming of national borders.*

Pope Francis: The Last Pope?

1. (C) Summary. Pope Benedict XVI's September 12 speech in Regensburg caused an unwanted firestorm in the Islamic world because of the pope's quoting, in passing, an insulting reference made by a 14th-century Byzantine emperor. The Holy See, and the pope himself, responded with statements of clarification and regret in the ensuing days. While the pope surely did not intend such an outcome, his own approach toward
Islam and toward interreligious dialogue is cooler than that of
his predecessor. Post expects further papal comments on the matter on September 20, unless the controversy has died down by
then, and will report further in the coming days. End summary.

2. (C) During his recent visit to Germany, Pope Benedict XVI gave a lecture to a gathering of academics on September 12 at
the University of Regensburg. The lecture, entitled "Faith, Reason and the University: Memories and Reflections", fairly long at roughly 3800 words, was of a learned sort, and focused

*FIG. 11. First page of a previously classified 14 page document put together by CIA section in Rome under the direction of Anna M. Borg sent to former U.S. Secretary of State **Condoleezza Rice** on the 18th of September 2006, from the U.S. Embassy in the Vatican regarding the international crisis that took place after Ratzinger's speech at the University of Regensburg.*

1. (C) Summary: Iraqi Ambassador to the Holy See Yelda, sees
severe consequences to western interests should radical Shia and
Sunni factions ever put aside their differences and unite.
Yelda, an Assyrian Christian, counseled the U.S. to take steps
now to combat this possibility by portraying Iran as an
anti-Arab Shia State bent on domination over Arab nations.
Yelda said radical Islamic elements were recruiting
western-looking women from Albania and Bosnia for nearly
undetectable suicide missions in western nations and how efforts
to recruit Arabic speakers by U.S.G. agencies were being
exploited to infiltrate those agencies. Yelda, whose
information sources are unclear, also discussed the presence of
an active former regime network within Iraq's MFA.

An Unified Islamic Front Cannot Be Permitted
----

2. (C) Iraqi Ambassador to the Holy See Albert Yelda warned
PolOffs in an August 28 meeting that the U.S. must take whatever
steps are necessary to prevent the formation of a unified
Islamic force throughout the world or we would all "suffer the
consequences". Yelda stated that the coalescing of radical
Sunni and Shia factions would be disastrous for the West,
leading to an onslaught of world-wide terrorism. While moderate
Shia and Sunni factions can cooperate without adverse
consequences, Yelda counseled that the U.S. needs to take
affirmative steps now to prevent the reality of a unified
radical Sunni and Shiite coalition.

3. (C) The key to keeping radical Shia and Sunni forces from
coalescing under a United Islamic Front said Yelda, is to
isolate Iran from the Arab States and to never permit Iran to
take a leadership role in the Islamic world. One way of

FIG. 12. First page of a previously classified top secret U.S. intelligence document regarding the threat of a unified Islam, denounced by the Iraq Ambassador at the Holy See Albert Ismail Yelda, previously responsible for saving the Vatican from a Islamic terrorist attack in October 2005. The informative was sent by the Roman section of the CIA in charge of the Vatican affairs on the 1st of September 2006.

Pope Francis: The Last Pope?

As a result, the Church is physiologically feel-good, putting on the same level, or putting the good of others before the good of the Church. Compromising the root of the concept of the common good. Finally, I note that the Church is physiologically tempted by evil, as with violation of public morality, since it requires behaviors that are in conflict with human nature. Behaviors such as priestly celibacy, abstaining from sexual relations outside of marriage, the indissolubility of marriage, in addition to the temptation of money. This more than any other factor drove me away from the Church's religious relativism. In particular its view on the legitimacy of Islam as a true religion, Allah as a true God, and Muhammad as a true prophet, the Quran as a sacred text and the mosques as a place of worship. It is genuine suicidal madness that John Paul II went so far as to kiss the Quran on May 14, 1999, followed by Benedict XVI who put his hand on the Quran, praying toward Mecca inside the Blue Mosque in Istanbul on November 30th, 2006, while Francis began exalting the Muslims 'who worship the one God, living and merciful.' I am convinced that, while respecting the Muslim as custodians, like all other people of their inalienable right to life, dignity and freedom. Islam is inherently a violent ideology, as it has been historically conflictual inside, and belligerent to its exterior. Even more so, I am increasingly convinced that Europe will eventually be submitted to Islam, as it has already happened from the Seventh Century on the other two sides of the Mediterranean. If the Church does have the vision and the courage to denounce the incompatibility of Islam with our civilization and the fundamental rights of the human being, then it will ban the Quran for its lack of apology for hatred, violence and death against non-Muslims. It will condemn the Sharia law as a crime against humanity, which preaches and practices the violation of the sanctity of all life, the equality of men and women and religious freedom. Finally, it does not block the spreading of mosques.

I am opposed to globalism that brings unconditional opening of all national borders on the basis of the principle that the whole of humanity must be conceived as brothers and sisters. The whole in its entirety should be conceived as a single land, at the disposal of all humanity. I am instead convinced, that the indigenous population has a reason to enjoy the right and the duty to preserve their culture and their heritage. I am opposed to the Church standing as ultimate protector for immigrants, including—especially—the illegal immigrants. I am for the reception of the rules. The first rule, is that in Italy, we must first ensure the good of the Italians, correctly applying the exhortation of Jesus' love your neighbor as you love yourself.

There have been some witnesses, those that make the claim that truth corresponds to the faith they believe in, and that this will result in the good works that they fulfill, to persuade me of the goodness, the charm, the beauty and strength of Christianity as the natural home of values. Values which are non-negotiable. The inseparable truths of reason and faith, truth and freedom, values and rules. And it is precisely at this moment, when all around me, the presence of authentic and credible witnesses is less and less, which is in parallel with the in-depth knowledge of the Catholic context of reference. My faith in the Church staggered.

I make this choice, in the suffering and in the inner-consciousness of disapproval that will generate in the home of Catholicism, because I feel a moral imperative to continue to be consistent with myself and with others in the name of the primacy of truth and freedom. I never resigned to lie and I was never subjected to fear. I will continue to believe in Jesus. I have always loved and proudly identify with Christianity, which as a civilization, more then any other, brings man closer to God. He who chose to become a man, and more than any other, embodied the essence of our common humanity. I will continue to defend the secular non-negotiable values, the sanctity of life, the centrality of the natural family, the dignity of the human person and freedom of religion. I will continue to move forward with my back straight and with my head up, contributing to the revival of values and the identity of the Italians. I will be a man of integrity within the total context of my humanity. [21]

What words of wisdom can I say about somebody, who I must confess, I was initially very skeptical about, especially after his sudden conversion to Catholicism? With his latest choice, he has demonstrated to be worthy of my respect, and hopefully yours as well.

CAUTION: ISLAM IS PRESENT AT THE TOP OF THE VATICAN HIERARCHY

Regarding this context of what we can define as the *"pro-Islamic Jesuitry,"* my close friend and journalist, Alberto Roccatano, told me he would one day like to ask Father Thomas Michel exactly what happened to the special vow of obedience he made to the Pope as a Jesuit? As some of you may know, after a certain period of service as priest, members of the Society of Jesus—*the Jesuits*—can be allowed to take a fourth vow of obedience to the pope with regard to the missions, like we saw Bergoglio do in the 1970's. The text of the vow is as follows:

I further promise a special obedience to the sovereign pontiff in regard to the missions, according to the same Apostolic Letters and the Constitutions. *(Constitutions S.J., N°527)*

The same text is being used today, just as it was in the days of Ignatius of Loyola. [22]

―――

21   http://www.ilgiornale.it/news/interni/bersani-ora-basta-899699.html ‡ Archived from the internet July 20, 2014.

22   http://en.wikipedia.org/wiki/Fourth_vow ‡ Archived from the internet August 30, 2014.

Pope Francis: The Last Pope?

FIG. 13. The Jesuit Father Thomas Michel, SJ along with Leo Zagami in Oslo, Norway in 2007.

In any case, I was able to witness this strange radical pro-Islamic stance from Father Michel when I personally met him in Oslo in 2007, thanks to the Gülen Movement. This is a dangerous and influential religious Islamic sect based primarily in Turkey, with schools and companies all over the world, which hides their real fundamentalist agenda behind a sort of moderate Islamic façade. They are controlled by the Turkish Muslim scholar Fethullah Gülen, born in Erzurum, Turkey, on April 27, 1941. Gülen is a philosopher and the author of over 60 books. Now based out of the USA, he has made his organization an important structure of the New World Order, and he is often used by the CIA, according to Nuri Gundes, a former Top Turkish intelligence official.

Jeff Stain wrote the following regarding the issue in *The Washington Post*, in an article called, *"Islamic Group is a CIA Front."* In the article the ex-Turkish Intel Chief states:

> *A memoir by a top former Turkish intelligence official claims that a world-wide moderate Islamic movement based in Pennsylvania has been providing cover for the CIA since the mid-1990s. The memoir, roughly rendered in English as 'Witness to Revolution and Near Anarchy,' by retired Turkish intelligence official Osman Nuri Gundes, says the religious-tolerance movement, led by an influential former Turkish imam by the name of Fethullah Gülen, has 600 schools and 4 million followers around the world. In the 1990s, Gundes alleges, the movement 'sheltered 130 CIA agents' at its schools in Kyrgyzstan and Uzbekistan alone, according to a report on his memoir Wednesday by the Paris-based Intelligence Online newsletter. The book has caused a sensation in Turkey since it was published last month. Gülen could not be reached for comment.*

Leo Lyon Zagami

Further on in the same article, Stein writes that Imam Gülen, *"whose views are usually close to U.S. policy,"* and *"according to Intelligence Online, favors toleration of all religions, putting his movement in direct competition with al-Qaeda and other radical groups for the affection of Muslims across Central Asia, the Middle East and even Europe and Africa, where it has also expanded its reach."* Gundes, who was Istanbul station chief for Turkey's MIT intelligence agency, and according to the newsletter's report in his memoir (which has not been translated into English) *"personally supervised several investigations into Gulen's movement in the 1990s."* The purpose of Gundes's investigation was not immediately clear. His own religious views could not be determined, but the influence of radical Islamist forces in Turkey swelled in the 1990s. The Imam left Turkey in 1998 and settled in Saylorsburg, PA, where the movement is now headquartered. According to *Intelligence Online*, he obtained a residence permit only in 2008, with the help of Fuller and George Fidas, described as head of the agency's outreach to universities.[23]

On February 9, 1998, Fethullah Gülen was received in the Vatican by Pope John Paul II.[24] The meeting was also attended by the Grand Master of the Sufi brotherhood Jerrahi Halveti, Gabriele Mandel Khan (1924 - 2010), who is a well-known member of the editorial staff of *Jesus*, the monthly magazine owned by *Edizioni San Paolo*, probably the most prestigious Roman Catholic publishing group. Mandel, of Italian-Turkish-Afghan descent, who I also knew personally, was a good guy at heart but was unfortunately used as an important pawn by the Jesuits in their geopolitical and religious strategies for the Middle East, much like other Muslim leaders. He was linked not only to Turkey and to Sufism at the highest levels, but also to the Vatican and Italian Freemasonry, where he was awarded an honorary 33rd degree of the *Ancient and Accepted Scottish Rite*. Gülen is not only a supporter of the Mondialist ideology, but, in the eyes of his allies, he is connected to this most influential Turkish businessmen. Even Bill Clinton mentioned and praised him publicly in 2008 with these words, *"You're contributing to the promotion of the ideals of tolerance and interfaith dialogue, inspired by Fethullah Gülen, and his transnational social movement. You do it through your everyday lives, and you are truly strengthening the fabric of our common humanity."*

Bill Clinton has not mentioned Gülen publicly again, but Gülenists would like us to believe that the prime motivating factor for Clinton's speech was a profound admiration for Fethullah Gülen's activities. Many have their doubts and believe the words in his speech were motivated mostly by the numerous contributions to Hillary Clinton's campaign made by the wealthy

---

23   http://voices.washingtonpost.com/spy-talk/2011/01/islamic_group_is_cia_front_ex-.html ‡ Archived from the internet August 30, 2014.

24   http://www.fethullahgulen.org/fethullah-gulens-life/dialogue-activities/meeting-with-the-pope-john-paul-ii ‡ Archived from the internet August 30, 2014.

businessmen of his movement.[25]

Gülen urges people to join without hesitation the *New World Order*. His 2006 book *"Toward a Global Civilization of Love & Tolerance,"*[26] whose preface is written by none other then Jesuit Thomas Michel, has a chapter unequivocally entitled, *"New World Order."* In an important speech he originally gave on the subject in 1995. Gülen writes, *"Everyone takes up the matter of a New World Order and evaluates it from a different point of view according to their own thoughts. This is quite natural."* Adding further on, *"Some of these developments follow a course based on religion. In relation to these it is possible to mention both organized and unorganized activities throughout various parts of the world. Unlike others they approach every matter from the principle that 'religion is basic.' Naturally they want to evaluate today's unsettled situation in line with their own way of thinking and manipulate and lead people to the position required by religion. In addition to this is the fact that the attempt by the powers which have exploited the world many times to take advantage of this period of restructuring seems normal from their own perspectives. Is there full agreement among these powers? Of course not. However it is widely believed that they are trying to come together and to reach an agreement as soon as possible. Britain does not think very differently on this matter from America."*[27]

But Gülen knows development of the New World Order is not going to be easy, so he gives a warning of sorts: *"There are some countries in which it is difficult to tell whether they are comfortable with the New World Order or not. It is quite difficult to understand the situation of these countries just as there are some diseases that are hard to diagnose. As a matter of fact they do not expect a share in the general advantages. In fact it is not obvious what they really want at the present time."*[28] Why does Gülen compare those countries that refuse the New Word Order to *"some diseases?"* He obviously feels he is a kind of doctor for the NWO—taking a very Jesuit approach, indeed. In December 2014, a Turkish court issued an arrest warrant for the influential cleric Fethullah Gülen, accusing him of leading an armed terrorist group, plotting to overthrow the Turkish government, and deposing he who once was his friend, now turned enemy, Recec Tayyip Erdogan.

"THE CONQUEST OF ROME"

What makes this unprecedented situation even more shocking with regards to the dangerous relations between Catholicism and Islam, was a statement made to me by a senior member on the board of Fethullah Gülen's movement, a close friend of Monsignor Luigi Padovese, Apostolic

---

25   http://turkishinvitations.weebly.com/why-bill-clinton-mentioned-gulen-at-the-tccny-dinner.html ‡ Archived from the internet August 30, 2014.

26   See. M. Fethullah Gülen, TOWARD A GLOBAL CIVILIZATION OF LOVE AND TOLERANCE, (New Jersey: Tughra Books, 2010).

27   *Ibid.* p. 251.

28   *Ibid.* p. 252.

Leo Lyon Zagami

Vicar of Anatolia, who died under mysterious circumstances in 2010. In a moment of extreme honesty during one of my visits to Turkey, he told me that Monsignor Padovese claimed that there were as many as 40 Vatican cardinals who had secretly converted to Islam and were secretly reciting the *Qur'an* in the Vatican. They all seem to like a particular text linked to Islamic belief. A text very dear to the Gülen movement, and in earlier times linked to the Risale-i Nur movement connected to Said Nursî (1877-1960), commonly known as Bediüzzaman, mostly known for his commentary on the *Qur'an* entitled the "Risale-i Nur Collection." The book in question, popular with both Sunni and Shi'a Muslims, is the *Jawshan Al Kabir*,[29] which means "the strong cuirass" (or breastplate). It is a supplication originally ascribed in a narration from Zayn Al-'Abidin, the son of Husayn, to his great-grandfather, the Prophet of Islam, Mohammed. Nursi who apparently recited the *"Jawshan regularly throughout his life, and as a source of reflective thought, said that in one respect, the Risale-i Nur had been born of it."*[30]

Some say it is a book of Islamic magic that Nursi used when, apparently, he killed Joseph Stalin with a psychic attack, and is considered the most powerful tool against the entities the Muslims call the *Jinn,* a subject I will go into depth about in the first volume of my *Confessions of an Illuminati* trilogy, as well as in the title *The Invisible Masters. All four books will soon be available in the English language thanks to the efforts of CCC Publishing.* Monsignor Padovese's shocking statements on the Vatican Curia and their Islamic practices began circulating in the alternative media on the internet, and I was one of the journalists responsible for the introduction of this material.

The powers that be in the Vatican and the various intelligence services certainly did not appreciate the divulgence of this terrible secret about the 40 cardinals that secretly converted to Islam, and who define themselves by using what are allegedly Padovese's own words: *"undercover converts to the faith of the Prophet Muhammad."*

Despite efforts by myself and other journalists to never mention his name, the poor priest was unfortunately killed in Iskenderun (Alexandretta), Turkey, by his driver, Murat Altun, who was later accused of having a mental disorder.[31] But the reality, of course, is very different. The driver, 26 years old at the time of the killing, replied at the end of the court process that he was, *"sorry for killing Msgr. Luigi,"* because *"he was the last person in my life who could harm me. But at that time I was not in control of myself."* It begs the question if Murat was not in control of himself, who was? He seems an ambiguous character,

29   See. Jawshan Al Kabir, English translation by Sukran Vahide, (Istanbul, Turkey, Sözler Publications, 2003).

30   *Ibidem* p.3

31   http://www.repubblica.it/esteri/2010/06/03/news/ucciso_monsignore-4543029/ ‡ Archived from the internet September 15, 2013.

and the light sentence he received for killing a priest, he will probably spend only six years in prison, is revealing. Many prelates and friends of Monsignor Padovese who had questions about Murat tried, in good faith, to learn more from the Turkish authorities, but their inquiries went nowhere. The disappointing trial of Mr. Murat has left many wondering,[32] especially considering Ali Agca, another *strange Turk* and the gunman who attempted to assassinate Pope Woytila. We have since become quite accustomed to handling the many lies of these killers *Made In Turkey* behind which lurk all the usual suspects. So, what are we to make of these revelations... disclosures made to me by a Gülen Movement senior activist?

FIG. 14. The Grand Master for Italy of the Sufi brotherhood Jerrahi-Halveti, Gabriele Mandel Khan (1924-2010) who was a psychologist, a writer, an artist, as well as a Freemason. Evidence of his membership is shown clearly in this image, present in a tribute article to his person that appeared in the Italian Masonic Magazine LA VOCE DELL'APPRENDISTA in November 2010.

The incredible news, if made public, could lead to an immediate schism in the Catholic Church. This at a time of weakness in the Church, when Islamic Prayers and readings from the *Qur'an* were apparently heard publicly inside the Vatican for the first time in history. In June 2014, it was said of Papa Bergoglio, *"Israeli and Palestinian presidents meet in an unprecedented prayer meeting with Pope Francis ... a gesture he hopes will 're-create a desire, a possibility' of eventu-*

---

32   http://vaticaninsider.lastampa.it/nel-mondo/dettaglio-articolo/articolo/turchia-turkey-turquia-21572/ ‡ Archived from the internet September 15, 2013.

ally relaunching the Middle East's stalled peace process."[33]

Instead, this functioned as a kick-start to the worst Middle East crisis in recent years. In the meantime, the Universal Church, a *nom de guerre* that can be traced back to 1958, continued forward with the ascension of Pope, and now St. John XXIII, who was the first Masonic Pope in history. The Muslim conversion of the 40 cardinals has been understood in secret by the leaders of Islam as well as senior Jesuits who are increasingly fascinated by Islam, as in the case of Father Thomas Michel.

It seems that Fethullah Gülen, while commenting on this unprecedented fact, even told his loyalists that *"the important thing is not to appear as Muslim converts for those who cannot show their real religious identity, but to actually be Muslim in their mind and in their actions."* Of course, as these words were reported by an inside confidential source, we cannot be certain. *However, if confirmed, it looks like a very Jesuit kind of view of this Vatican affair by Gülen.*

The Jesuits themselves seem to see these Muslim cardinals not as a threat or an intolerable heresy for the Church, but an added value during this time of impending Islamization of the West. I hope this information will make Pope Francis' position more evident for the reader, especially considering his unprecedented move during the second year of his Pontificate, where he not only allowed a Muslim cleric to pray in the Vatican, but allowed him to end his prayer with the phrase, *"Victory against the unbelievers."* Radio Vatican has disputed the fact that this was ever stated by the Imam, yet the historian and author Michael Hesemann confirms, on his Facebook page, the statements of the Imam, Hamed Abdel-Samad: *"The Muslims had 'cunningly deceived' the organizers, he writes. Apart from the harmless prayers which he submitted, the Imam began to quote from the second Sura of the Koran, in which Allah is implored to grant victory over the unbelievers. Hesemann explains Radio Vatican's disclaimer by the fact that no one there knows the Koran or speaks Arabic. The statements of the Imam are however documented in video footage and are verifiable. In conclusion, Hesemann expressed his thanks to those who had helped him in the disclosure and he hopes that this 'deceit' will contribute to seeing through Islam. When will our princes of the Church and the press finally face reality and regard Islam for what it is: A perfidious concoction of lies, deception and contempt for mankind in the garb of religion?"[34]*

Hesemann should be aware that some of the so-called *"Princes of the Church"* are probably traitors of their faith, as the growing Muslim infiltration of the Vatican hierarchy has only one final purpose—the conquest of Rome! This is why, in the summer of 2014, Abu Bakr al-Baghdadi, the self-proclaimed

---

33   http://nypost.com/2014/06/08/first-ever-jewish-muslim-christian-prayers-at-vatican/ ‡ Archived from the internet August 30, 2014.

34   http://gatesofvienna.net/2014/06/the-vatican-and-islamic-prayer/ ‡ Archived from the internet August 30, 2014.

Pope Francis: The Last Pope?

leader of the feared "Islamic State" (often known by its old name ISIS or ISIL) and stretching across Iraq and Syria, has vowed to lead the conquest of Rome, as he called on Muslims to join their Islamic State. He proclaimed, *"Rush O Muslims to your state. It is your state. Syria is not for Syrians and Iraq is not for Iraqis. The land is for the Muslims, all Muslims. This is my advice to you. If you hold to it you will conquer Rome and own the world, if Allah wills."*[35]

Believe it or not, at the time I heard this statement from Abu Bakr al-Baghdadi, it was already old news to me. Baghdadi had been implicated (with documented evidence) in the previously mentioned book of the Italian Masonic Grand Master Gioele Magaldi as being a member of the infamous *Hathor Penthalpa* Lodge, part of the transnational super lodges known as *Ur-Lodges*. I was reminded of the shocking words I heard years before, from another Sunni Muslim, a leader of the Gülen movement, Abdullah Aymaz, during a secret meeting he made with his disciples in Oslo stating, *"We Will Raise the Flag of Allah on the Vatican."*

It was also no surprise when news came through from more than one source that, contrary to general knowledge, the Turkish Secret Service was actively helping new ISIS recruits pass through Turkey. Turkey's 12th President, Erdogan, is also implicated by Magaldi as a member of *Hathor Penthalpa,* and, as of November 2014, ISIS is now in control of the coastal town of Derna and other Libyan cities from which the daily "invasion" of illegal Muslim immigrants continues into Italy and the rest of Europe. Illegal Muslim trafficking, a network using structured routes, seems unstoppable as they generate money for the mafia and the terrorist organizations involved, like ISIS. This scenario seem to fit perfectly into a secret plan by the New World Order called *The Coudenhove-Kalergi Plan,* that some in European right wing circles say was created for the systematic genocide of the people of Europe. This supposed plan was put together by an Austrian diplomat and known Illuminati member named Heinrich von Coudenhove-Kalergi (1894- 1972), with connections to the Byzantine family of the Kallergis, and who was the first proponent of a unified Europe back in the 1920's. For this reason, the Coudenhove-Kalergi European Prize is apparently awarded every two years to European leaders who have excelled in promoting what's beyond any political or religious ideology. It is actually a criminal plan that is becoming more evident every day. Among those awarded in recent times, for example, are Angela Merkel and Herman Van Rompuy, two of the top pawns in the Bilderberg Club.

The European political assets, those who are responsible for what can only be described as an "invasion," will ultimately be held accountable. Enza Ferreri, who is an Italian-born and London-based Philosophy graduate, prolific

---

35   http://www.telegraph.co.uk/news/worldnews/middleeast/syria/10939235/
      Rome-will-be-conquered-next-says-leader-of-Islamic-State.html ‡ Archived from
      the internet August 30, 2014.

Leo Lyon Zagami

author, and journalist for several Italian magazines and newspapers, including *Panorama*, *L'Espresso*, and *La Repubblica*, wrote about what we insist on calling, *"immigration,"* but should be actually called *"invasion,"* or even, *"ethnic cleansing."* Ferreri writes:

> *Invasion has three main meanings: a) the act of invading, especially the entrance of an armed force into a territory to conquer; b) a large-scale onset of something injurious or harmful, such as a disease; c) an intrusion or encroachment, an incursion by a large number of people or things into a place or sphere of activity. The latter is a perfectly apt description of what is happening in Western Europe. Even 'ethnic cleansing' could be used, since local populations are being replaced by different ethnic groups. London, for instance, is no longer a white-British-majority city, although mainstream media like the BBC and London's own paper, the Evening Standard, barely mention it, to say nothing of the city's mayor, Boris Johnson.[36]*

Here is the definition of ethnic cleansing from Wikipedia:

> *The official United Nations definition of ethnic cleansing is 'rendering an area ethnically homogeneous by using force or intimidation to remove from a given area persons of another ethnic or religious group.' ... Terry Martin has defined ethnic cleansing as 'the forcible removal of an ethnically defined population from a given territory' and as 'occupying the central part of a continuum between genocide on one end and nonviolent pressured ethnic emigration on the other end.' European native populations are being replaced because many locals, tired of being colonized, flee their countries, cities or neighborhoods.[37]*

If all this is not enough to break down Western civilization, there is the latest creation of the USA, Israel, and their friends in the oil rich Arab States, the previously mentioned **ISIS**. Such accusations don't come from your average conspiracy theorist, but instead from the official representative of the Melkite Greek **Catholic** Church in Rome, Father Mtanious Hadad, who is representing all the Eastern Church communities in the heart of Europe, as well as those in Iraq and Syria. His message in October, 2014, is strong and clear: *"ISIS is a monster created by USA, Israel and some Arab States. The objective is to take Bagdad and later bring down Assad."* This might be the initial plan, but these mercenaries of the NWO are aspiring for much more. In September 2014, the official spokesman for ISIS, Abu Nuhammed al-Adnani al-Shami, reiterated their interest in conquering Rome, stating during a 42 minute speech later published in the 4th issue of *DABIQ*, the official ISIS magazine: *"We will conquer Rome, break your crosses and we will enslave your women."* It is called

---

36   http://www.frontpagemag.com/2013/enza-ferreri/immigration-or-invasion/ ‡ Archived from the internet August 30, 2014.

37   http://en.wikipedia.org/wiki/Ethnic_cleansing ‡ Archived from the internet August 30, 2014.

"DABIQ" because this is the name of a town in northern Syria where ISIS believes Armageddon will begin. The magazine is published through their Al Hayat Media Center, and that follows the Islamic calendar. Maybe in a future edition they could tell us what they plan to do with the Vatican's *"Gay Lobby."* But that's another story we will cover later, as some priests seem to already be *in bed* with the enemy.

This looming threat is probably the reason why Pope Francis went to Turkey at the end of November 2014—in order to pay tribute to his Islamic brothers, and that includes his friend, Thomas Michel SJ. This trip defied previous warnings to Iraq's ambassador in the Vatican, Mr. Habeeb Al Sadr, who stated in September 2014, that there were strong indications of a more specific threat against Pope Francis by the so-called Islamic Caliphate.

THE ROSE-SHAPED CRYPT OF THE NWO NEO-TEMPLARS

There are forces operating within the Catholic institution that appear to be a tremendous betrayal, yet no one seems to want to stop them, perhaps because the stakes are too high and could jeopardize the very survival of the Church. If, one day, the Church is completely surrounded, it could cave in and embrace the so-called Islamic conversion, termed *"Chrislam."* This conversion has already begun, but before completion, there must be a final attempt to transform the Catholic Faith into a Universal Church for the New World Order. This Universal Church would be without a leader. To achieve this result, the divine nature of a pope must be completely distorted and minimized by a striking gesture, and that gesture began with *"the resignation,"* made in 2013, by Pope Benedict XVI. He would be the only pope in history that could retire with his whole staff intact. That is, perhaps, until 2019, in accordance with readying themselves for the final announcement of the establishment of the New World Order in 2020. The suggested timeline has more than a grain of truth upon which we should consider. The information was obtained directly from an inside source of some importance working at the Vatican. This timeline was articulated by Dr. Antonio Leonardo Montuoro, nicknamed, *"The Man of the Holy Spirit"* by the recently sainted Pope John Paul II. He was the right-hand man of the former Prefect Enrico Marinelli, whom the Polish pope called *"The General,"* and who for years acted as his head of personal security. Montuoro confirmed the potential destruction of the Vatican within the next few years, and for this reason they are creating an alternative site called *the Temple of the Work of the Holy Spirit*, currently under construction in Palestrina, a town near Rome. Palestrina is a sort of *Vatican 2,* set to be ready by 2019, and is intended to join into the Extraterritorial Rights afforded to Vatican City.

Leo Lyon Zagami

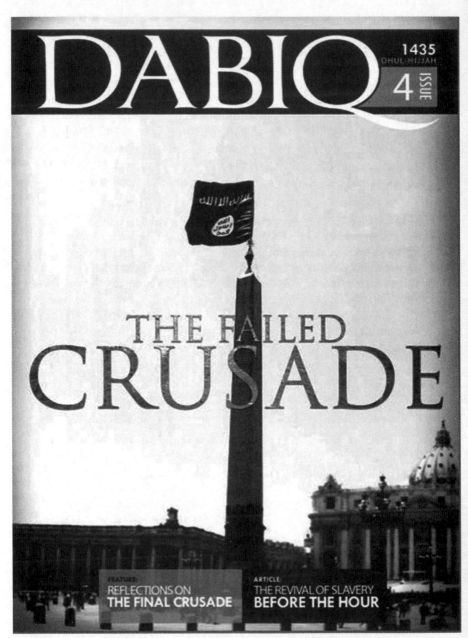

FIG. 15. *The cover of the 4th issue of* DABIQ, *published and distributed online by the self-declared Islamic State of Iraq and the Levant, is dedicated to The Conquest of Rome and discusses such comforting subjects as "The Final Crusade," and "The Revival of Slavery."*

FIG. 16. Pope Saint John Paul II on February 9, 1998 with Fethullah Gülen during their meeting. Photo take from: http://hizmetnews.com/5693/why-did-fethullah-gulen-visit-john-paul-ii/ ‡ Archived September 2, 2014.

The diocese where this temple is under construction is lead by another important figure of the contemporary Catholic scene, Bishop Sigalini, who runs the powerful Italian Catholic organization *Azione Cattolica*, a person I describe in depth in the third volume of my trilogy, *Confessions of an Illuminati,*[38] which also deals with the inter-religious work of the Neo-Templars in the Vatican. These individuals are linked in the past to John Paul II, who would obviously like to see all religions combined according to the infamous Jesuit-Masonic-Zionist NWO plan, in a temple common to all religions led by the Vatican, and dedicated to the Holy Spirit, to be inaugurated by 2019. If you visit the website created for the project, you can see the 3-D design of the Temple.[39]

The images speak for themselves: the circular shape of the Church not only has nothing remotely *"Christian"* about it, but strongly reminds us of the monumental megalithic sanctuary of Gobekli Tepe discovered in 1995 by German archaeologist professor Klaus Schmidt (1953-2014), and located approximately 6 km (4 mi) northeast of the town of Sanliurfa in Turkey, near the border with Syria.

---

38   *Le Confessioni di un illuminato Vol. III, Spionaggio, Templari e Satanismo all'ombra del Vaticano* originally published in Italy in November 2012 will be available in 2017 in the English language by CCC Publishing, San Francisco, CA.

39   www.spiritosanto.org ‡ Archived from the internet August 31, 2014.

The official dating of the Gobekli Tepe site goes back at least twelve thousand years, and such a discovery calls into question the expertise and the historical and archaeological knowledge of all the academic world that previously disregarded the place as a simple cemetery. Archaeologists have unearthed within the site the oldest example of a stone temple in the world, with estimates that place the construction around 9500 BC, and having required the work of hundreds of men over a period of three to five centuries. Without going too deep into the matter, we can not fail to notice the anomaly of such a architectural similarity between the *Temple of the Holy Spirit* and the Gobekli Tepe site.

According to the historical reconstruction of the ancient Turkish site by Venetian researcher Diego Marin:

> *The traditions of the groups (of initiated) tells us of the ancient meetings that took place 12,000 years ago in Urfa, in Turkey, where it has recently emerged an 'inexplicable' site of Gobekli Tepe. And yet they tell us of their meetings in the Sangam, the Indian academies destroyed by the waters of the flood. Even Atlantis and its inhabitants, the Pelasgians, were not strangers to their meetings.* [40]

It is difficult to find historical truth in the middle of all the various tales and legends transmitted through the ages. The sands of time have swallowed most relics of importance that could help us understand our true early history. Gobekli Tepe, however, has re-emerged fairly recently, and brought to light a period of history, and a civilization that we didn't previously know even existed. It leaves very little room for the conformist historical view and interpretation, usually manipulated to fit the *"official"* interpretation. Marin, however, informs me that the mysterious site of Gobekli Tepe, just outside of Sanliurfa, often pronounced simply as Urfa, is mentioned in the archives that belonged to Giacomo Rumor (1915-1990). Rumor was not only an important Italian politician who belonged to the Christian Democrat Party, and for this reason a Vatican loyalist, but he was also the cousin of five-time Italian Prime Minister Mariano Rumor. He was a person close to the *Azione Cattolica,* an organization that is now involved in the project for the construction of the Temple in Palestrina, along with their Assistant General Bishop, Domenico Sigalini. Marin writes:

> *The archive includes correspondence between Giacomo Rumor (cousin of the five-time Prime Minister Mariano Rumor) and the French Maurice Schumann, operating both in the committees convened by Roosevelt for the construction of the European Union. ... From what Paolo Rumor (the son of Giacomo) has transcribed in the book The Other in Europe it sug-*

40   Diego Marin, Il Segreto degli Illuminati, (Milan: Oscar Mondadori, 2013), pp. 13-14.

Pope Francis: The Last Pope?

gests the presence of an esoteric brotherhood that would design the birth and evolution of a supranational structure such as the UN and the EU. Rumor does not mention the name of the brotherhood, but stresses his ties with the major noble families of Europe, particularly with the Scottish family of Saint Clair (or Sinclair). Whether this is the All-Seeing Eye (Illuminati) is an easy and obvious conclusion. [41]

According to the archive of Rumor, this is the brotherhood that Marin presumes forms the original nucleus of the Order we now improperly call the *"Illuminati,"* and in possession of a document on its origins and traditions:

The document enclosed a list of personalities that became part of the structure in the last 2,500 years. It seems that in total there were 216 names, grouped in groups of 12, in turn gathered in units of 72. [42]

The archive of Giacomo Rumor, in fact, also contains the transcription of some archaeological findings, including a parchment discovered in the late nineteenth century in the synagogue of Nusaybin, near Urfa. The text of this parchment:

Refers to the three pyramids of Giza and some encryptions that you would find around there. ... Another passage speaks of the Flood, arguing that the term 'the long rains' was presented twice, at a distance of 'three thousand seasons' from one another, the first of which was in the age of Leo. The heavy rains have caused extensive flooding every time and the entrance of the sea inland. ... The document adds the description of various levels of coastal and geodetic points, highlighting six urban settlements of antediluvian foundation. Of these, five are listed as the first headquarters of the Brotherhood. [43]

So, in what we can now define as *"The Rumor document,"* there contains a list of names of affiliates of this Order, and even the meeting places or premises used by the Brotherhood throughout the various historical periods. Gobekli Tepe appears to be the first in order of time and in the area around Urfa, and is referred to as *the seat* in more recent times—around the fifth century BC. [44]

In light of this information, although not historically verifiable, the relationship between the architectural site of Gobekli Tepe and the project for the temple in Palestrina, which may become the new Vatican headquarters if the old is invaded or destroyed, is undeniable. This acquires another meaning, and allows me to assume that the design of the Temple of the Holy Spirit, if actually put together by the supporters of this New World Order, will reproduce the ancient headquarters of the Brotherhood—Gobekli Tepe. If it really

41   *Ibid.,* p. 73.
42   *Ibid.,* p. 82.
43   *Ibid.,* pp. 74-75.
44   *Ibid.,* p. 83.

was the primary site of a community that has been secretly passing down their initiated knowledge for thousands of years, this may be thanks to specific bloodlines within certain families, as Paolo Rumor, the son of Giacomo, points out. It would be 100% plausible that *The Temple of the Work of the Holy Spirit* in Palestrina could be largely inspired by the ancient temple design. It would not be so absurd if the Vatican Universal Church of the future global government reflected the original plan of the first post-diluvial seat of power of this mysterious Brotherhood.

As noted on the website *spiritosanto.org*, the cornerstones of the future Temple were placed, symbolically, on Pentecost Sunday, May 30, 1993 by the Pope of globalism himself, one Karol Wojtyla. The President of this important new facet of the Catholic Church, that includes various centers, and even an old folks home in Loreto, is the aforementioned Dr. Antonio Leonardo Montuoro, who founded it together with former Prefect Marinelli, who was, as mentioned earlier, the main person responsible for the safety of Pope Wojtyla. A new Knighthood order, *The Knights of the Temple of the Holy Spirit,* was born from the ashes of a pre-existing Neo-Templar Order, the Supremus Militaris Templi Hierosolimitani (*S.M.T.H.O.*/Ordine del Tempio). They are a mix between a Catholic Association of laymen working under the auspice of the *Azione Cattolica,* with Bishop Sigalini, and an order of chivalry operating under *"General"* Enrico Marinelli. This new reality was created in 2009 by Montuoro and Marinelli within the territory of the Vatican State to defend and promote the building of the Temple in Palestrina. The official headquarters are in Rome in a building owned by the Congregation for the Evangelization of Peoples (*Propaganda Fide*) and located in Via Venti Settembre, 98 / G. The Association may also refer to itself as the *"Order of The Knights of the Holy Spirit."* You can find a photo gallery on their website with very interesting images of their annual meetings, presided over by Montuoro and Enrico Marinelli.[45] There is even mention of a Mass conducted in 2012 in one of the main Churches in Rome, in memory of Cav. Rocco Zingaro. Marinelli's order, The Knights of the Temple of the Holy Spirit, however, originates from an external source, a Neo-Templar affiliation with the Portuguese nobility residing in Brazil, whose Italian representative was the above mentioned,Count Rocco Zingaro.

---

45   http: // www. cavalieritempiospiritosanto.it ‡ Archived from the internet August 31, 2014.

*FIG. 17. Photos of the stone temple found in the archaeological site of **Gobekli Tepe**. From http://maxlab.ca/research-projects-1/Gobekliphoto.jpg ‡ Archived from the internet June 6, 2014.*

FIG. 18. The ex-Vatican Prefect Dr. Enrico Marinelli and Pope Francis in May 2014. Photo from http://www.altomolise.net/notizie/attualita/4445/vaticano-enrico-marinelli-incontra-papa-francesco ‡ Archived from the internet December 31, 2014.

Leo Lyon Zagami

FIG. 19. Dr. Antonio Leonardo Montuoro, nicknamed "The Man of the Holy Spirit" by the recently sainted Pope John Paul II, and this book's author next to a model of the future Temple of the Holy Spirit.

Cav. Rocco Zingaro died in 2011 under circumstances that some of his friends and closest collaborators, including a character who I have spoken of previously, Luciano Sciandra of the Equestrian Order of the Holy Sepulcher, consider unclear, if not downright suspicious. Sciandra, who was also involved in running Zingaro's Templar order before the Marinelli-Montuoro takeover, speaks in particular of a phone call that he received from Zingaro a week before his death in which the Grand Preceptor of the Order of the Temple told him that he was in a life threatening situation and terrorized. A conversation in which he said: *"they want to kill me just like they did with Jacob De Molay."*

So who wanted to kill Rocco Zingaro and why? Most likely we will never reach a conclusive solution to this mystery. What is certain, however, is that on his death Dr. Montuoro, Marinelli and the Vatican inherited Zingaro's Neo-Templar lineage, namely that of S.M.T.H.O., of which Rocco Zingaro was the Grand Preceptor in Italy, and also found possession of a supposed *Holy Grail* (of dubious origin) as well as the ashes of the last Grand Master of the Knights Templars: Jacob de Molay, a relic of great importance, but also of great controversy if made public. According to Dr. Montuoro, who I met immediately following the death of Rocco Zingaro, these relicts have been

Pope Francis: The Last Pope?

secretly acknowledged as genuine by Peter Hans Kolvenbach, S.J., Superior General Emeritus of the Jesuits, and will be exhibited to the public only when *The Temple of the Work of the Holy Spirit* opens in Palestrina. This will happen in 2019, but Montuoro stated that nothing depends on him or Marinelli, but instead must be done following the Will of the Lord. This was indicated following their project in Palestrina, which may save the Church one day, and that is also in accordance with the visions of *Our Lady of Medjugorje*. One of the six visionaries who visited and stayed in Palestrina was invited personally by Montuoro. Due to the relic's exhibit, the Temple of Palestrina would assume a key role not only in the growing Neo-Templar organizations among the growing Marian Catholic movements, and within the future globalist religious plan set up by the New World Order, of which Zingaro was at least initially a strong supporter, as shown in a letter addressed to Pope Ratzinger after his election, and that I published in the third volume of my *Trilogy*.[46] It seems that in the end poor Rocco changed his mind on this controversial subject, and suggesting one more reason for his possible murder. The tradition dictates that the *Neo-Templars* who do not follow the Johannite faith were Catholics, especially those coming from the Brazilian lineage of the *Order of the Temple,* that originally arose from the Rosicrucian tradition present both inside and outside of Freemasonry, and mainly in the upper echelons of the various Masonic Rites thanks to the Jesuits. In the famous Ancient and Accepted Scottish Rite, for example, the teachings of the Rosicrucians are positioned in the 18th grade. *The Symbol of the Rose* is an important symbol for the initiated of a certain Christian mysticism. This is emphasized within the future structure of the Temple of the Holy Spirit, and verified in a video that shows a 3-D reconstruction of the crypt of the Temple, and still present on the internet.[47] The new Temple of Palestrina clearly shows that the structure evokes a rose with five petals, then joined by two larger petals and divided into three parts. As I have mentioned prior, the first stone was laid on May 30th by Pope John Paul II, a date considered by the ancient Romans to be within the dates of *the Feast of the Dead,* a period celebrated between the 11th of May and the 15th of July, and known also as the Festival of Roses, or *Rosalia*. This tradition is still present in some regions of Italy where the Sunday of Penticost is called the *"The Easter of Roses."* In Christian symbolism, the red rose was the symbol of the blood shed by Christ and the love of heaven, while the white rose was used instead as a symbol of death. The rose represents reality in the making and the manifestation of it. The rose in the West, and the lotus flower in the East, have the same meaning, that is, they represent the feminine side of creation. The great author and Freemason Rene Gué-

---

46   Leo Lyon Zagami, Confessioni di un Illuminato Vol. III, (IT ed.), p. 202.

47   The original site http://www.spiritosanto.org/media /movie/avi/video3d.avi is no longer active, but you can still view it on *YouTube*: http://www.youtube.com/ watch?v=FRkKPyzAJWM ‡ Archived from the internet August 31, 2014.

non (1886-1951), in his book *Symbols of Sacred Science*, wrote, "*In the myth of Adonis (whose name means 'the Lord'), our hero is hit to death by gritifo the wild boar, his spilled blood spreading on the ground giving rise to a flower that tradition identifies with as the rose.*"[48]

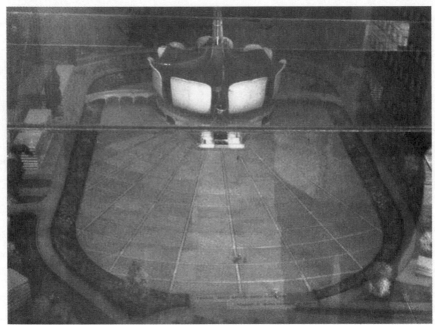

FIG. 20. A small-scale model of the future "Temple of the Holy Spirit."

The Greek myth corresponds symbolically to the death of Christ. That is, *Adonis the Lord* is brought to death by the spear of *Longinus*, but instead of the boar blood being collected in a cup, the Holy Grail, when it is dispersed on the ground the blood generates a flower. No coincidence here that when we speak of a "cup" it can be regarded as a flower. The symbolism used for this new Vatican project is pretty clear and obvious by the architectural design in place for Palestrina's future, the new *Temple of the Holy Spirit*. The Freemason author Guénon cites an article written by Louis Charbonneau Lassay (1871-1946), who writes, "*we see the blood of the wounds of the Crucifixion fall into droplets that turn into roses on the stained glass windows of the thirteenth century cathedral of Angers where the divine blood, flowing in streams, blossoms still under the form of roses.*"[49]

Guénon reminds us that the rose, like the lily, carries the same symbolic

48   René Guénon, Simboli della Scienza Sacra, (Milan: Adelphi, 1975, Original title: Symboles fondamentaux de la Science sacrée, 1962).

49   Article originally published in the French Catholic monthly magazine *Regnabit, Ibid.,* in René Guénon, *Simboli della Scienza Sacra,* p. 73.

meaning as the lotus in the East, each representing the passive or feminine principle of the manifestation as stated previously. Guénon explains the symbolism tied to the number of petals of the rose: *"It is represented with a variable number of petals, we'll just point out that the numbers five and six refer respectively to the 'microcosm' and the 'macrocosm,' moreover, in alchemical symbolism, the rose with five petals at the center of the cross represents the four elements, it is also ... the symbol of the quintessential, who plays on the other hand, relative to the bodily manifestation, a role similar to that of Prakriti."[50]*

The rose, due to its shape and its meaning, rejoins with the symbolic meanings of the spear, the pentacle, and the five-pointed star. The connection between the cross and the rose is the main symbol of *The Rose Cross Brotherhood,* referring to itself since its creation as, *"The Board of Wise Men,"* and which has the motto: *"Ad Rosam per Crucem; Ad Crucem per Rosam In eaeis gemmatus, resurgam Non Nobis, Non Nobis, Domine Sed nominis tui gloriae solae."* And in the second part of the motto you can clearly see the similarity with the Templar motto: *"Non nobis Domine, non nobis, sed nomini tuo da gloriam."*

The Rosicrucian philosophy has always been the true mystic side and the heart of Neo-Templarism and Freemasonry. These are the Neo-Templar Orders that are not particularly tied to the Occult, at least not in appearance. The Knighthood of Marinelli and his loyalists, as well as Montuoro, are experts in esotericism and magic of the highest level, together with the Jesuit controllers of the infamous Vatican Intelligence, that include both Montuoro and his boss Marinelli. The former Vatican prefect Marinelli, now Honorary President of the *Order of the Knights of the Temple of the Holy Spirit*, and Woytila, who I mentioned earlier, appeared to have a great friendship. We have Montuoro, Marinelli's right hand man, who was jokingly referred to by Woytila as, *"the man of the Holy Spirit,"* precisely because of this secret building project in the town of Palestrina. From the beginning he had the full approval of the Polish Pontiff. It would be interesting to see what Bergoglio thinks of this project. In any case, since their first official meeting at the Vatican in May 2014, Pope Francis and Marinelli have been getting along quite well, and they have a common friend in Father Alfredo Xuereb, the personal secretary of the Argentinian Pope. This means the project for the Temple in Palestrina, and the *Order of the Knights of the Temple of the Holy Spirit*, will continue in its present direction during the Pope Francis era.

In the third volume of my *Confessions* book I write the following observation:

> *The Neo-Templar Order of the Knights of the Temple of the Holy Spirit demonstrates now, without a shadow of doubt, that Neo-Templars of Jesuit origin are present at the top of the Vatican power structure. They have inherited in a*

---

50   La Theorie hidoue des cinq éléments *Ibid.,* in René Guénon, Simboli della Scienza Sacra, p. 75.

Leo Lyon Zagami

murky way the Holy Grail of poor Rocco Zingaro, who found himself despite all this, spending his last years in the old folks home defined officially as a 'Protected Residence' called 'Ave Maria Oasis' in Loreto, with the description 'Protected Residence.' It obviously says something more about the situation Rocco was in, then any other words. The CEO of the retirement home is the aforementioned Dr. Montuoro.[51]

Of course Palestrina is not the same as Palestine, occupied by Israel, but for the Vatican it is certainly closer and less dangerous for the time being, given that for many, including myself, Italy in the present stage is much closer to civil war and major unrest than you can imagine abroad. This includes the United States, where the population still has a romantic and euphoric view of Italy, typical of the postwar period and the so-called "Dolce Vita" made famous by Fellini's movies, but times have changed of course. Yet, in recent years, we are seeing disturbing signs of crisis from the Italian economy. By adopting the *Euro* currency, Italy has basically left their monetary sovereignty in the hands of the European Union. The country is now technically in the hands of the Germans, who seem to exercise total control over the fate of the so-called *"Euro Zone."* These troubling signals are also monitored very closely by the American Intelligence Agencies who are searching for new allies among the present-day political scene. I have found traces of this in a special report, sent by the American Embassy in Rome to the U.S. State Department in Washington, dated April, 2008. These are actually the minutes of a secret meeting between Beppe Grillo, a former comedian turned politician, the leader of a new political party also secretly tied to the Vatican and the Academy of the Illuminati in Rome, and the American ambassador at the time Ronald Spogli, who signs the report in question, a document entitled, *"NO HOPE FOR ITALY; AN OBSESSION WITH CORRUPTION,"* that has the protocol number C175860, and is part of a series of notes that American intelligence is analyzing not only for their new ally Beppe Grillo, but also for his new political entity called *"Movimento 5 Stelle."* The growing crisis that has involved Italy in recent years is a crisis that touches other Euro Zone countries, particularly those of southern Europe—the nations considered expendable by the Bilderberg Group—an organization originally co-founded by the Dutch Prince Bernhard, who was a member of the Nazi Party during World War II. He was specifically linked to the Northern European aristocracy in and around Germany, the country from which originated not only the infamous *Order of Illuminati* created by Adam Weishaupt, but also *The Order of Brothers of the German House of Saint Mary* in Jerusalem, commonly known as the *Teutonic Order*. This leads us to the black heart of the European aristocracy and their Royal Houses. Just think for a moment how the British royalty, probably the most powerful monarchy in the world, is now in the hands of the

51   Leo Lyon Zagami, Confessions of an Illuminati Vol. III (IT ed), *Ibid.*, p. 49.

Pope Francis: The Last Pope?

House of Windsor. In reality, the British Royal Family is the German House of Saxe-Coburg and Gotha, and prior to that, was in control by the German House of Hanover until Queen Victoria arranged a few strategic marriages with German royalty. In a few words, the elite of Germany, the heart of what was once called the Holy Roman Empire, has always ruled over Britain. Even if the Brits apparently can't stand the Germans, and waged war against Adolf Hitler, they still submit to them every day in a more subtle way by singing, *"God Save the Queen."*

A last note of interest regarding the Nazi connection and their sympathizers. I pose this question: Where do you think the most infamous German officers and other Nazi characters took refuge after their defeat? I'll give the answer: In Argentina, the home of Pope Bergoglio, whose flag is, among other things, similar to the symbol of the Jesuits. Both designs have a sun that radiates 32 solar rays with the same design pattern. All things considered, and knowing the colonial past of the Jesuits in South America, it's a little too close to be a coincidence, don't you think?

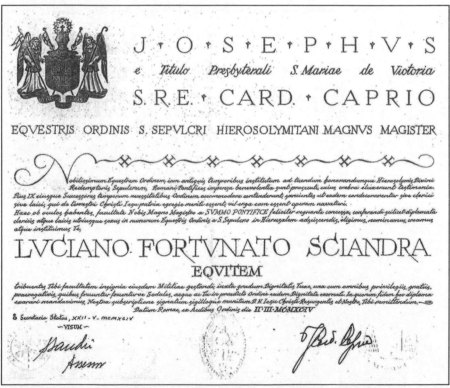

FIG. 21. *Diploma of appointment of Luciano Fortunato Sciandra to the Order of the Holy Sepulchre approved, sealed and signed by officials of the Vatican Secretariat of State and the Cardinal Grand Master of the Order in Rome.*

S. M. T. H. O.

Esimio Dott. LUCIANO FORTUNATO SCIANDRA
Vicolo di Casalotti, 19 C/D
00166 R O M A

Caro Luciano, ti ringrazio come al solito di esserti ricordato del povero
Cavaliere di Cristo, che oggi compie 67 anni con l'aiuto di DIO e della
Santa Vergine Maria Madre di Gesù.
Il mio Cavaliere errante Luciamo, oggi ha un compito ingrato , quello di
selezionare con oculatezza e coscienza, coloro che desiderano affiancarci
nel cammino periglioso di questo Mondo pieno di invidie e gelosie.

Dio onnipotente ed eterno ci darà la forza necessaria per continuare a
costruire il TEMPIO DI CRISTALLO come i nostri Padri.
La nostra coscienza e il nostro discernimento saranno il marchio indelebile
della nostra eterna Fede.

Benedetto XVI ci guarda, noi diciamo benedici questa nostra missione.
Abbi pietà di noi Padre Santo.

Un abbraccio

Il Maestro dei Templari
Rocco Zingaro di San Ferdinando

LORETO 29 Ottobre 2008
890* Fondazione Ordine

Gran Precettoria d'Italia -
www.web.cheapnet.it/smtho   smtho@tiscali.net.it

FIG. 22. Letter sent by Rocco Zingaro to Luciano Fortunato Sciandra on the 29th of
October 2008 shows the real intentions of the Grand Preceptor in appointing him as his
successor, not Montuoro.

Pope Francis: The Last Pope?

UNCLASSIFIED U.S. Department of State Case No. F-2009-07041 Doc No. C17586026 Date: 07/03/2012

ACTION EUR-00

```
INFO  LOG-00   EEB-00   AF-00    AID-00   CEA-01   CIAE-00  COME-00
      CTME-00  INL-00   DODE-00  ITCE-00  DOTE-00  WHA-00   DS-00
      EAP-00   DHSE-00  EXME-00  E-00     FAAE-00  UTED-00  VCI-00
      FRB-00   H-00     TEDE-00  INR-00   IO-00    MOFM-00  MOF-00
      VCIE-00  NEA-00   NSAE-00  ISN-00   NSCE-00  OES-00   OMB-00
      NIMA-00  EPAU-00  SCT-00   ISNE-00  DOHS-00  SP-00    IRM-00
      SSO-00   SS-00    STR-00   TRSE-00  FMP-00   CBP-00   BBG-00
      R-00     EPAE-00  IIP-00   DSCC-00  PRM-00   DRL-00   G-00
      SCA-00   NFAT-00  SAS-00   FA-00    SWCI-00           /001W
                    ----------------7EAF45  111235Z /38
```

R 111204Z APR 08
FM AMEMBASSY ROME
TO SECSTATE WASHDC 0133
INFO AMCONSUL FLORENCE
AMCONSUL MILAN
AMCONSUL NAPLES

RELEASED IN FULL

UNCLAS ROME 000457

SENSITIVE

E.O. 12958: N/A
TAGS: ECON, ETRD, KCOR, PGOV, IT
SUBJECT: LUNCH WITH ITALIAN ACTIVIST BEPPE GRILLO: "NO HOPE
FOR ITALY;" AN OBSESSION WITH CORRUPTION

REF: ROME 255

1. (SBU) SUMMARY: Italian political comedian-turned activist
Beppe Grillo began a recent discussion with EconOffs saying,
"There is no hope for Italy." He believes only a complete
replacement of the Italian political class can resolve
Italy's corruption problems. Grillo is eccentric, yet
appeals to Italy's downtrodden, reliably putting hundreds of
thousands into the piazzas in protest against the established
order. His comments were a striking contrast to those of
Post's other more conventional interlocutors on economics,
politics and particularly, corruption. END SUMMARY.

BACKGROUND
2. (U) Giuseppe "Beppe" Grillo is a politically outspoken
former comedian-activist who has achieved worldwide celebrity
by excoriating Italian politicians in his daily blog, and by
prompting a very well-attended (one hundred fifty thousand
plus by his count) public rally last fall protesting GOI
corruption. The subject of recent features in the New Yorker
and other American press, the UK's Observer rated him one of

REVIEW AUTHORITY: Martin McLean, Senior Reviewer

*FIG. 23. The first page of an unclassified document entitled "NO HOPE FOR ITALY;
AN OBSESSION WITH CORRUPTION," with the protocol number C175860, is part
of a series of notes that American intelligence is analyzing regarding Beppe Grillo and the
severe economic crisis that is sweeping Italy.*

Chapter: IV

HOMOSEXUALITY AND CHILD ABUSE IN THE VATICAN

"IMPROPRIAM INFLUENTIAM"
THE VATICAN GAY LOBBY AT WORK

In the third volume of *The Confessions of an Illuminati,*[1] I reveal what happened when Franco Bellegrandi, the former Chamberlain of Cape and Sword of His Holiness Pope Paul VI, as well as one of the journalists who contributed most to the foundation of the *"Osservatore Romano"* (still the official newspaper of the Vatican), wrote, in 1977, a very interesting and now very rare book entitled *Nichitaroncalli,* that was published posthumously in 1994.[2] It was accompanied by a great outcry from the National Press at the time of its first print. This was because among the people who took part in the book presentation, there was none other than one the most powerful cardinals of that time, Cardinal Silvio Oddi. For years, he was one of the leaders of the Roman Curia and the Vatican Intelligence. Oddi seemed happy to endorse what turned out to be a very controversial book. As revealed in this book, such a gesture is scandalous as it indicated, in a very explicit manner, the alleged homosexuality of Pope Paul VI. This brings us in contact with the highest level of hypocrisy in the Vatican, as homosexuality is still a thorny issue that fascinates and divides heterosexual and gay Christians and

---

1   Confessions of an Illuminati Vol. III, *Ibid.,* p. 299-300.

2   See. Francesco Bellegrandi, Nichitaroncalli, (Rome: Edizioni internazionali di letteratura e scienze, s.n.c, 1994).

Pope Francis: The Last Pope?

Catholics around the world. There was utter amazement at so much hypocrisy in the Vatican towards *their condition,* while at the top of the Holy See, they basically have done what they want in regards to their own sexuality since ancient times. Of course things are different now in the modern age, when such information is more easily revealed and spread without censorship. Thanks to inside sources, information is now being portrayed accurately, and a few courageous journalists who speculated in the past about this controversial subject are being exonerated. Homosexuality, of course, is not a crime, and it is considered very natural these days by the majority of people in the Western world. Unfortunately, homosexuality in the Vatican often involves pedophilia, and the protection of those involved are now labeled by the Italian media as the *"gay lobby"* of the Vatican. On the 11th of February, 2012, exactly one year before the resignation of Ratzinger, the Italian daily newspaper *Libero,* which belongs to the Berlusconi media empire, spoke openly about this "gay lobby" as possibly being the biggest danger facing the Vatican: *"Some well-informed sources indicate an even greater threat to the current structure of the Vatican. The business committee is shaking, but it is the gay lobby who feels terrified."*[3] Before that, in 2010, the continuing scandals in the Vatican brought another piece from Berlusconi's media portfolio, the weekly magazine *Panorama,* that put this unprecedented title on the cover: *"THE BRAVE NIGHTS OF THE GAY PRIESTS."*[4] This is perhaps a revenge piece, taken on at the time by the then Italian Prime minister Silvio Berlusconi, probably the most controversial Italian politician ever, mostly due to his own sexual scandals. At the time, he probably wanted to divert public attention from his personal conduct, considered nothing short of *libertine. Panorama* decided at the time to film and publish a series of revelations revealing the controversial practice of homosexuality in the Vatican. This also included male prostitution, a reality that many gays in the Italian capital knew about for years, but never dared to reveal for fear of what some insiders call *"The Vatican Gay Mafia."*

Interestingly, after the historic resignation of Pope Ratzinger in the first months of 2013, even the so-called "left wing" newspapers of Italy began to speak about the homosexuality issue. This included *La Repubblica,* with an article by Concita De Gregorio entitled, *"Sex, Career and Blackmail in the Vatican behind the resignation of Benedict XVI."*[5] At the time the hypothesis of the *"gay lobby"* landed in the *La Repubblica* newspaper, its owner was, among other things, a well-known Italian entrepreneur named Carlo De Benedetti. He works directly for none other than the Rothschild family, as is stated in

3   http://www.liberoquotidiano.it/news/italia/932534/Gay--massoni--gole-profonde.html ‡ Archived from the internet September 3, 2014.

4   http://italia.panorama.it/Le-notti-brave-dei-preti-gay ‡ Archived from the internet September 3, 2014.

5   http://www.repubblica.it/esteri/2013/02/21/news/ricatti_vaticano-53080655/ ‡ Archived from the internet September 3, 2014.

his online CV.[6] The article in *La Repubblica* spoke about Cardinal Julian Herranz, aged 83, who was a senior Spanish member of the Opus Dei, appointed by Ratzinger along with two other cardinals, to chair the commission of inquiry that the newspapers termed *"Vatileaks."* This produced a documentation known as the Vatican *"Relationem."* It revealed tidbits about the resigning Pope, something much more unusual than the usual *"bad apples"* angle that could be expected from within the Vatican walls. It refers to the existence of a secret network linked to the homosexual orientation of their members, or even worse, in some cases linked to pedophilia. Strangely, *La Repubblica* made no distinction between pedophilia and homosexuality in their article. That seemed like a serious mistake, especially for a newspaper considered to be "left wing," and they would later be criticized for doing so by the renowned Italian association for the defense of the rights of homosexuals called, *"Circolo Mario Mieli."* Here are the words of Concitta De Gregorio, from the article in question dated February 21, 2013, a few days before the final abandonment of the Petrine throne by Ratzinger: *"For the first time the word homosexuality has been pronounced, read aloud from a written text, in the apartment of Ratzinger. For the first time it as been said, although in Latin, the word blackmail: 'influentiam,' His Holiness. 'Impropriam influentiam.'"* De Gregorio continues her uproar, predicting the destiny of this key document for the future of the Church: *"The 'Relationem' now is there. Benedict XVI will deliver it into the hands of the next Pope, who should be strong enough, and young, and 'holy'—he hopes—to tackle the huge job that awaits him. Designed, in these pages, is a geography of 'improper influences' that a man very close to their author described in this way: 'Everything revolves around the non-observance of the sixth and seventh commandment.' Do not commit adultery. Do not steal. The credibility of the Church will be shattered by the evidence that its own members violate the original dictation. These two points, in particular."* [7]

"Relationem" is the name of the work created by these three cardinals. The aforementioned Julián Herranz Casado, Salvatore De Giorgi and Jozef Tomk, who at the time of the Polish Pope, were head of the Vatican secret counterintelligence unit. They had been recalled to duty by the German Pope to investigate, and possibly create, a *"360 degree"* view of the infighting and evil within the Roman Curia. In the end, they delivered the final result of their investigation directly to Pope Ratzinger on December 17, 2012. Their operation and their intelligence work continued even after Pope Benedict XVI's resignation. After February 26th, 2013, the day of their last papal audience with Ratzinger, the three grand inspectors, with ever greater insistence, made the results of their investigation outlining the wrong doings within the Curia available to the Conclave, as to provide useful information related to the election of the new pontiff. It was the secret files of the *"Relationem"* that

---

6   http://www.gruppoespresso.it/it/governance/management/curriculum/carlo-de-benedetti.html ‡ Archived from the internet September 3, 2014.

7   La Republica, *Ibid.*, 02/21/2013.

eventually caused the improvised resignation of Ratzinger, who now is re-ferred to as the *Pope Emeritus,* and who had an audience with the famous trio on the day of his resignation.

The *"Relationem"* seems to be a dossier of 300 pages which contains dis-turbing evidence, interviews, wiretaps, autographed letters, admissions, oaths and so on, about the scandals that took place over the last few years in the various institutions of the Vatican. In fact, the analysis appears to have many similarities with parts of the third volume of my trilogy, **soon to be released by CCC Publishing,** that mainly focuses on the corruption of evil inside the Vati-can. Some say this was another among the reasons why Ratzinger resigned. This is an accusation that can only flatter me.

Di Feo, a Vatican expert of the prestigious Italian weekly news magazine *L'Espresso*, another publication of the aforementioned Carlo De Benedetti, wrote in July 2013 about the investigation in a special article dedicated to the "gay lobby." *"At first they seemed just some cheap shots in an underground game of poison that overflowed from breaches of the Leonine walls. Then the suspicions have been consolidated in the little information leaking from the secret and shocking investi-gation ordered by Benedict XVI."* Di Feo states further on in the article, *"The new pope knows the 'Relationem,' the final report of the Curia cardinals drawn from the three investigators appointed by his predecessor."*

"RELATIONEM"

They say that Pope Francis has actively used the *"Relationem"* to clean up the Vatican scene. In September 2014, in an unprecedented move, the Vatican authorities arrested, in their own Vatican territory, the already laicized Archbishop Jozef Wesolowsky, with the charge of pedophilia, and who was found to have over 100,000 sexually explicit photos of children on his computer. He is a citizen of both the Holy See and Poland, and at one time he was the papal nuncio in the Dominican Republic. For the first time in history, the Vatican has (finally, in 2013) introduced the crime of pedo-philia into Criminal State Law, and is now proceeding directly against one of their own. The Holy See has been put under extreme pressure by the United Nations since February, 2014, in regards to the many crimes against minors committed by the clergy worldwide. The UN report noted: *"The committee is gravely concerned that the Holy See has not acknowledged the extent of the crimes committed, has not taken the necessary measures to address cases of child sexual abuse and to protect children, and has adopted policies and practices which have led to the continuation of the abuse by, and the impunity of, the perpetrators."* This report was announced by Kirsten Sandberg, who chairs the UN Committee on the Rights of the Child. Finally, we see a prosecution against the "gay lobby," but it seems like a drop in the ocean. The file, in fact, appears to be deliberately incomplete, with rather important omissions that will sooner or later bring Pope Francis to make bad and even embarrassing choices. Eventually, even the new Pope will suffer what the most widely-known Italian gossip blogger Roberto D'Agostino rightly calls a *"poisoned chalice."*[8]

This has occurred with the appointment of Monsignor Battista Mario Salvatore Ricca, for example, at the top of the IOR. Regarding this controversial decision, Sandro Magister wrote in the previously cited special edition of *L'Espresso,* dedicated in the summer of 2013 to exposing the gay lobby:

> *In the curia there is talk of a 'gay lobby.' And it is true, it's there. 'Let's see what we can do,' Francis said on June 6 to Latin American religious received in audience. And again: 'It is not easy. Here there are many of the pope's 'bosses' with great seniority of service,' he confided a few days ago to his Argentine friend and former student Jorge Milia. In effect, some of these 'bosses' have hatched against Jorge Mario Bergoglio the cruelest and most subtle deception since he was elected pope. They kept important information in the dark, that, if he had known it before, would have kept him from appointing Monsignor Battista Ricca the 'prelate' of the Institute for Works of Religion. With this appointment, made public on June 15, Francis intended to place a trusted person in a key role within the IOR. With the power to access all of the proceedings and documents and to attend all of the meetings of both the cardinalate commission of oversight and of the supervisory board of the disastrous Vatican bank. In short, with the task of cleaning house. Ricca, 57, originally from the diocese of Brescia, comes from a diplomatic career. He served for fifteen years in the nunciatures of various countries before he was called back to the Vatican, to the secretariat of state. But he won Bergoglio's trust in another guise, initially as director of the residence on Via della Scrofa at which the archbishop of Buenos Aries stayed during his visits to Rome, and now also as director of the Domus Sanctæ Marthæ in which Francis has chosen to live as pope. Before the appointment, Francis had been shown, as is customary, the personal file on Ricca, in which he had not found anything unseemly. He had also heard from various personalities of the curia, and none of them had raised objections. Just one week after appointing the 'prelate,' however, during the same days in which he was meeting with the apostolic nuncios who had come to Rome from all over the world, the pope became aware, from multiple sources, of some episodes from Ricca's past previously unknown to him and such as to bring serious harm to the pope himself and to his intention of reform. Sadness over having been kept in the dark with regard to such grave matters, and the intention to remedy the appointment he had made, albeit not definitive but 'ad interim.' These were the sentiments expressed by Pope Francis once he was aware of those matters.*

---

8   http://www.dagospia.com/rubrica-3/politica/monsignor-ricca-e-il-suo-vizietto-tenuto-nascosto-al-papa-la-polpetta-avvelenata-servita-59762.htm ‡ Archived from the internet September 5, 2013.

Pope Francis: The Last Pope?

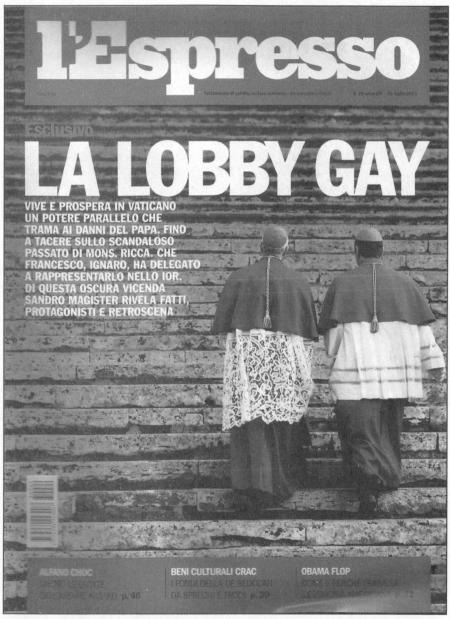

FIG. 24. Cover of the Italian weekly news magazine L'Espresso, no. 29 of 2013, on news-stands July 25, 2013, and dedicated to the infamous "gay lobby" of the Vatican, indicated as one of the primary enemies of Pope Francis.

Leo Lyon Zagami

The black hole in Ricca's personal history is the period he spent in Uruguay, in Montevideo, on the northern shore of the Rio de la Plata, across from Buenos Aires. Ricca arrived at this nunciature in 1999, when the mandate of the nuncio Francesco De Nittis was coming to an end. Previously he had served at the diplomatic missions of Congo, Algeria, Colombia, and finally Switzerland.

Here, in Bern, he had met and become friends with a captain of the Swiss army, Patrick Haari. The two arrived in Uruguay together. And Ricca asked that his friend be given a role and a residence in the nunciature. The nuncio rejected the request. But a few months later he retired and Ricca, having become the chargé d'affaires 'ad interim' until the appointment of the new nuncio, assigned Haari a residence in the nunciature, with a regular position and salary. At the Vatican, they let it go. The substitute for general affairs in the secretariat of state at the time was Giovanni Battista Re, a future cardinal, he too originally from the diocese of Brescia. The intimacy of the relations between Ricca and Haari was so open as to scandalize numerous bishops, priests, and laity of that little South American country, not last the sisters who attended to the nunciature. The new nuncio, Janusz Bolonek of Poland, who arrived in Montevideo at the beginning of 2000, also found that 'ménage' intolerable immediately, and informed the Vatican authorities about it, insisting repeatedly to Haari that he should leave. But to no use, given his connections with Ricca.

In early 2001 Ricca also got into a scrape over his reckless conduct. One day, having gone as on other occasions—in spite of the warnings he had received—to Bulevar Artigas, to a meeting place for homosexuals, he was beaten and had to call some priests to take him back to the nunciature, with his face swollen. In August of 2001, another mishap. In the middle of the night, the elevator of the nunciature got stuck and in the early morning the firemen had to come. They found trapped in the car, together with Monsignor Ricca, a young man who was identified by the police authorities.

Nuncio Bolonek asked that Ricca be sent away from the nunciature and Haari fired immediately. And he got the go-ahead from the secretary of state, Cardinal Angelo Sodano. Ricca, dragging his heels, was transferred to the nunciature of Trinidad and Tobago, where he remained until 2004. There as well he butted heads with the nuncio. Finally to be called to the Vatican and removed from diplomatic service on the ground. As for Haari, in the process of leaving the nunciature he demanded that some of his luggage be sent to the Vatican as diplomatic baggage, to the address of Monsignor Ricca. Nuncio Bolonek refused, and the luggage ended up in a building outside of the nunciature. Where it remained for a few years, until from Rome Ricca said that he didn't want to have anything to do with it anymore. Once the luggage was opened to get rid of its contents—as decided by the nuncio Bolonek—a pistol was found in it, which was handed over to the Uruguayan authorities, and in addition to personal effects, an enormous quantity of condoms and pornographic ma-

Pope Francis: The Last Pope?

terial. In Uruguay, the facts reported above are known to dozens of persons: bishops, priests, sisters, lay people. Without counting the civil authorities, from security forces to fire protection. Many of these persons have had direct experience of these facts, at various moments. But at the Vatican as well there are those who know about them. The nuncio at the time, Bolonek, always expressed himself with severity with regard to Ricca, in reporting to Rome. And yet a blanket of public silence has covered until today these past episodes of the monsignor. In Uruguay, there are some who respect the granting of silence out of scruples of conscience. Some for the duty of office. Some who are silent because they do not want to put the Church and the pope in a bad light. But at the Vatican there are some who actively promoted this cover-up operation. By blocking the investigations from the time of the events until today. By concealing the reports from the nuncio. By keeping Ricca's personal file immaculate. In this way they facilitated a prestigious new career for Ricca. After his return to Rome, the monsignor was integrated into the diplomatic personnel serving at the secretariat of state: initially, from 2005, in the first section, that of general affairs; then, from 2008, in the second section, that of relations with states; and then again, from 2012, in the first section, with a top-level position, that of nunciature advisor first class.

Among the tasks assigned to him was supervision of the spending of the nunciatures. And from this as well was born that reputation as an incorruptible moralizer which was assigned to him by the media all over the world, at the news of his appointment as 'prelate' of the IOR. Moreover, beginning in 2006, Monsignor Ricca was entrusted with the direction first of one, then of two, and finally of three residences for cardinals, bishops, and priests visiting Rome, including that of Saint Martha. And this allowed him to weave an intricate network of relationships with the highest levels of the Catholic hierarchy all over the world. The appointment as 'prelate' of the IOR was for Ricca the crowning of this second career of his. But it was also the beginning of the end. Because of the many upright persons who knew about his scandalous past, the news of the promotion was a cause of extreme bitterness, all the more keen because it was seen as a presage of harm for the arduous enterprise that Pope Francis has in the works, of purification of the Church and of reform of the Roman curia. Because of this some believed it to be their duty to tell the pope the truth. Certain that he would make the consequent decisions.[9]

One year after publication, Monsignor Ricca is still working in the Institute for Works of Religion (IOR) as one of the three key players in charge of what is the Vatican Bank.[10] Bergoglio has done nothing to correct his decision,

9   Article by Sandro Magister, published in *L'Espresso*, no. 29 of 2013. English translation by Matthew Sherry, Ballwin, Missouri, USA for http://chiesa.espresso.repubblica.it ‡ Archived from the internet, September 3, 2014.

10   http://it.wikipedia.org/wiki/Istituto_per_le_Opere_di_Religione ‡ Archived from the internet, September 3, 2014.

Leo Lyon Zagami

demonstrating his failure to oppose one of the top leaders of the Vatican *"Gay Lobby."* Why then did Pope Francis say: *"Non è facile. Qui ci sono molti 'padroni' del papa e con molta anzianità di servizio."* This can be translated in two ways: *"It is not easy. Here there are many of the pope's 'bosses' with great seniority of service,"* or *"It is not easy. Here there are many 'owners' of the pope with great seniority of service,"* Who then are these *"bosses,"* or even worse the *"owners,"* of the Pope? Isn't he supposed to be a free man and the top of the Vatican power structure? Apparently not. It would appear that God's representative on Earth has more terrestrial controllers, if we are to believe his own words.

In the same historical piece published by *L'Espresso*, Di Feo wrote, *"Now the information that did not reach Pope Francis regarding the past of Monsignor Battista Ricca seem to close the circle, in a design pattern that has something diabolical: the gay lobby in the Vatican exists, strong, rooted around the management of business and blackmail."* The reason why Pope Francis can still trust Msgr. Ricca to serve him in one of the most delicate positions of power within the Vatican, especially after the scandal broke in the Italian media, remains a mystery to this day. There must be something more to the real power this figure holds, who is clearly a senior representative of the infamous *"gay lobby."* Most Italian media articles pointed this out after he was nominated for the top job at the IOR, perhaps hoping, as Magister and Di Feo had, that Pope Francis will eventually make him resign. Unfortunately, this did not occur.

The picture emerging is that the Church of today is made of sexual scandals, pedophilia and blackmail performed by clergy and Vatican workers at all levels. There is a "mafiosi" protection of sorts, exercised by powerful and respected cardinals, bishops and archbishops of the infamous "lobby." Many of the orgies organized continuously in the Vatican and villas on the outskirts of Rome, are often the result of actual Black Masses. On the 27th of May, 2014, on his way back from the Holy Land, Pope Francis stated, *"Pedophilia is like black masses."* This should remind us of an Italian book that came out in the 90's entitled, *SATAN AT THE GATES OF ROME a Journey in the World of the Black Masses.*[11] This book is an in-depth investigation, written by Enrica Cammarano and Letizia Strambi, that reveals, among other things, that such rituals are often carried out in proximity of the Papal Palace of Castel Gandolfo, based in the town of Castel Gandolfo, located 15 miles (24 kilometers) southeast of Rome in the Lazio region of Italy. The authors write:

> *But there is another factor to be taken into consideration for the choice of the Castelli Romani: the Pope has taken his summer residence in Castel Gandolfo. The devotees of evil find the Pope's choice is not random and prefer these lands because they are trodden by the footsteps of many popes. Finally, everywhere the fear is spreading on the advent of a new era. In history everything seems*

11   See. Enrica Cammarano, Letizia Strambi, Satana alle porte di Roma, (Rome: Ed.Mediterrannee, 1995).

to collapse except Rome, the Eternal City. However, there are many prophecies that see in the year 2000, the beginning of a new aeon characterized by an attack on the church ... in their own home. [12]

We must also remember that in the period immediately after the resignation, Castel Gandolfo had been, albeit temporarily, chosen as the residence of *Pope Emeritus* Joseph Ratzinger, who has been accused by more than one person to have participated in black masses himself.

It seems that the older cardinals did not vote in the election of Bergoglio because of their advancing age. This would have left evidence that the three Inspectors General of the Holy See, if we want to call them in this way, knew of these terrible practices.

To sum up the *"Relationem,"* it gives particular emphasis to the non-observance of two commandments in particular. They include the Sixth Commandment, "Thou Shalt Not Commit Impure Acts," and the Seventh, "Thou Shalt Not Steal." These are the two main problems today in the Vatican: First the *Gay Lobby,* and second the IOR, the infamous Vatican bank. They are the constant source of scandals and criminal activities, and from an inside source that has observed Bergoglio closely from his installation to the Throne of Peter, it seems that whatever he is doing on the surface to fight these two delicate issues in the eyes of the public is just merely a show, not a real act of significant change. Sad but true, a Jesuit in the end is always a Jesuit, no matter how white his liturgical clothing gets. Pope Francis, the Jesuit, is unfortunately disappointing many, including this author, who thought for a brief time that real change was at hand in the heart of Christianity.

THE QUEEN OF FREEMASONRY ARRIVES ... A YEAR LATE

On August 31, 2013, we find the strange and sudden departure of Cardinal Bertone when Pope Francis officially accepted his resignation, for reasons of age, from the all-powerful position of Secretary of the Vatican State. This also coincides with the forced resignation, a month before, of another friend of Bertone, the IOR Director General named Paolo Cipriani. Both actions seem to originate from the suspected violations of the international anti-recycling laws by the two prominent figures and their bank clients. Apparently the true identities of the many owners of mysterious and top secret bank accounts held in the Vatican Bank are mentioned in the previously discussed *"Relationem."* Such secret accounts belong to many influential people, some of whom may be prominent Italian politicians never previously investigated, seemingly because of the usual lack of interest from both the Vatican and the corrupt Italian Republic. Not surprisingly, there was

---

12   *Ibid.*, p. 24.

also mention of accounts of mafia bosses, drug traffickers, so-called terrorists, and secret agents of the CIA. They would use their accounts at the IOR to put away huge sums of money originating from money laundering, drugs, political corruption, and even funds for terrorist operations to be used for bribes, in the Vatican bank.

According to Giorgio Bongiovanni, a very controversial character because of his claimed stigmata, and some say New Age religious delusions, there may be even much more in the documents contained in the *"Relationem."* A controversial figure, he constantly fights against corruption of the Vatican by the Mafia in the magazine *Antimafia Duemila* that he courageously runs from his headquarters at Via Asti 23 in the Italian city of Porto S.Elpidio. Bongiovanni makes reference to a scandal involving 229 million euros that was put on deposit with the IOR. Apparently arranged by APSA, the most important financial institution of the Vatican State, this money was secretly routed toward accounts in London during the final years of the pontificate of Ratzinger, and discovered later by Italian prosecutors based in Rome. [13]

To have a clear idea of the function of APSA, here is the Wikipedia definition on the subject:

> *The Administration of the Patrimony of the Apostolic See (Italian: Amministrazione del Patrimonio della Sede Apostolica, abbreviated APSA) is the office of the Roman Curia that deals with the 'provisions owned by the Holy See in order to provide the funds necessary for the Roman Curia to function' Pastor Bonus, 172 as revised by the 8 July 2014 motu proprio of Pope Francis on the transfer of what had been the Administration's Ordinary Section to the Secretariat for the Economy. In its reduced form, it acts as the Treasury and central bank of Vatican City and the Holy See. It was established by Pope Paul VI on 15 August 1967. [14]*

This secret financial operation mentioned by Bongiovanni is judged by experts in the field as another huge money laundering scandal orchestrated by the Vatican with no respect for international laws, an operation that even disrupted the powerful Freemasons of the Bank of England.

I myself was initiated years ago into the United Grand Lodge of England (Kirby 2818). Founded with the help of the Bank of England Lodge, I know very well the figures of power residing in the City of London, who are based in a specific area widely referred to as *The City*, the business heart of London. They operate when things get out of hand, and this happened when another

---

13   http://www.antimafiaduemila.com/2013022341367/giorgio- bongiovanni / rela-tionem-shadow-dellanticristo-in-vaticano.html ‡ Archived from the internet July 3, 2013.

14   http://en.wikipedia.org/wiki/Administration_of_the_Patrimony_of_the_Apostolic_See ‡ Archived from the internet September 4, 2014.

important banking institution called Monte dei Paschi di Siena (MPS), the oldest in Italy, was involved in illegal operations with the IOR when they illicitly sent a couple of billion to London. At this point, the direct intervention of Queen Elizabeth II was requested by her loyal Freemasons of The City. During this time, the financial police in Italy expanded their investigation into what is now believed to be a 90-million-euro fraud at MPS, including new investigations in several Italian cities including Siena, Rome, and Milan. The latest search in 2014 is part of a broader probe targeting alleged members of the so-called *"5% gang"*—a name given to ex-bank managers suspected of taking 5% payoffs on banking operations under a previous management.[15]

Most of the managers of this so-called "5% gang" are Freemasons linked to Stefano Bisi, a well-known journalist and communication expert from Siena, Italy. Bisi is a person who once collaborated with the MPS and was elected to succeed Gustavo Raffi on April 5th, 2014, as Grand Master of the Grand Orient of Italy. This is the only Masonic obedience recognized by their American counterparts in the various States of the Union.

Meanwhile, the investigating judge of the court of Siena announced that the file had been suddenly closed into the supposed suicide of David Rossi, the bank's communication manager of MPS, and a close collaborator of Stefano Bisi. He jumped, or was probably forced, from a window of the MPS headquarters in March, 2013, exactly one year before Bisi became Grand Master of the Italian Freemasons. The family of Rossi had their doubts on his suicide, and strongly opposed the archiving of this case from the start.[16]

The journalist and Masonic expert, Rita Pennarola, in March 2014, wrote of the many connections between Bisi, Rossi, and MPS, wondering if there was the involvement of what she called the "illuminated" hand of Bisi and his influential Freemasons from Siena, in the 30-meter fall of poor David Rossi.[17] Rossi's office computer was also apparently hacked and manipulated by an unknown individual soon after his death.[18] But this is Italy, and the case was closed in March, 2014, due to the influence of the people involved, including the new Grand Master, Stefano Bisi.

15   http://www.ansa.it/web/notizie/rubriche/english/2014/03/05/New-operations-probe-scandal-hit-MPS_10186123.html ‡ Archived from the internet September 4, 2014.

16   http://www.corriere.it/cronache/13_settembre_26/mps-rossi-suicidio-famiglia_3cb06b3e-269a-11e3-a1ee-487182bf93b6.shtml ‡ Archived from the internet September 4, 2014.

17   http://www.corriere.it/cronache/13_settembre_26/mps-rossi-suicidio-famiglia_3cb06b3e-269a-11e3-a1ee-487182bf93b6.shtml ‡ Archived from the internet September 4, 2014.

18   http://www.freemasonry.london.museum/os/wp-content/uploads/2010/12/Royal-Masonic-Hospital.pdf ‡ Archived from the internet July 3, 2013.

FIG. 25. A smiling Queen Elizabeth on March 4, 2013 walking unassisted from King Edward VII Hospital, accompanied by a nurse that graduated from the Royal Masonic Hospital. Photo by Andrew Winning (Reuters).

Pope Francis: The Last Pope?

Let us return to the arrival of Queen Elizabeth II at the Vatican, and her secret mission on behalf of the Freemasons of "The City." Worried about the disturbing news coming from the Vatican and the Italian financial sector, this meeting was originally scheduled to occur at the beginning of March, 2013, and would have coincided with what we can define as the Masonic murder of David Rossi. This was yet another improbable death of a prominent banker, just like the 1982 "suicide" of Roberto Calvi, who was called "God's Banker," who was found hanging from scaffolding under London's Blackfriars bridge the day after he went missing from Rome. The Queen's previous journey had been delayed a year, as on March 3, 2013, she was rushed to and remained at a hospital for 24 hours, due to what was officially reported as a severe gastrointestinal problem. Until 2002, the hospital in question was called The Royal Masonic Hospital. Despite her medical problems, as she was leaving the hospital, *The Queen of the Craft,* as she is traditionally referred to in English Freemasonry, launched a very subtle, yet a strong and unequivocal signal to "The Brothers" involved. Always attentive to the symbolic details, the Queen was accompanied to the exit of the hospital with a nurse wearing a huge buckle with the symbols of Freemasonry, which was in use at the hospital only until 2002.[19]

The Queen of England finally arrived at the Vatican for a meeting with Pope Francis on April 4th, 2014. This was a visit of very strategic importance from what is not only a head of state but also the supreme leader of the Anglican Church, and protector of English Freemasonry, which is only present in the Vatican via the Duke of Kent, cousin of *Her Majesty,* and the Grand Master of the United Grand Lodge of England. This brief visit by the Queen, originally intended to sort out the various financial problems detected by her Freemason bankers, and eventually, to take the pulse of the Conclave for the election of the Pope in 2013, happened in 2014, and focused instead on the growing crisis in the Ukraine, the Middle East, and Israel, where the Pope went to visit in May, 2014. This was the beginning of the worst crisis in decades, so Francis was dispatched to instruct his Jesuit agents on the coming conflicts and their plans of action for the area. The Queen of Freemasonry had, to a certain extent, influenced the nomination of Pope Francis, as is true with previous nominations, beginning with the first Masonic and Rosicrucian Pope in 1958, Pope John XXIII.

She must have been very pleased with the work of Pope Francis, who has been cleaning up the mess of his predecessors, at least in the public eye. With the help of Shimon Peres of Israel, another key player in Freemasonry, he is now planning what will became the world parliament of religions, the final stage of the plan devised by the New World Order. Peres said before meeting

---

19   http://www.ilfattoquotidiano.it/2014/02/24/monte-paschi-il-computer-di-david-rossi-e-stato-manomesso-dopo-il-suicidio/892691/ ‡ Archived from the internet September 4, 2014.

Pope Francis on the 4th of September, 2014: *"The UN has done its time, what we need is an Organization of the United Religions, a UN of the religions."*[20]

FIG. 26. Detail of the huge Masonic buckle, worn by the nurse photographed with Queen Elizabeth II during her exit from the hospital on March 4, 2013.

THE PARALLEL INVESTIGATION TO PROTECT THE LOBBY OF BERTONE AND THE ILLUMINATI

Over the years, the Vatican has kept hidden the largest tax evasion of all time, which has never been denounced by any government. Their crimes go unpunished because of the sovereign state status held by the Vatican, where obviously it is not the Holy Spirit that reigns, but rather the spirit of Satan, along with his gang of pedophiles, satanists, mafiosi, and Masonic businessmen that are leading the Church of Rome into an inexorable decline. Let's not forget that it was the son of a mobster, the controversial Massimo Ciancimino, who revealed not too long ago, that he had accompanied his father Vito to the offices of the Vatican bank to deposit briefcases containing billions of lire. And then there was the testimony of Vincenzo Calcara, who became a traitor to the mafia, a so-called *"pentito,"* but also a precious informer to the investigating authorities. He stated that he delivered, in person, to a high prelate, the sum of 10 billion lire. This large sum of money was the result of criminal trafficking by some say the current head of Cosa Nostra, the Sicilian *"Boss of Bosses,"* Matteo Messina Denaro, also known as *Diabolik*.

20   http://www.ansa.it/sito/notizie/topnews/2014/09/04/peres-a-papa-fondiamo-onu-religioni_d3e714f1-4555-49e6-9347-8970b43cff95.html ‡ Archived from the internet September 4, 2014.

Pope Francis: The Last Pope?

These revelations are just the tip of the iceberg. If we went much deeper than that, and we could prove our findings, it would probably mean the end of the Church. Here we have, in the age of information technology, a person who could very well be considered the *last Pope*.

I would call him a *"technical"* pope, in the period before complete collapse, a sort of *"Governor"* of the Church who reminds me of the ex-Italian Prime Minister and economist Mario Monti, a proud Jesuit student and a member of the Bilderberg directorate, who rose to power in Italy without being elected, kicking out Berlusconi in 2012 thanks to the Bilderberg and the Vatican. With a sort of technical *coup d'etat* to save the stability of the NWO Euro Zone, Pope Francis and his team are a kind of *"insolvency service"* set up by the Vatican Jesuits. As the aforementioned Beppe Grillo said, given the situation and the decline facing the whole of Italy and the Church of Rome, it's a dominatrix.

Francis needs to be a sort of ferryman, who would ferry the Vatican ship to the end of its time on earth, preparing for the advent of the so-called Universal Church in 2019. The same Beppe Grillo is now very close to the former Secretary of State Tarcisio Bertone, as they are both linked to the Academy of the Illuminati in Rome, and their President/Grand Master, Professor Giuliano Bernardo. After his first face-to-face meeting with Bertone, Grillo had initially hoped that Bertone would be elected as Pope, going so far as to publicly announce it on his website, specifying that Bertone was the last Pope of the Malachi prophecies, the famous *Petrus Romanus*.[21] This explanation came together partly because Bertone was born in Romano Canavese, a small town in the province of Turin, hence the link with the name *Petrus Romanus*. Grillo suddenly changed his mind after the resignation of Benedict XVI, and instead of announcing the advent of Bertone, he stated: *"Maybe the next one will be a black Pope,"*[22] indicating later on, that it could be a Pope of possible African descent. Some say to this day, that Pope Francis is the so-called *"black Pope"* of the prophecies, simply because he is a Jesuit.

This sudden change in Bertone's status with Beppe Grillo (and contrary to some people's perception, Grillo remains a powerful man of the system), was probably related to the fact that the earliest revelations of Ratzinger's butler, the so-called *"Crow"* of the Vatican, the now-infamous Paolo Gabriele, were about the *"gay lobby"* and Bertone, who was portrayed as the biggest loser due to these revelations that ruined his public image forever. It seems that Bertone had even initiated a secret investigation in 2011, in order to protect his colleagues from the "gay lobby," which included, some inside sources say,

---

21   http://www.beppegrillo.it/2009/08/bertone_lultimo_papa.html ‡ Archived from the internet September 4, 2014.

22   http://www.ilfattoquotidiano.it/2013/02/11/grillo-tsunami-a-rovigo-magari-prossimo-sara-papa-nero-video/496131/ ‡ Archived from the internet September 4, 2014.

Leo Lyon Zagami

Ratzinger himself, as well as the former Grand Master of Ceremonies of the Pope, Monsignor Camaldo, as previously mentioned and indicated by Julian Assange of Wikileaks, as an agent of the CIA involved in homosexual activities monitored by *The Agency*.

> *For more than a year, email, phones, meetings and discussions have been meticulously put under observation, on behalf of Cardinal Tarcisio Bertone, the Vatican Gendarmerie led by General Domenico Giani, a former Italian intelligence officer, that in the coming weeks could lead the Holy See to a new assignment at the United Nations.*

The Italian edition of the *Huffington Post* reported this in an article in the weekly *Panorama,* on February 28, 2013. The article anticipated and highlighted the content[23] of what will be revealed on the day Ratzinger abandoned the Vatican theater, to become *Pope Emeritus.* He did not come down from the cross as Jesus would have probably done, but is *"going up the hill,"* instead. Ratzinger, in fact, took the helicopter to his Castel Gandolfo summer residence, which I mentioned earlier, in the area infested by satanists in Castelli Romani, in the hills near Rome. This is where he retired for a few months before returning to his current residence, a monastery inside the Vatican walls. Regarding General Domenico Giani, who began the investigation instigated by Bertone, it is worth mentioning that he is still at the service of the new Pope every day. He never departed for the UN as wrongly predicted by journalists, most likely because he is from Arezzo, the city of the Past Worshipful Master of the infamous P2 Masonic Lodge, the late Licio Gelli, was a friend of Giani and also a very special friend of the Vatican. He collaborates with them as an expert on intelligence and a Commander of the Order of the Holy Sepulcher of Jerusalem, as well as a Grand Officer of the Order of St. Sylvester Pope. According to the first statement from the *Panorama* article, this top secret investigation issued by Bertone and his associates was dated until 2012, but then later corrected it to 2011.

> *When the first letters of threats to Bertone began circulating (revealed by 'Panorama') with the first leaks of confidential documents, they were put in place as the most massive and widespread work of interception ever made to date in the Sacred buildings which, according to some, continues to this day.[24]*

Of course, there remains a lot of confusion, even in the media, between this parallel investigation and the main *"Relationem"* conducted by Vatican intelligence cardinals: Herranz, De Giorgi and Tomko. What followed has been defined as *"Vatileaks,"* the main investigation conducted by Vatican au-

23   http://www.huffingtonpost.it/2013/02/27/vaticano-panorama-da-un-anno-tutta-la-curia-e-sotto-controllo-per-ordine-del-cardinal-tarcisio-bertone_n_2772689.html?utm_hp_ref=italy ‡ Archived from the internet September 4, 2014.
24   *Ibid.*

Pope Francis: The Last Pope?

thorities officially released when the *"Crow"* scandal broke in the press, to investigate such leaks and arrest the suspects. In the end there was only one suspect, the butler, the classical scapegoat. Bertone's original investigation began much earlier in 2011, which was initiated by Bertone as a result of the threats received personally and by other members of what appear to be the *"Gay Lobby."* In a letter named the *"Great funerals at court,"* it soon became Bertone's personal attempt to save his position when the *"Vatileaks"* investigation was taken over by the Vatican Judicial authorities. Later the intelligence operatives of the *"Relationem"* began their own operation, and to this day, we don't know how much of this previous investigation was passed on and used for both *"Vatileaks"* and *"Relationem,"* and how much was omitted and used to save and preserve the powerful *"Gay Lobby,"* as in the case of Monsignor Ricca, who was conveniently left out so he could reach his new position in the new IOR of the Pope Francis era. Regarding the conclave that elected Bergoglio, it was controlled by the usual foreign intelligence services normal to the Vatican. In recent history, we have seen throughout the period of the Cold War, with the United States and Russia in the lead, attempts to steal secrets and effect the choice of Pope. This happened to poor Cardinal Siri, for example, as far back as 1958, when he was forced to renounce because of Roncalli's choice. This was made by the powerful Masonic lobby at the time, as it prepared the stage for the Second Vatican Council.

Since the last Conclave there has been a clash between inside lobbies. Above it all we find Cardinal Bertone and his associates, ready to use sophisticated methods and technology to gather information, and set in motion the eventual blackmail methods traditionally used by modern intelligence agencies. All this merely to defend the interests of the Vatican *"Gay Lobby,"* under attack by the Italian media, and under investigation by the Vatican authorities of *"Vatileaks"* and the Vatican intelligence trio responsible for the *"Relationem."* This internal struggle has worried many concerned, especially those who reside within Vatican territory. In addition to emails and phone calls that have been archived by the *"Vatileaks"* investigators, Bertone's men put together a list of all those who entered and exited from the Leonine Wall after 9 PM. A list containing what some say include many names of men and women engaged in prostitution activities inside the Vatican walls, as well as drug deals of cocaine and other contraband used by workers and clergy alike. A parcel addressed to the Vatican containing cocaine-filled condoms was seized by German customs officers in March, 2014. The package was sent to the Vatican from a South American country, and contained 14 condoms filled with £33,000 worth of liquid cocaine.[25] Two men were also detained in September, 2014 by French police after the discovery of four kilos of cocaine, and between 150 to 200 grams of cannabis, that were discovered hidden inside an official Vatican car

25   http://www.theguardian.com/world/2014/mar/23/vatican-cocaine-condoms-parcel-seized-package ‡ Archived from the internet September 4, 2014.

with diplomatic license plates. As you can see, there is a constant demand for these kind of substances at the Vatican's so-called *"Party Time"* events. The only statement to the press made about the unprecedented initiative of the Vatican ex-Secretary of State, Tarcisio Bertone, was made by the official spokesmen, Jesuit Father Federico Lombardi, at the end of February, 2013, and just before Ratzinger left the picture. In the heat of the moment, it went nearly unnoticed: *"In the context of Vatileaks that may have been authorized by the prosecution, and not by the Secretary of State, (there were) a number of interceptions and some controls. I can assure you that it is not a large investigation or generalized."* So the Vatican spokesman, Father Federico Lombardi, downplayed the initiative of Cardinal Tarcisio Bertone and even said, *"Two or three phone utilities may have been put under control,"* followed by *"To say that this case involves an extensive investigation across the board that creates the atmosphere of fear or distrust, and now affects the Conclave has no affinity with reality."* The statement by the magazine *Panorama*, revealed on their website that same day, seems to state something different, *"This thorough investigation has been ordered to the Vatican Gendarmerie, coordinated by the master Domenico Giani, on the request of the Secretary of State. The months following the publication of confidential documents from the Secretary of State and from the Papal States, led the Gendarmerie to strengthen their efforts in the investigation. These have been the subject, in February 2012, of a specific measure authorized by the promoter of justice, Nicola Picardi. The trials of Paolo Gabriele and Claudio Sciarpelletti, celebrated in the months of October and November 2012, and concluded with a sentence for both defendants, have not stopped the investigative work of the Gendarmerie, which has instead continued—and it is not yet defined—with particular reference to the following alleged offenses: crimes against the state, crimes against the powers of the state, insulting state institutions, slander and libel, the inviolability of secrets. It should also be noted that the body of the Gendarmerie, under the control of the Governorate of Vatican City State, in its capacity as police and judicial protection of public works closely with the first section of the Secretariat of State 'Section of the General Affairs' under the responsibility of the Substitute (art. 13th, c.3 L. CCCLXXXIV of 16 July 2002 on the Government of the State of Vatican City, and art. c.1 41, the Apostolic Constitution, Pastor Bonus)."*[26]

With this note, *Panorama* made a reverse statement of sorts, confirming that the then-Secretary of State Tarcisio Bertone and his deputy were, therefore, *"ex officio,"* and were kept abreast of investigations and protection of the public order carried out by the Vatican Gendarmerie, and had access to the relevant documents by way of their work, thus justifying their investigation, deemed 100% legal according to Vatican law. Or maybe this is what they would like us to think.

We can only speculate why Lombardi insisted on making the following comment during a press conference on the 28th of February, 2013, *"In the*

26   http://news.panorama.it/cronaca/intercettazioni-vaticano-cardinale-bertone
‡ Archived from the internet September 4, 2014.

Pope Francis: The Last Pope?

context of Vatileaks, they may have been authorized by the prosecution, and not by the Secretary of State." The Vatican law states that in this case, *"the Gendarmerie, under the control of the Governorate of Vatican City State, in its capacity as police and judicial protection of the public, work closely with the first section of the Secretariat of State."*[27] On the vastness of the surveillance controls, *Panorama* finally makes clear that the operations room of the Vatican Gendarmerie has been archiving a huge mass of data, mainly phone and web activity, by a large amount of people inside the Vatican, not the 2 or 3 intercepted phone lines falsely stated by Father Lombardi.

All this information is still available to the investigation department and the Group of Rapid Intervention (GIR) of the Vatican Gendarmerie.[28] And finally, for those who are thinking after all this that the Vatican and Freemasonry are at war, the ex-Grand Master of Freemasonry at the time of the infamous P2 Lodge, Armandino Corona, received for his final departure in 2009, a *"syncretistic funeral,"* mixing the two traditions. This ceremony was held in Cagliari, in the Basilica dedicated to Our Lady of Bonaria, protector of Sardinia, visited the year prior by Pope Ratzinger. On this occasion he bestowed the honor of a Golden Rose to the Basilica.[29] The mixture of the two rites, apparently antithetical to each other, would obviously be judged blasphemous by non-Masons, especially in the Catholic world. The people involved do not have such concerns, having the power and the knowledge of both the esoteric and the occult that bind them secretly in a church very different from what has always been portrayed. A Church that has in their knighthoods the point of contact with the upper echelons of Freemasonry (which are more than willing to enlist in the Knights of the Holy Sepulcher) as well as those in the Sovereign Order of Malta, *or other less important, even if not officially recognized by the Vatican.*

THE DUTCH CATHOLIC DISASTER

In 1993, the head of the diocese of Rotterdam unexpectedly left his post and retired to the Benedictine abbey of Chevetogne in Belgium. Years later, the reason for his sudden departure became public and the Dutch Church received another blow to their already precarious image. It was revealed that Prelate Philippe Bär, who had led the diocese of Rotterdam for ten years, had been accused of giving organizational support to a pedophile association. The well-known Vaticanists insider, Giacomo Galeazzi, wrote in December 2011, *"Bishop and leader of a 'gang' of pedophiles: the prelate Philippe Bär (who headed the most important diocese in the Netherlands from 1983 to 1993) is suspected of offering organizational support to an association which intended to sexu-*

---

27   *Ibid.*

28   *Ibid.*

29   http://en.wikipedia.org/wiki/The_Basilica_of_Our_Lady_of_Bonaria ‡ Archived from the internet September 4, 2014.

Leo Lyon Zagami

ally abuse minors and to take part in such acts."[30]

Galeazzi's observations seemed to open the inquiring eye of the mainstream media. Three months later, in March 2012, the Dutch evening newspaper *NRC Handelsblad* published an article[31] in which they accused the Catholic Church of having ordered and organized in the fifties, the castration of a dozen men to apparently *"cure"* them of their homosexuality. In reality, castration was often a punishment for revealing too much about their sexual encounters with the clergy. The UK newspaper *The Telegraph* reported on the Dutch article cited above, and stated that, *"At least 10 teenage boys or young men under the age of 21 were surgically castrated 'to get rid of homosexuality' while in the care of the Dutch Roman Catholic Church in the 1950s."* The article was written by Joep Dohmen, a journalist of *NRC Handelsblad,* who was among the first to investigate cases of child abuse within the Dutch Church in 2010. This was before the government decided to open an official investigation into the abuse. His newspaper is headquartered in Rotterdam and is one of the most widely read newspapers in the Netherlands. After the publication of these articles, some Dutch parliamentarians called for the opening of a new survey and asked to interrogate Weim Deetman. He was the figure responsible for an independent commission to investigate the pedophilia cases, but failed to mention the castration cases.[32]

The article by Dohmen became extremely popular in March 2012, and was cited by many newspapers around the world, ranging from *The Daily Beast*[33] to *The New York Times.*[34] The new articles basically revolved around the story of a young Dutch citizen named Henk Heithuis. Mr. Heithuis was first locked up in a psychiatric hospital run by the Catholic Church and then surgically castrated in 1956. He was sent there after he reported to the Dutch police the abuse he suffered between 1950 to 1953 at the Harreveld Catholic boarding school in the province of Gelderland, in Holland. *"This case is especially painful because it concerns a victim who was victimized for a second time,"* said **Peter Nissen,** a professor of the history of religion at Radboud University in the Netherlands. *"He had the courage to go to the police and was castrated."*[35]

30   http://vaticaninsider.lastampa.it/en/inquiries-and-interviews/detail/articolo/olanda-netherlands-holanda-pedofilia-pedophilia-10958/ ‡ Archived from the internet September 5, 2014.

31   http://www.nrc.nl/nieuws/2012/03/17/jongens-binnen-r-k-kerk-gecastreerd-we-gens-homoseksueel-gedrag/ ‡ Archived from the internet September 5, 2014.

32   http://www.ilfattoquotidiano.it/2012/03/17/olanda-nuovo-scandalo-pedofilia-nella-chiesa-vittime-religiosi-venivano-castrate/198196 ‡ Archived from the internet September 5, 2014.

33   http://www.thedailybeast.com/articles/2012/03/22/dutch-castration-scandal-how-journalists-broke-the-story.html ‡ Archived from the internet September 5, 2014.

34   http://www.nytimes.com/2012/03/21/world/europe/dutch-church-accused-of-castrating-10-young-men.html?_r=0 ‡ Archived from the internet September 5, 2014.

35   The New York Times, *Ibid.*

Pope Francis: The Last Pope?

The journalist Robert Chesal, who reported for *The Daily Beast* on how his colleague and collaborator Joep Dohmen uncovered the Dutch castration scandal wrote that, *"he was a colleague who I worked with to break the story of Dutch church sex abuse back in 2010. Dohmen and I, working for our respective media outlets but sharing information, uncovered a series of scandals in boarding schools and parishes that led hundreds of abuse victims to step forward and tell their story. Our work led the Dutch bishops to install a commission of inquiry that completed its work last December."*

FIG 27. *Former Secretary of State of the Vatican Cardinal Tarcisio Bertone and Beppe Grillo the leader of the "5 Stars Movement" the new political reality tied in with the Italian Academy of the Illuminati and supported by the Vatican.*

FIG. 28. On the right is the Inspector General of the Vatican Domenico Giani (b.1962), notice the Knights of Malta (SMOM) jewel on his collar.

So how did these two investigative journalists, who had already revealed dirt on the Catholic Church in the Netherlands in 2010, receive such shocking information regarding Henk Heithuis? It was from a friend of Henk named Rogge who apparently helped them, as Chesal writes, *"Rogge, a 79-year-old sculptor living in a converted farmhouse near the Dutch city of Zutphen, showed me a stack of letters from the 1950s. Some were in his own hand; others were from his brother, their deceased mother, and their friend, Henk Heithuis."*

Since he is such a central figure in all this, let's try to understand better the incredible story of Henk Heithuis from the words of Robert Chesal: *"In 1956, Henk, then 20-years-old and legally a minor, reported the clerical abuse to the police. Hearing about the abuse, the police treated him as if he were insane, bringing him to a Roman Catholic psychiatric hospital where he was involuntarily committed. People there told detectives Henk was 'a homosexual, untrustworthy, a liar and mentally disturbed.' One month later, at St. Josephs Hospital in the southern Dutch town of Veghel, Henk was surgically castrated or 'eugenized,' as the hospital records put it, using a term previously attributed to the Nazi program of systematically sterilizing the mentally and physically handicapped. In one of his letters, Henk wrote about how he was 'maimed.' The surgeon, he told Rogge, played records to calm the other boys who were in the hallway, waiting to undergo the same procedure. 'I didn't believe him,' Rogge said. But when Henk took off his pants to show him, he was shocked to see the truth. 'When he undressed I saw that, indeed, there was nothing left there where his testicles used be. It blew us away to see that this was not a joke. He was mutilated.' 'Henk said the monks there preyed on the boys,' Rogge told Dohmen. 'When he was seventeen he became the* *brother superior's play thing.' In a series of articles for his paper, Dohmen reconstructed how Henk tried to get his life back on track after his discharge from St. Josephs. In April 1957, with nowhere to live, Henk joined the crew of a Dutch cargo ship headed for Indonesia. But on board, his body swelled up grotesquely and he had wild mood swings caused by the hormonal imbalance following his castration. When the ship docked in Kobe, Japan, Henk went ashore and sought help. With the help of the Dutch consul there, he found Ysbrand Rogge, Cornelius's brother. Ysbrand, a merchant banker in Kobe, arranged for Henk to fly home to Amsterdam by KLM jet, and he ensured that his mother Thea would be waiting for Henk when he got there. Thea took him in and got him medical help. Thea Rogge wrote in one of the letters her son kept that the lawyers and doctor who'd helped Henk had found nine more cases—another nine boys who'd been castrated in similar circumstances. Dohmen found documents that show that there were more castrations, and he knows the identity of at least one more person, but suspects there could be many more. Using Thea Rogge's letters, Dohmen traced the rest of Henk's story. He discovered that Henk, once nursed back to health, had moved out of her house and found a place of his own. Lawyers acting for Henk had filed suit against the psychiatric institution and the child welfare board that approved the minor's involuntary commitment and castration, demanding 150,000 guilders or about $100,000, at the time, in damages. A few weeks after Henk reported brother superior Gregorius to the police, Gregorius was spirited out of Harreveld boarding school. Records in the Dutch state attorney's office reveal that he was never prosecuted, for 'lack of evidence.' His congregation quickly moved him to New Glasgow, in Nova Scotia, where he helped set up a home for the mentally handicapped and worked for many years, according to a Dutch newspaper. Gregorious, whose given name was Gregory van Buuren, died in 1993 of natural causes, at the retirement home of his congregation in the Netherlands."[36]*

Henk Heithuis died in 1958 in a mysterious car accident, and some monks were later convicted of sexual abuse, but the story of his castration never surfaced until many decades later, and according to Dohmen, there is evidence that at least nine other boys were castrated. This is particularly disturbing because as it was reported in *Time* magazine, *"The revelations are especially shocking given the long-standing Dutch traditions of openness and tolerance, notably regarding homosexuality. Same-sex relations have been legal in the Netherlands since 1811, and the country was the first in the world to legalize same-sex marriages in 2001. Perhaps most disturbing, however, is the fact that the castration claims were also missed by an official investigation into sexual abuse in the church published last year. The investigation—headed by Wim Deetman, a former Dutch Education Minister and mayor of the Hague—looked into 1,800 reports of sexual abuse by clergy or volunteers within Dutch Catholic dioceses from 1945 to 2010. While the 1,100-page final report concluded that tens of thousands of children had been abused over 40 years, it did not delve into the castration claims, saying, 'There were few leads for further research."* [37]

36   The Daily Beast, *Ibid.*

37   http://content.time.com/time/world/article/0,8599,2109795,00.html ‡ Archived from the internet September 5, 2014.

Leo Lyon Zagami

The author and journalist Giacomo Galeazzi, back in 2011, wrote, "*The independent inquiry commission presided over by former minister Wim Deetman, reached a shocking conclusion, identifying 800 perpetrators of abuses (priests and lay staff), of whom 150 are still living. One in five minors who came into close contact with Church structures, in the Netherlands, between 1945 and 2010, were forced to suffer abuse.*"[38]

The Deetman Commission, promoted and supported officially by the Catholic Church, only seemed interested to investigate cases that occurred from 1945 to 1985. They probably left out the more recent cases to the scrutiny of the public, as to not upset the present hierarchy of the Dutch Catholic Church, and again they failed to make any mention of the castration cases.[39] The investigation officially ended in December of 2011, which was led by Willem Joost "Wim" Deetman, who was born 3 April 1945 in The Hague. He was a Dutch politician of the Christian Democratic Appeal (CDA), a statesman, former minister of education and mayor of The Hague, and currently a member of the Dutch Raad van State (Council of State).[40] Needless to say, in recent times the CDA has been the dominant political party in the Netherlands. It is a pro-Vatican party, however several groups of activists have criticized the work of the Commission of Inquiry controlled by Deetman, accusing the Catholic politician of covering up many abuse cases committed by the Church. In the end Deetman has been criticized by the Dutch parliament for failing to include evidence of the castrations of at least ten minors.[41] *Radio Netherlands Worldwide* even went as far as stating: "*We now know that former Dutch cabinet minister Wim Deetman did not meet the expectations he raised when he chaired the Commission of Inquiry into sexual abuse in the Roman Catholic Church. He did not get to the bottom of the abuse scandal or reveal all of the horrors that took place behind church doors in the Netherlands.*" The radio station made mention that journalist Dohmen found something even more important during his investigation, "*He discovered that the Deetman Report failed to mention a certain political figure who tried to secure a royal pardon for Gregorius and other convicted Catholic brothers from Harreveld. That was Victor Marijnen, a former Dutch prime minister and leading member of the Catholic People's Party (KVP). The KVP later merged with Protestant parties to form the Christian Democrats (CDA)—the political party of inquiry commission chairman Wim Deetman. Victor Marijnen was in an extraordinary position in the 1950s. Not only was he a rising star in his political party, he was also vice-chairman of the Dutch Catholic child protection agency, and—most pertinently—director of Harreveld boarding school. The Deetman Commission was aware of these connections and the potential conflicts of interest they represent. The commission was aware of Marijnen's letter to the*

38   La Stampa, Vatican Insider, *Ibid.*

39   Il Fatto Quotidiano, *Ibid.*

40   http://en.wikipedia.org/wiki/Wim_Deetman ‡ Archived from the internet September 5, 2014.

41   *Ibid.*

Pope Francis: The Last Pope?

Queen on behalf of sexual abusers, too, but omitted these facts in its report. Reacting to Dohmen's revelations, the Deetman Commission explains that it did not mention Marijnen because it did not detail any cases that could be traced back to an individual, for the sake of protecting privacy. However, elsewhere in the same report we see numerous mentions of cases that can be traced back to individuals, even highly-placed figures such as bishops Ad Simonis and Philippe Bär. The commission did not shy away from slapping these men on the wrist. It's not unreasonable to conclude that the Deetman Commission refrained from investigating the castration because it knew this would inevitably lead to closer scrutiny of the Harreveld situation, exposing the role of Victor Marijnen and showing Mr. Deetman's own political party in a very negative light indeed." [42]

The Italian television network *LA 7* picked up the story for a TV special, and stated that in this tragedy of chemical castration there was, *"not even a hint in the final report by the Commission."* [43] As per the usual, the Deetman Commission was controlled and manipulated by the Vatican Jesuit stooges who responded to the media accusations by saying they had been aware of the case of Henk Heithuis (of course they were!), but they were simply not able to arrive at a definite conclusion based on a supposed lack of evidence, showing once more that the Catholic hierarchy and their politicians are liars with no heart.

FIG. 29. Pictured above is Henk Heithuis, the Dutch citizen who was castrated in 1956 by the Catholic Church. Photo: omroepbrabant.

42   http://www.rnw.nl/english/article/time-truth-about-catholic-sex-abuse-netherlands ‡ Archived from the internet September 5, 2014.

43   http://tg.la7.it/vaticano/pedofilia-chiesa-bimbi-castrati-in-ospedali-cattolici-in-olanda-17-03-2012-61436/ ‡ Archived from the internet September 5, 2014.

Leo Lyon Zagami

THE VATICAN AND THE NETHERLANDS OF HORRORS

In May of 2013, more shocking revelations were revealed from Holland with the statements of Toos Nijenhuis, alleged victim of pedophilia by priests and people in high places. She is described by a known blogger as, *"a fifty-four-year-old physiotherapist and mother of five from Holland, who was tortured, raped and used experimentally from the age of four years old by wealthy and powerful men around the world, including top officials of churches and governments. And, Nijenhuis claims, these crimes are continuing today, including the ritual sacrifice of children in rural Holland. On May 7 (2013), Ms. Nijenhuis accompanied Kevin Annett, Mel Ve and other investigators to a forested site near to Zwolle where such child murders took place as recently as November, 2010, according to Ms. Nijenhuis. Among the perpetrators who are named in these crimes and who allegedly assaulted Toos Nijenhuis are Prince Bernhard of Holland, who was the grandfather of the newly-crowned Dutch King Alexander, and a founder of the Bilderberg Group; Catholic Cardinal Bernard Alfrink of Utrecht; and members of the British Royal Family."*[44]

Ms. Nijenhuis is not alone. Supporting her extraordinary claims is another eyewitness of the events, a man who was a regular participant in the dark rituals of the pedophile cult, including the supposed killing of children. We find him in a video next to Nijenhuis saying, *"I saw Joseph Ratzinger murder a little girl at a French chateau in the fall of 1987,"* stated the witness who was a regular participant in the cult ritual torture and killing of children. *"It was ugly and horrible, and it didn't happen just once. Ratzinger often took part. He and (Dutch Catholic Cardinal) Alfrink and (Bilderberg founder) Prince Bernhard were some of the more prominent men who took part."*[45]

Ms. Nijenhuis is now hoping for some kind of binding legal action against the Church on her behalf by the ITCCS, the International Tribunal into Crimes of Church and State, a legal entity that is now moving in this direction. I therefore hope that sooner or later we will all receive clarification on what has really happened in the Netherlands. It's safe to say that as a democratic nation there must have more honesty and transparency from both its clergy and its politicians.

Regarding Ratzinger, he is perhaps not the monster described by Ms. Nijenhuis and her friend, but we can't be certain of these incredible allegations until we have further evidence. *Pope Emeritus*, more than any other, taking into account his previous position of power during the pontificate of John Paul II, and who was Prefect of the Congregation for the Doctrine of the Faith, is certainly guilty of having acted for years in a conspiratorial role at the top of the Vatican hierarchy, often to cover up the wrong-doing of his pedophile

44   http://aangirfan.blogspot.it/2013/05/child-sacrifice-and-royalty.html ‡ Archived from the internet September 5, 2014

45   http://www.youtube.com/watch?v=-A1o1Egi20c ‡ Archived from the internet September 5, 2014

priests. He could have initiated a process of transparency and renewal of the Church if he was a different man, without waiting to reach this level of shameful decline that possibly lead to his resignation. During the reign of the now-sainted John Paul II, Ratzinger was in charge of the *"Faith,"* and pedophile priests were not only tolerated in the Vatican, but often rewarded by the Polish Pope. It has been proven, without a shadow of a doubt, that these are the serial pedophiles at their very worst. There is Father Marcial Maciel Degollad (who died January 30, 2008), founder of the Legionaries of Christ, a pedophile involved in numerous sexual scandals that came out only after the death of Pope Wojtyla, and were finally acknowledged publicly by Ratzinger only after his death. Jimmy Savile, the now-deceased pedophile BBC presenter, who in 50 years had molested more than 200 victims and, according to a witness, had even boasted of turning into jewelry the glass eyes stolen from bodies in a morgue in which he often gave himself to acts of necrophilia. *"A glass eye stolen from a corpse by Jimmy Savile, which he then made into a trophy necklace, was sold at a charity auction for £75 shortly after his death. It is believed to have been worn by the pedophile DJ as he co-presented the final episode of 'Top of the Pops' at BBC Television Centre in 2006, where he also groped a child. An official NHS report revealed yesterday, Savile had bragged about stealing glass eyes from the sockets of the dead at Leeds General Infirmary, and had them made into rings and medallions."*[46]

This infamous monster known as Jimmy Savile, who until his death on October 29 of 2011, was never charged with anything because he was protected in high places, having received in his hands personally by the so-called Saint, John Paul II, an important acknowledgment when he was nominated Knight of the Pontifical Equestrian Order of Saint Gregory the Great, in 1990.

So the next time people speak of how good of a man Wojtyla was, let them read this book and maybe then they will begin to understand what kind of person he really was.

THE "BABY PROSTITUTION RING" AND THE CHURCH OF COMPROMISE

In November 2013, yet another big scandal erupted in Italy with clear links to prominent political figures and the Vatican. A few months after the election of the new Argentinian Pope, the Italian police discovered a child prostitution ring that was operating in the Parioli neighborhood in the north of Rome, one of the most exclusive areas of the Italian capital. This latest pedophilia scandal shook Italy to its core. It was not only the result of the present decay of morals, which now rages in our Western society, but was secretly controlled for years by the forces imposed on us by the New World Order.

---

46   http://www.dailymail.co.uk/news/article-2672395/Glass-eye-stolen-corpse-Savile-necklace-sold-charity-auction-75-wore-final-Top-Pops-groped-child.html#ixzz3CTXlqX4c ‡ Archived from the internet September 5, 2014

Leo Lyon Zagami

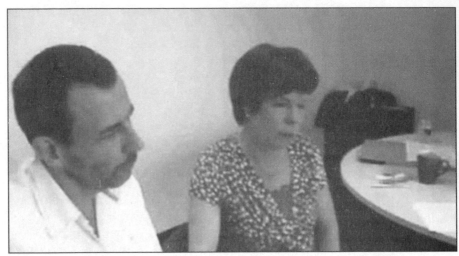

FIG. 30. A frame from the video interview showing Toos Nijenhuis, alleged victim of pedophilia by priests and people in high places, along with another alleged super witness.

FIG 31. Pope John Paul II together with the infamous pedophile Jimmy Savile, during his appointment as Knight.

It is also the inevitable result of compromise and hypocrisy reigning within our current society. A society which, beyond measure, tolerates deplorable conduct. It pretends not to see what is really going on, often out of laziness, or perhaps to keep up the appearance of a quiet life around them.

Pope Francis: The Last Pope?

Even in an exclusive neighborhood of Rome, the meetings of these young prostitutes went on for years undisturbed before finally being discovered by the police. The public was initially shocked while television programs bombarded its viewers with improbable *"Talk Shows"* and *"News"* on this sad story. The paradox is that the more you dig into this cross-section of today's society, the more it opens into the world the proverbial "Pandora's Box" in which the prevailing squalor ends with the discovery of more and more *customers* from the so-called elite of our society. These include professionals, military officers, politicians, and even Mauro Floriani, director of *Trenitalia,* and husband of Alessandra Mussolini, the granddaughter of fascist dictator Benito Mussolini *(Il Duce),* and the niece of Sophia Loren. Shortly after this story broke and the names began to leak, the newspaper articles and various broadcasts about this delicate subject suddenly stopped. This occurred after investigators discovered evidence that certain employees of the Vatican were also involved in this child prostitution ring.[47] The apparent *loyal customers* of the *"Baby Prostitutes"* as they were called, also include what could be important prelates.

After these revelations, and as far as the mass media was concerned, the case was closed. For the public, going deeper into the story would have been too much for the Catholics of Italy to handle, a culture still somewhat submissive to the Church. After all, the public is consumed at present with a sort of Pope frenzy, created by Bergoglio and his Jesuits, to manipulate the masses further. In any case, 40 people, potential clients of the ring are still being investigated. The girls involved were aged 14 and 15. When the press exposed the Vatican involvement, the online edition of the Roman newspaper, *Il Tempo,* always loyal to the Vatican, quickly wrote, *"It could not be priests involved, but civilians."*[48] In a later print edition of the same newspaper, reported by the website *Gazzettino.it,* a police investigator admitted: *"We are also investigating priests and politicians who could be involved in the case."*[49]

The following period witnessed the absolute silence of the Italian and the international media on this delicate case. The first convictions arrived in the summer of 2014, which of course did not include the politicians, the priests, or the Vatican employees involved. This was yet another demonstration of the power of the Holy See, which said nothing on the matter, even in the supposed new era of Pope Bergoglio, who just preferred to ignore the whole thing. A month before the scandal erupted, in October 2013, another abuse case involving the Church was brought to light, and this time it involved Pope

47   http://www.fanpage.it/baby-squillo-preti-politici/ ‡ Archived from the internet September 6, 2014.

48   http://www.iltempo.it/cronache/2013/11/17/baby-squillo-tra-i-clienti-dipendenti-del-vaticano-1.1190392 ‡ Archived from the internet September 6, 2014.

49   http://www.ilgazzettino.it/ITALIA/CRONACANERA/baby_squillo_roma_preti_politici/notizie/361817.shtml ‡ Archived from the internet September 6, 2014.

Francis directly. Erik Zattoni from the city of Ferrara in northern Italy told his story to reporters of an Italian television program, *Le Iene,* broadcasted by Berlusconi's TV channel *ITALIA UNO.* The poor Zattoni knew from an early age that he was the product of rape by a priest. When his mother was aged 14, she was abused by a priest that housed her and her family in the parish. He was born from this terrible act of violence 33 years earlier, and now in 2013 he finally demanded justice from the *"new"* Church of Pope Bergoglio. But the media outlets of Ferrara focused their attention on the reaction of the present Bishop Luigi Negri, which was truly shocking and not in line with the supposed Christian values of the Bishop. At the microphone of *Le Iene,* the Bishop made it clear that he did not have too much to say about Zattoni's case, or the priest responsible for it.

When a journalist from *Le Iene* asked how a priest could remain in his position even after a "crime of this nature," Negri glossed over the question by stating: *"You want to teach the Church how to be the Church? Certainly it is fair to say that there were reasons why the Church believed that he should be dismissed. Rape is not enough. For the monetary compensation I don't know who you should ask, but not me. These things are civil matters, not ecclesiastical. Stop it, because I am getting upset."*[50]

I think these unrepentant words by a Bishop are more than enough to understand the current situation within the Church. So how does Pope Francis fit in Zattoni's case in particular? When he was still a Cardinal, a mere four days before his Pontifical election, he was interviewed on the case by the same TV show.[51] Quite annoyed, with an attitude far removed from what we see today as the *"good"* Pope Francis, he dismissed the case and left in a hurry. It is quite paradoxical that in early December, 2013, Bergoglio received with a smile a book on the Inquisition from the Israeli Prime Minister Netanyahu.[52] Perhaps he should use it as inspiration for his work with the group of Cardinals denominated the "C8" that he has put together, which I will discuss in a moment. The news that was broadcast on April 13th, 2013, exactly one month after his election, stated that eight cardinals were chosen to advise the Pope, *"in the government of the universal Church"* to consider a draft revision of the Apostolic Constitution *Pastor bonus* on the Roman Curia. *"I think that the consultation is very important,"* said Francis in an interview with the Jesuit publication *Civiltà Cattolica.* He stated, *"The consistories and synods are, for example, important places to make real and active consultation. We must, however, make them less rigid in form. I want to consult them in a real way, not formal. The consultation of*

50   http://www.ilfattoquotidiano.it/2013/10/18/prete-pedofilo-stupro-mia-madre-papa-francesco-faccia-giustizia/748792/ ‡ Archived from the internet September 6, 2014.

51   https://www.youtube.com/watch? V = Df-fhHjLUkA ‡ Archived from the internet December 3, 2013.

52   http://www.ilgiornale.it/news/esteri/netanyahu-visita-papa-porta-regalo-libro-sullinquisizione-972739.htm ‡ Archived from the internet September 6, 2014.

Pope Francis: The Last Pope?

the eight cardinals, this outsider advisory group, is not only my decision, but the result of the will of the cardinals, as it has been expressed in the general congregations before the conclave. I want it to be a real consultation, not just formal."[53]

The C8 group that is apparently assisting him in his mission of *"purifying"* the Church in the eyes of the public is composed of Cardinals from all continents: Giuseppe Bertello (the only Italian particularly linked to the Knights of the Holy Sepulcher), Francisco Javier Errazuriz Ossa (the only *emeritus* of the group), Oswald Gracias, Reinhard Marx, Laurent Monsengwo Pasinya, Sean Patrick O'Malley, George Pell, and Andrés Rodríguez Maradiaga. The latter also plays the role of coordinator, while the function of secretary has been entrusted to Marcello Semeraro, the Bishop of Albano, which is a town near Rome. Their official level function has focused on the administration of the Vatican machine, which is not treating in any consistent way, the increasing demands for compensation by victims of pedophilia perpetrated by the clergy. Since their appointment, the cardinals in question have been in contact with each other where they exchange ideas, proposals, collected materials, and cited instances from the Bishops Conferences to which they belong. With the new Secretary of State Pietro Parolin, the C8 has also worked with the so-called *Council of 15* for the Study of Organizational and Economic Problems of the Holy See (Meisner, Rouco Varela, Pengo, Carera Rivera, George, Fox Napier, Cipriani, Scola, Toppo, Pell, Vallini, Urosa Savino, Ricard, Odilo Scherer, Tong Hon). *The Council of 15* was created at the time by John Paul II to create greater collegiality in the approval of the financial statements, budgets and accounts of the Vatican. At the center of the debate, "the mission of the IOR" is inserted in the wider mission of the Church as seen from *not only* the *"economic operational side."* The Cardinals officially consider a *"limited horizon,"* but I have to wonder, do they really? In the end it seems that the IOR will not close its doors after the arrival of Pope Francis, as many of us were hoping. The final decision, of course, is not really up to the Pope, but to the Roman Curia, the first and most direct collaborator to the Pope. They were not excluded from this process of *apparent* transformation to the administrative structure of the Vatican.

All the heads of the various departments in fact, have submitted proposals to reform, or otherwise improve, the coordination between the curial offices and their activities. There are two main issues that the eight cardinals from the C8 are dealing with, in particular, together with the Pope, since their appointment to this new office. To begin with, there are questions on the life within the Church: collegiality: the relationship between the center and the particular churches; the relationship between the Curia and the Bishops' Conferences; and the possible reform of the Synod of Bishops. On

---

53   http://vaticaninsider.lastampa.it/vaticano/dettaglio-articolo/articolo/vaticano-curia-28215/ ‡ Archived from the internet September 6, 2014.

this, much material and many requests and suggestions were collected by the Bishops' Conferences of various continents. The second major theme is the reform of the Roman Curia.

On the roadmap, there are cases to streamline the Curia itself, which has often been perceived as a central governing body of the Church, as opposed to a service to the universal ministry of the Bishop of Rome. Streamlining could go through the amalgamation of several pontifical councils, some of which, for example, could be embodied in a new Congregation for the Laity. Another issue concerns the structure of the Secretariat of State that was, as we know, in the hands of the infamous Cardinal Bertone. Lost in such bureaucracy, who knows if the Pope and his team will eventually manage to save the dignity of the Church before his departure from earth. Let me say that I have my doubts. Meanwhile, in early December, 2013, more shocking news began to unfold in the media regarding the possible resignation of Pope Francis himself at some point in the near future. Such a possibility was first hinted by Guillermo Marcò, *"After Benedict's gesture it will not seem too strange if Francis gave up, after having done what he thought was right to do and if he feels that his strength is weakening."* Marcò also stated during a radio interview, *"To be able to resign, as the bishops do, would be positive, since it would then appoint younger people."* Obviously, by doing so, Francis will be giving in to the New World Order project to destroy any *divine presence* in the various religions before the *One World Religion* comes to life. French journalist Caroline Pigozzi, who with the Jesuit Henri Madelin, authored a book on the figure of Francis, called *Ainsi fait-il*. In an interview given to the website *Infobae*, he stated that the tradition of the Society of Jesus would support the Pope's future decision to resign, and this must be taken into account: *"I believe that Francis had a vision of his own power, a Jesuit vision and personal. He arrived late for his mission but wants to accomplish it and knows what he is doing."* He then adds, *"the day he feels that he can not go further, that the forces are deserting him, he should leave, as did his predecessor."* According to Pigozzi this could become *"a new rule in the Vatican. If Francis also resigns he would create in this way a historical precedent, which would become part of the tradition in the Vatican."* Religious political fiction? Not really. In August 2014, on his way back from Korea, Pope Francis confirmed what his ex-spokesmen Guillermo Marcò had suggested, that he may one day resign the papacy. Marcò stated, *"The pope said that his predecessor Benedict XVI has opened the door for papal resignations with his decision to stand down last year, the first example since Pope Gregory XII in 1415. Some theologians may say this is not right, but I think this way."* In a lighthearted exchange with reporters returning to Rome from a trip to South Korea, Pope Francis noted, *"Let us think about what (Benedict XVI) said, 'I have become old, I do not have the strength.' It was a beautiful gesture of nobility, of humility and courage."* He added: *"But you could say to me, if you at some time felt you could not go forward, you should do the same."* Asked about his immense popularity, the 77-year-old joked that he would probably die soon so he should not get too proud: *"I know this will last a short time, two or three years, and then I go to the house of the Father."* Pope Francis also said he had some nerve problems that he treated with a South American tea-like drink called Mate, and that he had not taken a vacation away from home since 1975.[54]

Comments like this naturally lead Catholics—and the general public alike—to begin to wonder with some apprehension, what then will happen after Ratzinger's resignation if another Pope leaves the Chair of Peter voluntarily? The continuous indispositions of Bergoglio in the internal wars for the ultimate control of the Vatican bank are worrying to many insiders who say the Pope is fed up.[55]

In short, Francis could very well resign, but by doing so it will mean the definitive and final end of what is left in the Sacrality of the Papacy, as well as fulfilling the NWO aspirations. Whatever excuse Pope Francis gives, it is not justified in a religion based on the ultimate sacrifice of its founder: *Jesus Christ.*

54   http://www.nbcnews.com/news/world/pope-francis-i-could-quit-benedict-or-even-die-2017-n183721 ‡ Archived from the internet September 6, 2014.

55   http://mentiinformatiche.com/2014/06/francesco-e-stanco-e-nello-ior-torna-la-guerra-di-poltrone.html ‡ Archived from the internet September 6, 2014.

Chapter: V
PROPHECIES AND MORE...

THE END TIMES ALWAYS HAVE A NEW BEGINNING

The crisis looming over the Catholic Church has long been a constant theme of prophecies—some very old, and others from reputed seers in the last few decades. Consistent with biblical prophecy, almost 900 years ago the Irish Saint Malachy predicted that the last pope will be called *Petrus Romanus,* or "Peter the Roman," and would preside over the destruction of Rome. Catholic prophecies also tell of an "Antichrist" who will betray the faith. In more recent times, the apparitions of Our Lady of America—a partially-approved apparition—warned in 1981 that certain "priests and consecrated virgins" were caught in a "web of evil" which included "unnatural acts," while others were teaching "false doctrines" and "repudiating" the sacraments, raise even more eyebrows. [1]

In light of the many prophecies, current events, and the mass sensitivity of Catholics, we find ourselves divided amongst those who try to recall the numerous—and sometimes puzzling—prophecies of *"The Last Pope,"* and others who are dazzled by the rich background and charismatic history of Christianity. Then there are those who wish to delve deeply into the shocking circumstances of Ratzinger's resignation. In light of the dramatic political

---

[1]   http://cathnews.acu.edu.au/204/96.php ‡ Archived from the internet September 6, 2014.

and human crisis that now involves the whole world, for many the arrival of an *"End of Times"* scenario is confirmed. Despite what some might believe, the impression that emerges from the prophecies and Christian apocryphal writings is not simply a bunch of religious *"mumbo jumbo."* To the contrary, they demonstrate a precise story line of great proportions, at times dramatically true, predicting episodes of importance from the recent past. The *"End of Times"* scenario we seem to be living in, these new dark ages, as defined by the decadence of the Church infected by apostasy, should later give birth to the infamous *"Reign of the Antichrist"* narrative, who in the view of many Christian eschatologists, has already risen to power. The persecution and martyrdom that the Church will have to face in this terrible period for mankind will be followed by a possible *"rebirth."* And this could correspond to the predicted and increasingly-real project to establish a One World Religion, complete with the Temple in Palestrina that we analyzed earlier. The messages of the prophets are clear: There will be a dramatic period of *"tribulation"* and divisions, a possible schism, infighting within the clergy, and apostasy within the ranks of the faithful. Those who will not side with the growing evil and stay true to the path of Christ will eventually be rewarded for their strong faith. The possibility of a sort of diagram on the basis of these prefigurations is clearly of a Hermetic nature: *Passion-Death-Resurrection*. It is the same pattern that we find in the exemplary life of Jesus, and the true significance of mystical Christianity. This brings us to the rebirth stage of true awareness and understanding—*but only after a period of profound tribulation*. In some traditionalist interpretations, the mystical visions will lead to the *"construction"* of the faithful's soul. That is, only those who follow the pure path of practice and prayer will be able to *"save"* their soul from death and dissolution.

THE EMMERICH VISIONS

The Christian prophecies accepted by the Vatican seem to allude to the resignation of Ratzinger as a major turning point, and more generally, they are addressed to this specific period in history. We find it in the words of the Virgin from the cycle of Rue de Baruch, La Salette, and Fátima, and the visions of the Blessed Catherine Emmerich (1774-1824). Born at Flamske in Westphalia, Germany, on September 8, 1774, Catherine Emmerich became a nun of the Augustinian Order at Dulmen. She had the use of reason from the time of her birth and could understand liturgical Latin even from her first time at Mass. During the last 12 years of her life, she could eat no food except for the Holy Eucharist, nor take any drink except water, and thus subsisting entirely on the Holy Communion. From 1802 until her death, she bore the wounds of the Crown of Thorns, and from 1812, she apparently received the full stigmata, including a cross over her heart and the wound from the lance. Anne Catherine Emmerich seemed *"to have possessed the gift of reading hearts, and she saw, in actual visual detail, the facts of Catholic belief that most of us simply have to accept on faith. The basic truths of the catechism—angels, devils, Purgatory, the life of Our Lord and the Blessed Mother, the Real Presence of Christ in the Eucharist, the grace of the Sacraments—all these truths were as real to her as the material world."[2]*

A book entitled *The Life of Anne Catherine Emmerich* written by Rev. Carl Schmoeger, C.SS.R., was published in English in 1870, and reprinted in 1968 by Maria Regina Guild based in Los Angeles, California.[3] The truly remarkable visions that were seen, or *channeled* to use a more modern term, by Emmerich between 1820 and 1822, spoke of a false church in Rome built against every rule, in which they would find and shelter heretics of every kind, and giving rise to division and chaos. For the first time, along with this premonition, is introduced the theme of twin popes, and the false ecumenical Church established in Rome. The latter reference sounds very much like the previously mentioned *Temple of the Work of the Holy Spirit,* a truly *"strange, and extravagant Church"* created by what are becoming the zombies of the New World Order, the ones Emmerich says in her visions work *"mechanically."*

Let us directly examine some of her most interesting visions:

> *I saw also the relationship between two popes ... I saw how baleful would be the consequences of this false church. I saw it increase in size; heretics of every kind came into the city of Rome. The local clergy grew lukewarm, and I saw a great darkness.*

> *I had another vision of the great tribulation. It seems to me that a concession was demanded from the clergy which could not be granted. I saw many older priests, especially one, who wept bitterly. A few younger ones were also weeping. But others, and the lukewarm among them, readily did what was demanded. It was as if people were splitting into two camps.*

> *I saw that many pastors allowed themselves to be taken up with ideas that were dangerous to the Church. They were building a great, strange, and extravagant Church. Everyone was to be admitted in it in order to be united and have equal rights: Evangelicals, Catholics, sects of every description. Such was to be the new Church ... But God had other designs.*

> *I saw again the strange big church that was being built there in Rome. There was nothing holy in it. I saw this just as I saw a movement led by Ecclesiastics to which contributed angels, saints, and other Christians. But there in the strange big church all **the work was being done mechanically according to set rules and formulae.** Everything was being done according to human reason.*

2   http://www.olrl.org/prophecy/emmerich.shtml ‡ Archived from the internet September 6, 2014.

3   http://ourlady3.tripod.com/emmerick.htm#(1) ‡ Archived from the internet September 6, 2014.

I saw all sorts of people, things, doctrines, and opinions. There was something proud, presumptuous, and violent about it, and they seemed very successful. I did not see a single Angel nor a single saint helping in the work. But far away in the background, I saw the seat of the cruel people armed with spears, and I saw a laughing figure which said: 'Do build it as solid as you can; we will pull it to the ground.'

I saw again the new and odd-looking church which they were trying to build. There was nothing holy about it ... People were kneading bread in the crypt below ... but it would not rise, nor did they receive the body of our Lord, but only bread. Those who were in error, through no fault of their own, and who piously and ardently longed for the Body of Jesus were spiritually consoled, but not by their communion. Then my Guide (Jesus) said: 'This is Babel.'[4]

Regarding this subject, there is also a similar prophecy by Nostradamus in one of his famous quatrains, numbered *II.30,* and entitled,

The New Mass of Many Languages, the Antichrist:

One whom the infernal gods of Annibal
Shall be reborn to terrorize mankind
Never greater horror have been reported
One shall come due to the Babel
Mass given to the clergy.[5]

The vision of the two popes seems incredibly accurate in relation to Ratzinger and Bergoglio, but it also continues to be accurate in reporting that the priests would have surrendered to every kind of obscenity; from gambling to sex, just as is done in the Vatican today. Emmerich continues:

I saw deplorable things: they were gambling, drinking, and talking in church; they were also courting women. All sorts of abominations were perpetrated there. Priests allowed everything and said Mass with much irreverence. I saw that few of them were still godly ... All these things caused me much distress.

Then I saw an apparition of the Mother of God, and she said that the tribulation would be very great. She added that people must pray fervently with outstretched arms, be it only long enough to say three 'Our Fathers.' This was the way her Son prayed for them on the Cross. They must rise at twelve at night, and pray in this manner; and they must keep coming to the Church. They must pray above all for the Church of Darkness to leave Rome. ... These were all good and devout people, and they did not know where help and guidance should be sought. There were no traitors and enemies among them, yet they were afraid of one another.

---

4   *Ibid.*
5   *Ibid.*

*I saw more martyrs, not now but in the future. ... I saw **the secret sect** relentlessly undermining the great Church. Near them I saw a horrible beast coming up from the sea. All over the world, good and devout people, especially the clergy, were harassed, oppressed, and put into prison.* [6]

In the prophetic dreams of Don Bosco (1815-1888), the Church also appears divided toward a possible schism. Don Bosco was the founder of the now powerful Salesians of Don Bosco, known also as the Salesian Society. Most of the prophecies associated with Don Bosco came to him during his dreams, just as Matthew's Gospel describes the process of Joseph as being instructed by angels during dreams. It is clear that Don Bosco's experiences were more than the type of dreams most of us have while asleep. Most of Don Bosco's dreams were concerned with the direction that he and his Order, the Salesians, were to take in the future—and in particular—with the students who lived at his oratory in Turin. He would often speak to them just before they went to bed, sometimes predicting that one of their number would die within a certain period, but without indicating who.

On the 30th of May, 1862, during one of his "Good Night'" talks, Don Bosco told his boys and the young clerics that he was training, about a dream he had a few nights previously. He stated: *"Very grave trials await the Church. What we have suffered so far is almost nothing compared to what is going to happen."* [7]

This seems to echo what Anne Catherine Emmerich said only a few decades earlier, on October 1st, 1820: *"The Church is in great danger. We must pray so the Pope does not leave Rome; there would be innumerable evils if he did. Now they are demanding something from him."*

What is most striking in this prophetic scenario is the explicit reference made by Emmerich to the *"Secret Society,"* which would set out a plan for the destruction of the Church. Who and what is she referring to? Perhaps the Illuminati and their Ecclesiastical Freemasonry? Even Mother Agnes Steiner and Blessed Anna Maria Taigi spoke respectively of a church without a pastor and of the Holy Father being forced out of Rome: *"They will have to leave their monasteries, monks and nuns will be uprooted from their convents, especially in Italy. ... The Holy Church will be persecuted. ... Unless people with their prayers obtain the pardon, the time will come that will see the sword and death, and Rome will be without a shepherd. ... The religion ... will be persecuted, and priests massacred. The churches will be closed, but only for a short time. The Holy Father shall be obliged to leave Rome."* [8]

---

6   *Ibid.*

7   http://www.theotokos.org.uk/pages/Fátima/donbosco.html ‡ Archived from the internet September 6, 2014.

8   http://profezie3m.altervista.org/ptm_c2-2.htm ‡ Archived from the internet September 6, 2014.

ARE THE PROPHECIES TRUE?

Can the visions described above be defined as authentic? Of course their authenticity is not merely a matter of formal approval by the Church—that may or may not accept them as genuine. There are a variety of extremely popular visions that have made their way into the hearts and faith of millions, even without formal acceptance. Yet the intentions of the few in charge at the top of the Vatican hierarchical structure still count on the ultimate Pontifical approval, as in the case of *Our Lady of Medjugorje,* also known as the Queen of Peace. To be considered as part of the official and recognized visions of the Church, as is typical for all claims of private revelation that the Catholic Church must follow as a standard criterion for evaluating apparitions. There are two possible judgments: *constat de supernaturalitate,* or *"it is confirmed to be of supernatural origin,"* and *non constat,* or *"it is not confirmed."*[9] The Catholic Church has made successive comments on the status of the Medjugorje apparitions, and each has been declared *non constat,* that is, it cannot confirm the supernatural nature of the apparitions.[10]

The Vatican commission set up to study the Medjugorje prophecies concluded their work on January 18, 2014, but its results have remain unpublished.[11] Of course, this begs the question why? They could simply be slow to publish them, but in reality, due to the strange behavior of some of the visionaries involved, there are still many doubts on their authenticity. Inside the Vatican, that is, the NWO lobby of Marinelli, Montuoro and company, are those trying their best to promote the Marian cult, as there are also economic and geopolitical interest in the matter.

In order to have a clear perspective on this particular matter for non-Catholics or non-Christians alike, I will let the Catholic American blogger Glenn Dallaire from Bristol, CT, who specializes in the extraordinary mystics and visionaries of the Church,[12] articulate a good explanation on the subject:

Some might ask if there are authentic mystics, visionaries and prophets in the world today? Judging by history the answer would have to be a most resounding 'yes.' Beginning in the Old Testament, we see the holy Prophets arise, inspired by the Holy Spirit to enlighten God's people, and to reveal and set forth God's laws. And throughout the centuries, we see the Catholic Church

9 http://www.vatican.va/roman_curia/congregations/cfaith/documents/rc_con_cfaith_doc_19780225_norme-apparizioni_en.html ‡ Archived from the internet September 6, 2014.

10 http://www.cbismo.com/index.php?mod=vijest&vijest=101 ‡ Archived from the internet September 6, 2014.

11 http://www.news.va/en/news/commission-to-submit-study-on-medjugorje ‡ Archived from the internet September 6, 2014.

12 http://www.mysticsofthechurch.com/2009/11/who-i-am-and-origins-of-this-site.html ‡ Archived from the internet, September 7, 2014.

Leo Lyon Zagami

inspired and strengthened by Her holy mystic Saints and visionaries, who by the express will of God, become extraordinary instruments in His hands and special 'channels' for the Holy Spirit. Mystics and Visionaries as specially chosen souls have a variety of missions within the Church such as: (1) they inspire devotions like the Sacred Heart and Divine Mercy devotions; (2) through their lives as victim souls they make reparation to God for the conversion of sinners, and remind us to make sacrifices and do penance; (3) they enlighten us concerning the evils of the world and reveal to us the horrors of sin; (4) through their sufferings willingly accepted and offered to God, they remind us of our call to participate in the redemption of all of humanity through the offering of our own sacrifices, and through our sufferings willingly accepted.

In the book Mystics of the Church *by Evelyn Underhill, we see that no century has been without its Mystics throughout the history of the Church. And certainly our most recent century has been enriched by some of the most extraordinary mystics in the history of the Church, such as St. (Padre) Pio (1887-1968)—the first Priest confirmed to have had the sacred Stigmata, St. Faustina Kowalska (1905-1938) of the Divine Mercy devotion, and the extraordinary lay Mystic and Stigmatic, St. Gemma Galgani (1878-1903), just to name a few. There are certainly a good number of persons in the world today who are said to be mystics, and to a much lesser extent, there are a number of persons who are said to be stigmatics. The difficulty of course lies in the discernment as to whether a mystic or visionary is authentic or not. It is of course much easier for the Church (i.e. normally the local Bishop) to discern the authenticity of a mystic after their death, thus being able to discern and judge their entire life and the presence (or absence) of heroic virtues. Apart from any glaring theological errors, the Church normally does not make any judgments until after their death, and even then, a good number of them are never formally investigated by the Church.* [13]

Glenn Dallaire adds to the point in regards to *"the spiritual dangers of mystics and visionaries,"* when he clarified the following:

Although on the one hand Scripture states that we are not to despise prophecy, on the other hand the Church and the Saints advise us to be extremely careful and prudent in such matters, because perhaps more often than not, the origins of some alleged mystical graces can in reality be the devil in disguise. The extraordinary Mystic St. Paul of the Cross says that for every 100 persons said to be mystics; there is perhaps only one or two that are truly authentic and inspired by God—and this is coming from someone who was not only an extraordinary Saint and religious founder, but who himself was a authentic Mystic! Certainly we should heed his wise advice.

13   http://www.mysticsofthechurch.com/2010/01/mystics-and-visionaries-in-world-today.html ‡ Archived from the internet, September 7, 2014.

We need to remember that the devil does not counterfeit copper or tin, but only gold. And all that glitters is not necessarily gold. Just because a visionary en- courages such things as Eucharistic devotion, the Rosary, Confession, etc, this does not mean they are authentic mystics. After all, the devil does not appear with horns and cloven hooves suggesting that we follow or imitate him. If he showed himself the devil, who would follow or be inspired by him? He is the deceiver, and his deceptions are oh so very subtle. Let us not pride ourselves into thinking that we are wiser than the demon by making ourselves judges and entrusting our spiritual lives to our own poor judgment.

Little by little, a false visionary or mystic will very subtly, almost impercepti- bly, introduce false devotions and doctrines, which on the surface seem logical and spiritual, but really are a means to instill spiritual pride in those affected, by thinking that they have 'additional' knowledge that other Catholics do not have, and / or by reciting special prayers and practicing special acts of devotion that other Catholics do not know of, thinking that they are specially graced through their association with the alleged mystic or visionary, and through the additional knowledge, prayers and acts of devotion that are not known or practiced by other Catholics. Once this spiritual pride takes root, then sooner or later comes spiritual disobedience to the Church, that is, usually the local Bishop, who will often test the spirit of the mystic by conveying certain sanc- tions upon the mystic and the followers, to see if they submit in obedience their alleged graces to the Church. [14]

1951 ‡ THE CROSSROADS OF PROPHECY
AND THE RISE OF THE ANTICHRIST

On September 19, 1846, near the village of La Salette-Fallavaux in southeastern France, there was a Marian apparition reported by two children, Maximin Giraud and Melanie Calvat, that was given the name of *Notre-Dame de La Salette,* or "Our Lady of La Salette." [15] Over 150 years later, in April 2002, the French Fayard Publications released a book entitled *Discov- ery of the Secret of La Salette,* by Fathers René Laurentin and Abbé Michel Cor- teville. This book was intended to be read only by the general public because the subject was considered taboo to modern Catholics. The book endorses nothing less than an elucidation to the question of the authenticity of the Secret of La Salette. The 2002 authors are especially renowned for the latest version of an old theme, one that happens to be the longest interpretation to date, and has received the Imprimatur of Bishop Zola, Bishop of Lecce in It- aly. The reason for this book was to summarize and popularize another book published in 2000. An enormous thesis of more than a thousand pages, also

---

14   *Ibid.*

15   http://en.wikipedia.org/wiki/Our_Lady_of_La_Salette ‡ Archived from the in- ternet, September 7, 2014.

penned by Father Michel Corteville, called *La Grande Nouvelle des Bergers de la Salette*, or "The Great News of the Shepherds of La Salette," and examining the Order of the Mother of God in the second part. Sections of the "secrets" remain to be published. It is Father Corteville who, in October 1999, discovered the original *Secret of La Salette* given to Pope Pius IX in 1851, buried for more than a century in the Vatican archives. This thesis was written to defend the divine authenticity of the many secrets.[16]

The biographer of Melanie Calvat has amazing things to say about the general opinion of the French clergy concerning the Apparition of La Salette and the child witness Melanie herself, during the years following the Apparition:

> *(In 1860, Melanie) returned to Marseille and the Convent of Our Lady of Compassion. There Melanie tried to get her Secret published, as the Blessed Virgin had instructed her. But the Bishop of Marseille reacted just as had the Bishop (Ginoulhiac) of Grenoble. He flew into a fury, scolded Melanie, then took the pages on which the Secret was written, crumpled them into a ball and threw them into the fireplace. As he watched them burn, he said to Melanie, 'This is how I will publish your secret!' Melanie knew then that she would not be able to get the Secret published in France. She said, years later, that if the Apparition of La Salette and its Secret had been accepted by the French clergy, all the miracles that were done at Lourdes had occurred also at La Salette. Melanie also said that the de-Christianization of France occurred because of the hostility of the bishops towards the appearance of the Blessed Virgin at La Salette.*[17]

Beyond the controversies and the doubts of authenticity, the visions and prophecies of the Lady of La Salette have uncanny similarities with most of the others. In a universal theme, the predictions of the decadence of the Church and the advent of the Antichrist are echoed over and over. In one of these visions, the Virgin of La Salette predicts the assassination attempt on a Pope, claiming: *"The Pope will be persecuted on every side, they will shoot on him, they will want to put him to death, but they can do nothing."* After analyzing the passage, some researchers, including Antonio Socci, identified it with the assassination attempt on Pope John Paul II in St. Peter's Square on May 3, 1981. Even the Italian mystic Teresa Musco, a remarkable seer and stigmatic, who like Jesus died at age 33, in September 1971, ten years before the Turkish killer Ali Agca would attempt the life of Pope John Paul II, while she was reliving the passion of Christ, had an ecstatic vision of the wounding of the Pope and said: *"Stop! What are you doing? Why do you want to kill him? They want to kill the Pope! This happens in St. Peter's Square."*[18]

---

16 http://www.sspxasia.com/Newsletters/2003/Jul-Dec/Secret_of_La_Salette.htm ‡ Archived from the internet, September 7, 2014.

17 http://www.salvemariaregina.info/SalveMariaRegina/SMR-168/LaSalette4.htm ‡ Archived from the internet, September 7, 2014.

18 Antonio Galli, Scoperti in Vaticano i Segreti de La Salette, (Milan: Sugarco, 2007), p. 68.

Pope Francis: The Last Pope?

Teresa Musco was born in the little village of Caiazzo near Caserta, in Italy on June 7th, 1943. She was one of ten children, four which died during childhood in a typical poor southern Italian family.[19] When Teresa was five years old, she had her first *"divine"* experience when she saw her first shower of large hail stones, falling fast toward her. She ran, half-dressed, out of the house, unaware of the danger. She lifted her arms and tried to catch the hail stones. Her worried father saw what was happening and immediately ran after her, slapped her face, and pulled her forcibly back into the house. Soon afterward, a *'very beautiful lady'* appeared to Teresa. It was the Mother of Jesus, and when Teresa told the Lady about the beating she had got from her father, the Lady told her very gently, *'Look, little daughter, your father meant well and didn't mean you any harm.*[20] It is believed that this was the first appearance of the Blessed Virgin Mary in Teresa's life, and later the presence of the Madonna became more and more frequent. One can rightly describe Teresa's early life as being heavily influenced and guided by the Holy Mary.

Two years before her shocking vision about the attempted assassination of the Pope, on Holy Thursday, April 3, 1969, at 10 am, Teresa received the stigmata. When she saw the Holy Mary dressed in black wearing a black veil from head to foot with tears that seemed to be running down of her face, telling her: *"Teresa, my beloved Son desires to give you His wounds."*[21] Curiously, one of the two shepherd children from La Salette, Melanie also received the stigmata as Teresa Musco had.

Stigmata seems to be a frequent event in the life of Catholic mystics and visionaries. So does the theme of abandonment of the faith by top officials. In a passage of the visions of La Salette, transcribed and sent by Melanie to the Pope on July 6, 1851, the Virgin says: *"There will also be the ministers of God and the brides of Jesus Christ who will abandon themselves to the riots and, this will be a terrible thing; in the end a hell will reign on earth; it will be then that the Antichrist will be born from a religious person, but beware, many people will believe him because they will say he came from the sky; the time is not far distant, will come to pass twice in 50 years."*

The message, as I stated, dates back to 1851. This implies that *"twice in 50 years"* will take us to 1951. On this front, the date of 1951 appears as a point of convergence between the visions of the Blessed Emmerich and the eight preserved writings of the secret of La Salette (three by Maximin, five by Melanie) that the Virgin transmitted to these two shepherds in La Salette, and that were later transcribed and sent to Pope Pius IX in July 1851, yet mysteriously disappeared until 1999. Rightly so, Mons. Antonio Galli, author of a book on the subject published in Italy, points out that *"those one hundred years would take*

---

19   *Ibid.*

20   http://www.mysticsofthechurch.com/2012/01/teresa-musco-stigmatic-mystic-victim.html ‡ Archived from the internet, September 7, 2014.

21   *Ibid.*

Leo Lyon Zagami

us to 1951, there is now a well-known prophecy of the Blessed Catherine Emmerich, who died in 1827, according to which fifty or sixty years before the year 2000, swarms of demons from hell would be set free to roam the earth. We must unfortunately note, at our expense, in the second half of the twentieth century, Satan is really going wild, plunging the world into an abyss of horror and darkness." [22]

Let us remember that in the 1950's the methodical Masonic infiltration of the Vatican began in earnest. It was soon afterward that a Freemason named Roncalli became the first Masonic Pope, who is now considered Saint John XXIII. The dramatic infiltration by Freemasonry into the Vatican is filled with hypocrisy, and endures to this day with disastrous consequences. In an attempt to save the Church, in 1956 Padre Pio secretly appointed Don Luigi Villa to fight Ecclesiastical Freemasonry, a subject I investigate in depth in the third Volume of my, *"Confessions."* In the eschatological message, [23] Melanie adds further details in paragraph 26 regarding the advent of the Antichrist and his origins: *"During this time (of the false peace) the Antichrist will be born, from a religious Jew, a false virgin who will communicate with the old serpent, the master of impurity."* Interestingly this diabolical figure that Melanie defines: *"in a word, he will be the devil incarnate."*

Of course we can't be sure if these visions are genuine or not, and we also have to take into account the period in which they were circulated and put together, when Jews were not so close and accepted as they are now by the Catholics (especially since the Second Vatican Council). What was revealed at La Salette is still quite incredible in relation to the coming of the Antichrist, though the shepherdess did not reveal a possible date for his birth, as did others, in more recent times, for example the American seer, Jeanne Dixon. According to Dixon, the Antichrist will be born in 1962 and will cause the ruin of the Church through the creation of a *"false humanism, through which man will worship himself."* Jeane L. Dixon (1904-1997) was one of the best-known American astrologers and psychics of the 20th century, mostly due to her syndicated newspaper astrology column, some well-published predictions, and a best-selling biography. [24] Jeanne Dixon accurately foretold the assassinations of Mahatma Gandhi, Martin Luther King Jr., John F. Kennedy, and his brother Robert. Mrs. Dixon predicted the launch of Sputnik and the sinking of the submarines USS Thresher and Scorpion. Her successful predictions include the political defeat of Dewey by Harry Truman, the landslide election of Dwight Eisenhower, the demise of Nikita Kruschev, and the plane crash

---

22   Scoperti in Vaticano i Segreti de La Salette, *Ibid.,* p. 56.

23   **Eschatology** *is a part of theology concerned with what are believed to be the final events of history.*

24   http://en.wikipedia.org/wiki/Jeane_Dixon ‡ Archived from the internet, September 7, 2014.

that killed UN Secretary Dag Hammarskold.[25]

Of course, many of Dixon's predictions proved incorrect, but she was followed by the most prominent Illuminati Republicans of her day. President Richard Nixon followed her predictions, for example, *and was a member of the Bohemian Grove.* Dixon even gave advice to Nancy Reagan, wife of another Bohemian Grove member, U.S. President Ronald Reagan.

She wrote, *"A child born somewhere in the Middle East shortly before 7:00 am (EST) on February 5, 1962 will revolutionize the world. Before the close of this century, he will bring together all mankind in one all-embracing faith. This will be the foundation of a new Christianity, with every sect and creed united through this man who will walk among the people to spread the wisdom of the almighty power."[26]*

Could this child be *Barack Obama*? He was born in August, 1961, not 1962, and he was apparently born in Hawaii, USA, not the Middle East, but a lot of speculations have been circulating for years on the internet and various publications in regards to his real place of birth and his Muslim origins. There is evidence he could have been born in either Kenya or Indonesia, both being countries with large Muslim populations. The Rev. Robert Jeffress, a Dallas megachurch pastor, came out with a book in 2014 that claims President Barack Obama is clearing the way for the Antichrist. Jeffress, head of the 11,000-member First Baptist Church of Dallas, writes in his book, *Perfect Ending,* that he does not believe Obama is the Antichrist, yet he links Obama's support of gay marriage to the coming of the Antichrist. *"For the first time in history a president of our country has openly proposed altering one of society's (not to mention God's) most fundamental laws: that marriage should be between a man and a woman,"* Jeffress continues, *"While I am not suggesting that President Obama is the Antichrist, the fact that he was able to propose such a sweeping change in God's law and still win reelection by a comfortable margin illustrates how a future world leader will be able to oppose God's laws without any repercussions."[27]*

Regarding the timing of Obama's birth and rise to power, in a letter written by Melanie in 1892 and addressed to Canon de Brandt, she writes: *son temps de paraître n'est pas très éloigné,* or "the time to look is not very far." Deconstructing this phrase in his book, Galli seems to think that this wording in French signifies an exact distance in time: *"The Distance (as advocated by Melanie) that can be between 60 or 70 years, taking into account the clarification contained in the message: 'During this time.' The time of the false peace, before the third world conflict and the triumph of the Immaculate Heart of Mary. If so, the Antichrist would*

25   http://powerpointparadise.c om/endworld/othrpred/jeandixn.htm ‡ Archived from the internet, September 7, 2014.

26   *Ibid.*

27   http://www.religionnews.com/2014/01/08/pastor-obama-paving-way-antichrist/ ‡ Archived from the internet, September 7, 2014.

already be among us.[28] In fact Maximin, the other visionary of La Salette, in his secret letter sent to Pope Pius IX on the 3rd of July, 1851, mentions the fact that this great evil should have manifested in full force against the Church *"at the latest around the year 2000 or soon after."* Michel de Notre Dame (1503-1566), also known as Nostradamus, who predicted several occurrences from 1555 to 3797, also spoke of the coming of the Antichrist, that will cause years of terror and blood before the new Golden Age begins.

This age would allegedly re-establish the correct balance on Earth. In Quatrain 72, *Century X,* Nostradamus says: *"In the year 1999, seventh month: From the sky will come a great King of Terror. To bring back to life the great king of Angolmois, Before and after Mars is to reign by good luck."* The date clearly refers to a solar eclipse that occurred in August 1999, (the difference of one month is due to the change of the Gregorian Calendar made in 1582). According to Nostradamus, that year saw the coming of the Antichrist whose kingdom will last 27 years, before the beginning of the Golden Age.[29]

THE "UNOFFICIAL" PROPHECIES

Next to the prophecies recognized by the Church, there are also a cycle of non-recognized prophecies, as in the case of those made in more recent times made by Jeanne Dixon, or a few centuries back, by the now-legendary Nostradamus. They are often called "apocryphal," as their origins are not always easy to prove at an academic level and on which, therefore, I can only suspend further judgment on their genuineness. Interestingly, most of these prophecies seem to trace the same language and apocalyptic images contained in the prophecies officially recognized by the Church. It is therefore at least worthwhile to examine them. The Apocalypses of Ephesus Prophecy, for example, were supposedly dictated to a hermit in the XIV Century by a angel from the Church of Ephesus. The following passage speaks upon the arrival of a new celestial body:

Over the mountains of blood ... shall fall the stars, whilst the Sun shall swallow the Moon and then two new lights will throw up.

Earth's wounds shall still be bleeding ... but the flood will no longer be of water, but of fire ... All shall turn into a sea of blood.

It will be on these days of universal madness that the Antichrist will come ... from the East, bearing signs of righteousness and wellness.

Many shall follow Death, confusing it with the Lamb of Peace ... and Many shall desert, when terror ... will fall upon Rome.

Whilst the sky will show the signs of the Great Day, that are the Cross (Chris-

28   http://it.wikipedia.org/wiki/Nostra_Signora_di_La_Salette ‡ Archived from the internet, September 7, 2014.

29   http://www.thexplan.net/english/nibiru/prophecies.htm ‡ Archived from the internet, September 7, 2014.

tianity), the half moon (Islamism), and the beheaded eagle (the Antichrist).

In the marked time the Sun will be ordered to cry ... and the tears of the Sun shall fall upon Earth

Huge Sparkles shall then spring up from different places on Earth ... and each Sparkle shall turn into a plague.

And each plague shall bleed salty water and bones' dust ...

Rome, in this time, shall change its name ... and the legion of the Antichrist will march through Rome.

And the ground of Rome shall move as the wave of the sea. And the sea will come to Rome ... The seed of life shall stand in the Glen of the Four Saints.

From there the history shall start again ...

Within the new garden ... new laws ... time shall have ... dimensions.

And the Sun shall give a different warmth."

Are we to believe the Earth, and to an extent that the Moon, would both collapse? Perhaps this is a metaphor, or a description of some kind of new physical reality? The *"days of universal madness"* could refer to the imbalance of the planets, while the "crying Sun" could suggest an intense radioactive solar-rain that will lead to the overheating of the atmosphere, and would increase aridity upon Earth. The passage describing *"... the ground of Rome shall move as the wave of the sea,"* could refer to violent earthquakes that would be produced, and that could even sink the Eternal City, followed by, *"And the sea will come to Rome ..."*

The outcome of this chain of catastrophic events predicted by the Apocalypse of Ephesus would be a complete reshaping of our planet, which perhaps will spin through a different orbit, or experience a pole shift where continents rise and fall. The line *"And the Sun shall give a different warmth,"* could even refer to a new Solar System.[30] In 1600, on the seventeenth of February, Giordano Bruno (1548-1600), an Italian Dominican Friar, philosopher, mathematician and astronomer, was ceremoniously burned at the stake in Rome's Flower Market by the Roman Inquisition. His end is brutal to our modern sensibilities, but not exceptional to the Vatican standards of his day. But Bruno's death stands out, mentioned in passing in most popular and even academic surveys of the emergence of modern science. Specifically, Bruno was linked to modern science by his advocacy of a version of Copernicus' heliocentric planetary hypothesis and the idea that our universe is infinite, with many suns and planets.[31]

---

30   http://www.thexplan.net/english/nibiru/prophecies.htm ‡ Archived from the internet, September 7, 2014.

31   http://jamescungureanu.wordpress.com/2013/04/04/myths-about-science-and-religion-that-giordano-bruno-was-the-first-martyr-of-modern-science/ ‡ Archived from the internet, September 7, 2014.

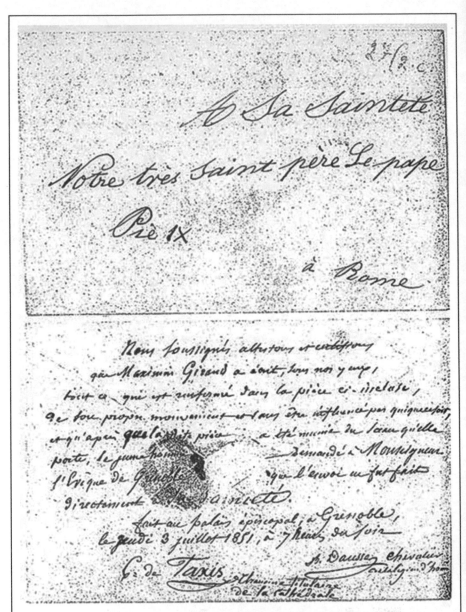

Doc. B. Enveloppe du secret de Maximin Giraud, adressé par lui au Pape Pie IX, contresignée par C. de Taxis et B. Dausse, à l'évêché de Grenoble, le 3 juillet 1851 à 7h du soir. SOLS fasc. 27 (ACDF).

FIG. 32. The envelope of the secret of Maximin Giraud addressed to Pope Pius IX on the 3rd of July 1851.

Pope Francis: The Last Pope?

Giordano Bruno has left some notes upon the future of Mankind:

Man shall travel the cosmos and from cosmos, he shall learn about the day of the ending ...

Just when the man will believe to be the lord of the Universe, many wealthy cities will end.

A black sun will swallow in the space the sun, the moon, and all the planets orbiting around the sun ...

Here the black sun could refer to a planet bearing so great a mass to be compared to the sun. The black sun could even refer to the *"twin"* of the sun, a *Nemesis*, a name given by Richard A. Muller for this celestial body. This new planet/dark sun, whose existence has been suggested recently as Planet X, Nibiru, Wormwood, and other names, but whose existence cannot be ruled out. Muller explains *Nemesis* would be a red dwarf sun, whose discovery has yet to come. As such, *Nemesis* would not generate light. Following the theory of our Solar system as a binary system, the prophecy could describe *Nemesis* as *"swallowing"* the sun. [32] In this context, some of the most interesting modern prophecies are those of the Nun of Dresden, and a German monk known as the "Black Spider." Both, however, have a common origin: their alleged discoverer was Renzo Baschera. This ex-professor, born in Casacco in the province of Udine in 1930, left his teaching job to devote himself full-time to the profession of writer and researcher of the prophetic texts. He published several books and discovered many unknown sources of prophecies, such as the Russian Monk Basilio, or the anonymous writers of the *Prophecies of the Shroud*. The fundamental problem in his work, and one which casts doubt, is that Baschera is not a historian. In many cases, he has been careful not to reveal certain details concerning the origins of these prophecies that he has supposedly identified. Although his books always contain bibliographies, they only contain historical sources used to verify the accuracy of the forecasts, but not their origins. It is never mentioned whether they are the original sources transcribed by him, from which library, or archive where they are found, and so on. Without knowing the origin of the texts it becomes impossible to even check if there are errors in his translations, that is, if the originals of these texts even exist! For this reason, the manuscripts of the Nun of Dresden and the *"Black Spider"* have never been studied by traditional academic means, but as I will show you now, they are still very interesting for their content.

The *"Black Spider"* is said to be a German monk who lived in the XVI Century, and who provides a list of occurrences and yearly prophecies. The year 2000, that he calls *"Glory of the Fire,"* represents a crucial turn in the history of mankind, a starting point towards a new spiritual path that will mark radical and physical changes:

---

32   http://www.thexplan.net URL.cit. ‡ Archived from the internet, September 7, 2014.

Leo Lyon Zagami

When mankind will reach the end of the Millennium, it will have climbed over the hilltop,

And from up above it shall see the wreckage of a time and the path, which leads to the new Earthly Heaven.

The first generation walking on that path will be a generation in pain, for hard shall be the path to regain the joy of the spirit.

According to the monk, mankind shall have to walk *"under the bridge of the five pains"* before reaching the *"joys of the spirit."* The prophecy speaks of 50 years of plagues that are deemed necessary to the conquest of the *"Earthly Heaven."* Between 2000 and 2010 there will be *"the time of fears,"* followed by *"the decade of madness," "the decade of settlement,"* and *"the decade of resumption."* The 1990-2000 decade represents *"the time of the Antichrist,"* but also the decade of the *"new commanders of the spirit."* The Black Spider claims that: *"Christ dies along the Tiber and arises on the Volga."*[33]

It seems that Christianity is doomed to be wiped out of the Mediterranean region—where it arose—to return further North in the present territory of the Russian Federation, where *Orthodox Christianity* is now reliving a period of growing faith and expansion. The expanding Islamic population of the European countries, especially those on the Mediterranean, seem to confirm the fears of the Black Spider on the possible disappearance of Christianity in these areas in the not so distant future.

The Russian and Greek Orthodox churches are also the only ones who have objected in recent times to plans in both countries (Russia and Greece) to introduce electronic national identity cards intended to streamline bureaucracy and, in the case of Greece, facilitate integration into the diabolical European Union. In reality, this is a trap set up by the New World Order to control and manipulate even further. The Catholic Church seems to even embrace such evil, where on the contrary, the Orthodox Church officials have been demanding, since 2011, a close study of these cards and the technology around them, and asking authorities to make them optional. They say that the personal and financial information that would be consolidated on the microchips in the cards could be manipulated to discriminate against believers.[34] Obama, AKA *"The Antichrist"* in the USA, is *(*of course) all for it, in what used to be *"The Land of the Free."* In an interview with *Rossiiskaya Gazeta,* an official government newspaper, Metropolitan Hilarion of Volokolamsk, chairman of the Moscow Patriarchate's Department of External Church Relations, said: *"Credit cards, which a person uses to take money from a bank machine or for payment in a store, are one thing, but a personal card in which all the information about a person's life and activities will be entered, about his bank accounts, health and travels is a*

---

33   *Ibid.*

34   http://ww w.christiancentury.org/article/2011-04/
       orthodox-churches-object-national-identity-cards

different matter. These are different grades of state control over people."

Conservative and nationalist wings within the churches had held demonstrations in Athens and Moscow back in 2011, as they rightly claimed that the cards will compromise national and religious identity. Many have gone so far as to say that identity numbers such as 666 are the *"Mark of the Beast"* from the Book of Revelation, the final book of the New Testament.

At a demonstration in Moscow on the 16th of April, 2011, Orthodox nationalists joined forces with members of the Communist Party of the Russian Federation, and even the Communists, to oppose the *Universal Electronic Card* (UEC) that was scheduled to be introduced in Russia in 2012.

Segodnia.ru, an Internet publication that often covers religious and nationalist issues, commented on the demonstration, and said, *"the introduction of the UEC makes it possible to build an unheard of, super-totalitarian electronic dictatorship, in which each individual person becomes a remote-controllable bio-object, for all practical purposes, a robot with a bar code on his body or a microchip implanted under his skin."*

Patriarch Kirill II of the Russian Orthodox Church spoke at a meeting of the Bishop's Council of the Russian Orthodox on February 2011, stating that, *"The church understands the position of people who do not wish to be subject to control that makes it possible to gather all-encompassing information about their private life, and could in the long-term be used to discriminate against citizens based on their world view."*[35] On the 27th of March, 2011, thousands of Greek Orthodox priests, monks, nuns and lay people marched through Athens to the Greek Parliament building in protest, but the international media ignored the news.

In April 2011, the Synod of Bishops of the Church of Greece expressed its concern about issuing the cards, and said it would hold meetings with top government officials. Religious leaders of the metropolitan regions Prokopios of Philippi, Neapolis and Thasos, that chair the Synod's Committee on Dogmatic and Canonical Questions, reported that the result of preliminary talks with the Greek government concluded that the church had received assurances that, amongst other things, the numerals 666 would not appear on the cards in any form.[36]

It's no wonder then, after all this opposition towards the infamous NWO plans to further control and eventually microchip us with what the Christians call *"The number of the Beast,"* that Greece is continuing its decline among its partners in the European Union. Meanwhile Barack Obama, the *"Black Prince,"* and his allies have begun a new Cold War in 2014, pitting the new Ukrainian government against Mother Russia. The term *"Black Prince"* is specifically used to define the Antichrist by the German Monk known as *"The Black Spider."*

---

35   *Ibid.*

36   *Ibid.*

Here is the passage of his prophecies making reference to *The Black Prince:*

> *There will be a new voice that the temple will demolish.*
>
> *Here he comes! (the Antichrist) descends from the sunny road standing on a carriage dragged by four black horses. He bears the color of the snow. His voice bears the force of thunder. Firm is his hand, a command is his gesture.*
>
> *There, among the stones of the last amphitheater the blood flows.*
>
> *The tablets of the law shall be thrown in the dust and stamped on by the horses' iron.*
>
> *Men! Pitiful, crawling creatures, the Prince gives you his law: rejoice until drunkenness and you will be happy; Worship Caesar and you will be exalted; steal, and you will be honored.*
>
> ***The Black Prince*** *shall hold a banquet in the hall of the Great Dome and thousands of fishermen shall incense his hand: a hand which holds the power of life.*
>
> *And death, a hand which destroy and creates, a hand which will bless and annihilate.*
>
> *Cry, mothers! Throw your bowels in the fire. Tear your womb apart.*
>
> *Man shall no longer be born from woman, for He came, the last son of Osiris. So it was written ... yet do not cry ... It's time for eyes to shut. Because the vine shall no longer give wine.*
>
> *And the earth shall no longer produce wheat. So it will be, until the new day we shall seek in the infinite.*
>
> *This will be the chant of the six legions crossing the river. Beware of the swamp, Here shall fall the last hope of the little Caesar.*
>
> *There will be signs from the sky. There will be the voices of the dead. There will be the moans of the living.* [37]

The Black Spider reminds us of how *"signs from the sky"* and *"other phenomena"* will trouble the peaceful. Could this be reference to the so-called UFO phenomenon? The monk's prophecies end with the passage: *"Humanity has been marked by three floods: the first was made of water, the second will be of fire, the third shall be made of stars ... at the third flood,"* which is dated circa 2500-3000 AD. The similar reference *"the sky shall go off forever"* is from the Apocalypse of Ephesus, which speaks identically about the "Flood of Fire." [38]

In German, *Schwarzer Spinner,* or "The Black Spider," was the first apocryphal prophet *"discovered"* by Baschera. He was a monk from the Bavarian Order of Cistercians, who presumably lived around the second half of the sixteenth century in Regensburg, Germany, and other locations. His name is supposedly derived from the seal, in the form of a black spider, with whom he penned his

---

37   http://www.thexplan.net URL.cit. ‡ Archived from the internet, September 7, 2014.

38   *Ibid.*

cards containing a long list of prophecies that would terminate on June 7th, 3017 AD. The provisions of the Black Spider are arranged in chronological order, and as thus they have a Christian origin for their clarity and do not require a particular comment, as opposed to the quatrains of Nostradamus. It is in these writings we find an explicit reference to The Decade of the Tribulation (*"the decade of madness"*), which would begin in 2011, and that would lead to the emergence of the Antichrist as head of the Church. Coincidentally, in 2011 Barack Obama began campaigning for a second term as President of the United States.

The expression *"the decade of madness,"* could indirectly make reference to the tribulation period spoken of in the Old and New Testament under different names, a concept that is widely developed in *the Apocalypse of St. John*. Emmerich also spoke in her visions of the *"tribulation"* that will face the Church, stating that, *"When the Church had been for the most part destroyed by the secret sect, and when only the sanctuary and altar were still standing, I saw the wreckers enter the Church with the beast."*[39] This "secret sect" is what we usually call the Illuminati. More than ever before, it is operating with the goal of destroying what little is left of the sacrality of the Church of Rome and its original values.

How close to this vision are we really? *"The Satanic hierarchy will rule upon Earth, lead by a demon who will speak the tongue of Attila but will wear the dress of Caesar,"* said the Nun of Dresden. Little is known of the Nun of Dresden, aside that she lived in a convent near the Elba River in Germany between 1680 and 1706. She experienced various ecstatic moments, although she could barely read or write in her native language. However, during these moments, she could speak Greek and Latin perfectly. The Nun of Dresden spoke about the time when Lucifer would arrive, which shall occur between 1940 and 2010.[40] So apparently he is already here.

TWO DECADES OF TRIBULATION

In May 2010, an interesting report was produced by The Rockefeller Foundation and The Global Business Network. Incredibly enough, this memorandum resumes the theme of the *"tribulation"* in the same time frame I discussed in the second volume of my *Confessions of an Illuminati,*[41] which includes an in depth analysis of this memorandum. The 53-page document issued by the Rockefeller Foundation, entitled *Scenarios for the Future of Technology and Interna-*

39   http://ourlady3.tripod.com URL.cit. ‡ Archived from the internet, September 7, 2014.

40   http://www.thexplan.net URL.cit. ‡ Archived from the internet, September 7, 2014.

41   Leo Lyon Zagami, Confessions of an Illuminati VOL II, (San Francisco: CCC Publishing, 2016).

tional Development, was published in PDF format on their Foundation website.[42] The document outlines a scenario in the next two decades that appears so catastrophic, it seems to be written along the same lines as the apocalyptic literature I have shown you in this chapter. The apocalyptic scenario envisioned by the global elite seems to resemble more the dystopian vision of a dark and violent totalitarianism as illustrated in George Orwell's *1984*, but also along the lines of the society envisioned by Aldous Huxley in *Brave New World*, which represents the model of a soft dictatorship. This is where the population willingly accepts the rules imposed from above, mainly because it has been manipulated and conditioned from birth to accept it without rebelling, as is happening currently in the United States and most of the Western world. What is striking is that the Rockefeller Foundation and their associates are *"scenario planning,"* suggesting an exorbitant amount of deaths that humanity is to expect in the coming years. For these individuals, our current and future disasters are within *"a range of future possibilities."* Read, below, their ideology to understand their mindset:

> *Scenario planning is a methodology designed to help guide groups and individuals through exactly this creative process. The process begins by identifying forces of change in the world, then combining those forces in different ways to create a set of diverse stories—or scenarios—about how the future could evolve. Scenarios are designed to stretch our thinking about both the opportunities and obstacles that the future might hold; they explore, through narrative, events and dynamics that might alter, inhibit, or enhance current trends, often in surprising ways. Together, a set of scenarios captures a range of future possibilities, good and bad, expected and surprising—but always plausible. Importantly, scenarios are not predictions. Rather, they are thoughtful hypotheses that allow us to imagine, and then to rehearse, different strategies for how to be more prepared for the future—or more ambitiously, how to help shape better futures ourselves.[43]*

According to a passage contained in this document, the world will suffer from a mysterious pandemic. The contagion should hit 20% of the population, killing at least 8 million people, in just seven months. Is this pandemic the same as the growing threat of the Ebola virus that the population of world began to fear starting in 2014? The 2010 report shows striking similarities:

> *The pandemic that the world had been anticipating for years finally hit. Unlike 2009's H1N1, this new influenza strain—originating from wild geese—was extremely virulent and deadly. Even the most pandemic-prepared nations were quickly overwhelmed when the virus streaked around the world, infecting*

---

42   http://www.rockefellerfoundation.org/uploads/files/bba493f7-cc97-4da3-add6-3deb007cc719.pdf ‡ Archived from the internet September 8, 2014.

43   The Rockefeller Foundation, GBN GLOBAL BUSINESS NETWORK, *Scenarios for the Future of Technology and International Development*, New York-San Francisco, May 2010, p.9

Pope Francis: The Last Pope?

nearly 20 percent of the global population and killing 8 million in just seven months, the majority of them healthy young adults. The pandemic also had a deadly effect on economies: international mobility of both people and goods screeched to a halt, debilitating industries like tourism and breaking global supply chains. Even locally, normally bustling shops and office buildings sat empty for months, devoid of both employees and customers.

The pandemic blanketed the planet—though disproportionate numbers died in Africa, Southeast Asia, and Central America, where the virus spread like wildfire in the absence of official containment protocols. But even in developed countries, containment was a challenge. The United States's initial policy of "strongly discouraging" citizens from flying proved deadly in its leniency, accelerating the spread of the virus not just within the U.S. but across borders. However, a few countries did fare better—China in particular. The Chinese government's quick imposition and enforcement of mandatory quarantine for all citizens, as well as its instant and near-hermetic sealing off of all borders, saved millions of lives, stopping the spread of the virus far earlier than in other countries and enabling a swifter post- pandemic recovery.[44]

Thanks to this epidemic the people will be forced to surrender their sovereignty to the NWO, as the document makes clear:

During the pandemic, national leaders around the world flexed their authority and imposed airtight rules and restrictions, from the mandatory wearing of face masks to body-temperature checks at the entries to communal spaces like train stations and supermarkets. Even after the pandemic faded, this more authoritarian control and oversight of citizens and their activities stuck and even intensified.[45]

A more authoritarian and more globalist government, a New World Order, in fact, will result in growing control over all aspects of our lives, and will include what the Rockefeller memorandum described as, *"technology that could literally see right through you."*[46] This includes the feared RFID chip, an implanted biometric identification chip made mandatory for all citizens. Instead of rebelling against such tyranny, the report predicted we will actually become eager to surrender our sovereignty, brainwashed as we usually are, by the elite and their corrupt media circus:

In order to protect themselves from the spread of increasingly global problems—from pandemics and transnational terrorism, to environmental crises and rising poverty—leaders around the world took a firmer grip on power. At first, the notion of a more controlled world gained wide acceptance and approval. Citizens willingly gave up some of their sovereignty—and their pri-

---

44 The Rockefeller Foundation, *Ibid.* p. 18.

45 *Ibid.*, p. 19.

46 *Ibid.*, p. 40.

*vacy—to more paternalistic states in exchange for greater safety and stability. **Citizens were more tolerant, and even eager, for top-down direction and oversight,** and national leaders had more latitude to impose order in the ways they saw fit. In developed countries, this heightened oversight took many forms: biometric IDs for all citizens, for example, and tighter regulation of key industries whose stability was deemed vital to national interests.[47]*

Initially, Obama's healthcare reform tried to introduce the biometric ID with the implementation of *Electronic Health Records* (EHR) for all Americans by 2014. But having failed, they opted instead to include the biometric ID into immigration reform. David Kravets wrote for *Wired* in May, 2013:

Buried in the more than 800 pages of the bipartisan legislation is language mandating the creation of the innocuously-named 'photo tool,' a massive federal database administered by the Department of Homeland Security and containing names, ages, Social Security numbers and photographs of everyone in the country with a driver's license or other state-issued photo ID. Employers would be obliged to look up every new hire in the database to verify that they match their photo. This piece of the Border Security, Economic Opportunity, and Immigration Modernization Act is aimed at curbing employment of undocumented immigrants. But privacy advocates fear the inevitable mission creep, ending with the proof of self being required at polling places, to rent a house, buy a gun, open a bank account, acquire credit, board a plane or even attend a sporting event or log on the internet. Think of it as a government version of Foursquare, with Big Brother cataloging every check-in. 'It starts to change the relationship between the citizen and state, you do have to get permission to do things' said Chris Calabrese, a congressional lobbyist with the American Civil Liberties Union. 'More fundamentally, it could be the start of keeping a record of all things.'

For now, the legislation allows the database to be used solely for employment purposes. But historically such limitations don't last. The Social Security card, for example, was created to track your government retirement benefits. Now you need it to purchase health insurance. 'The Social Security number itself, it's pretty ubiquitous in your life,' Calabrese said. David Bier, an analyst with the Competitive Enterprise Institute, agrees with the ACLU's fears. 'The most worrying aspect is that this creates a principle of permission basically to do certain activities and it can be used to restrict activities, he said. 'It's like a national ID system without the card.'[48]

For this reason alone, both the Greek and Moscow Patriarchates rightly consider inadmissible the forced application of such a diabolical technology, and Vladimir Putin seems to still listen to his people, more than the Greek

47   *Ibid.*, p. 19.
48   http://www.wired.com/2013/05/immigration-reform-dossiers/ ‡ Archived from the internet September 8, 2014.

government at least, which has submitted to the European Union's rules and regulations. Wake up Americans! The danger is imminent, even NBC predicted on their evening news that, *"We Will All Have an RFID Chip Under Our Skin by 2017,"*[49] and it will not be easy to avoid such a danger when the Vatican not only ignores it, but being part of the NWO, secretly approves of it. In September 2014, the new NFC (Near Field Communication) microchip has made its first public appearance in the media after an advertising director from Australia had the microchip injected into the webbing of his hands so he could use it in connection with some of the latest smart phones. This new kind of microchip can be used with any device that contains this technology, and, contrary to the RFID chip it can not only store data but collect it, and, as such, becomes an even more diabolical tool in the hands of the NWO. In synthesis, according to the Rockefeller Foundation's *"scenario planning,"* the coming virus pandemic would spread even more violence into Africa, Asia and Central America, where the protocols for containment would be less efficient, if not absent, as we have already seen happening with the Ebola outbreak in Africa. The only exception, from the passage cited, is China. The government would put in place a strict quarantine for the population, and activate a rigid control of the masses typical of their present approach, but similar restrictions will gradually be adopted by other countries. The control system resulting from such a crisis, in the end, becomes *the Orwellian scenario* in the year 2025—the year in which our illusion of democracy will come to an end. This climate of totalitarianism will cause many conflicts and hot beds of guerrilla warfare in various countries. In fact, the document predicts that: *"By 2025, people seemed to be growing weary of so much top-down control and letting leaders and authorities make choices for them."*[50] Fortunately, the demented Rockefeller report is not correctly predicting everything that has come to pass. Of course, there was the possible *"2012 Olympic bombing, which killed 13,000,"*[51] included on page 34 of the memorandum that did not happen, and this brings us back to reality regarding the content of the document. The question naturally arises ... *if such disinformation might have been inserted deliberately to scare the curious, or to simply confuse the population with news altogether fanciful, than what was included as truthful reporting?* Still, this uneasy expression included on the same page of the memorandum, *"The years 2010 to 2020 were dubbed the 'doom decade' for good reason,"*[52] leaves us wondering if this could possibly refer to the apocalyptic, and at times occult tones, used in globalism? As I fully explain in my *Confessions of an Illuminati* trilogy, this mentality was born and developed in the context of millenarian and apocalyptic prophecy within the Protestant

---

49   https://www.youtube.com/watch?v=1YJsxMcAJoA ‡ Archived from the internet September 8, 2014.

50   The Rockefeller Foundation, *Ibid.,* p. 21.

51   *Ibid.,* p. 34.

52   *Ibid.*

Reformation. The aim of the Rockefeller document seems to incorporate a form of psychological terrorism that intends to influence and intimidate the masses, with the sort of *"prophetic"* expectations held by those who were employed to draw it up. The doctrine of the architects of the NWO, who seem to await the second coming of Christ—*or rather the arrival of their Messiah (who most likely will be the Antichrist)*, penetrates deep within the message of the prophecies. The predictions of a dramatic crisis, the decline of the Church, an emergence of the Antichrist, and the return of Christ the Judge, look to be the pinnacle of the most dramatic moment for humanity. Now, the prophecies contained in the biblical texts, in particular, the Apocalypse of St. John, need to come to life, the same as the *"End of Times"* scenario plays a role in Islamic and Jewish traditions. Let us just say that the apocalyptic tone of this document comes directly from the doctrines of the architects of the NWO.

MARK OF THE BEAST ‡ "THE END TIMES" AND THE THIRD SECRET OF FÁTIMA

Electronic chips have became so *"ordinary"* nowadays that we don't even think about them anymore. Yet they are everywhere—in our calculators, our computers, and even in our household appliances. For the last few years, we also find chips embedded in our ATM, social security and credit cards, and even in our state-issued driver's licenses and passports! Microchips are also implanted under the skin of animals, and contain medical data such as the pet's name, and vaccination records, that allow them to be identified, localized, and tracked in the event the animals are lost or escape. One of the first identification microchips was the TX1400L transponder made by a company from St. Paul, MN, called Destron Fearing. It was originally designed for animals, but a commercial promoting its use states that, *"Although it was designed to be injected in animals, this transponder may be used for other applications requiring an identification tag!"*[53] Is Destron Fearing, a subsidiary of Applied Digital Solutions, the company that initially developed the technology for the *VeriChip,* now rebranded as *PositiveID,* working to make it more acceptable and less obvious to the consumer? Until now, everything I have shown you in this book helps explain the numerous anomalies that would otherwise have no significance toward the implementation of the *PositiveID,* that, incidentally, is the only human-implantable microchip approved by the Food and Drug Administration (FDA).[54] The *Radio Frequency IDentification* (RFID) chip is part of the family of *Automatic Identification and Data Capture* (AIDC) technologies that include 1-D and 2-D bar codes. RFID uses an electronic chip, smaller than a grain of rice, that is usually applied to a substrate to form a label that is affixed to a product, case, pallet or other pack-

53   http://www.freewebs.com/nochip/ ‡ Archived from the internet September 9, 2014.

54   http://en.wikipedia.org/wiki/VeriChip ‡ Archived from the internet September 9, 2014.

Pope Francis: The Last Pope?

age. The information it contains may be read, recorded, or rewritten.[55] With the growing possibility of such technology being used on the human population on a large scale, some individuals have grown to fear the loss of rights it may produce. Some even conceptualize a future that may result where every movement is tracked by the government.[56] According to ZDNET, critics believe that this technology will lead to tracking individuals' every movement, and thus will become an egregious invasion of privacy. For security reasons, it is likely that the RFID reader (called an interrogator) will require a secondary means of validating a person's identity. That validation might occur through using a fingerprint or iris scan, at the same time the RFID microchip is implanted in your right hand or forehead. In the security realm, both forms of biometrics are already routine. Is it mere coincidence that the Book of Revelation describes the "Mark of the Beast" as being in the hand or on the forehead?[57] Why these two places? Why not the left hand or arm? Putting aside the popular spiritual interpretation that our foreheads represent our thoughts, and our hands represent our actions, this may provide a good starting point regarding the spiritual realm. Presented alone, it falls short of the true physical implications of *"a mark"* that is required to buy and sell in the near future. The truth is that inserting a chip in the front of your head will enable the altering of the hormonal level of the population because of the vicinity of the pituitary gland, or hypophysis, as explained by many researchers and scientists. You must ask yourself where is the most logical place to put a tiny microchip that is injected under the skin, used for payment, and only operates within a couple inches of a reader? The hand is the obvious answer. It would literally allow payment at the wave of a hand—as it is already being implemented in some nightclubs around the world.[58]

The choice of the right hand in particular is explained further, by its reference in *Revelation 13*—one of the best-known passages of the Apocalypse: *"And he causeth all, both small and great, rich and poor, free and bond, to receive a mark in their right hand, or in their foreheads: And that no man might buy or sell, save he that had the mark, or the name of the beast, or the number of his name."*

The implementation of this project on a global scale could well become the trademark described by St. John in *Revelations.* Such technology will also be used as a substitute for money and credit cards, just as it is now occurring in many countries, with so-called smart phones, and especially the new iWatch and iPay by Apple, which allows automatic payment by swiping a device over

55   http://en.wikipedia.org/wiki/Radio-frequency_identification#cite_note-117 ‡ Archived from the internet September 9, 2014.

56   *Ibid.*

57   http://www.ridingthebeast.com/articles/666-hand-or-forehead/ ‡ Archived from the internet September 9, 2014.

58   http://www.wnd.com/2004/04/24179/ ‡ Archived from the internet September 9, 2014.

a receiver. First with *Obamacare*, and then with *Immigration Reform*, one way or another, the chip is already planned, but not yet rendered enforceable by the U.S. government. It will eventually find its way to the mainstream population. A majority of people are not only willing to accept what Christians call *"The Mark of the Beast,"* many are actively endorsing and promote its use as a tool of modern innovation. This is, of course, without understanding the dramatic consequences for their life and their supposed freedoms. Following this direction, we are lead by the latest product of a leader in the bioengineering field, named Somark Innovations.[59] This company has developed a tattoo based on RFID technology placed precisely with numbers and bar codes, that will substitute for the chip and be on the hand or on the forehead, thus fulfilling the scriptures *in totality*. The tattoo of Somark—tested since 2007 on rats—remains invisible to observation, but readable using the company's instrumentation. Bill Christensen on *Live Science* wrote:

> The Somark ID System creates a 'biocompatible ink tattoo with chip-less RFID functionality.' The RFID ink tattoo does not require line of sight to be read, as is the case with other RFID devices (making them better than a barcode for some applications). RFID ink tattoos also solve the annoying problem of ear tag retention. Conventional RFID ear tags sell for about $2.25; about 60-90 percent of them eventually fall off. Also, Somark claims that the biocompatible RFID ink system will improve readability rates as well. **Humans next? Somark Innovations co-founder Mark Pydynowski noted that the RFID ink is fully biocompatible and was safe for use in humans.** He noted that RFID ink tattoos could be used to track and rescue soldiers. 'It could help identify friends or foes, prevent friendly fire, and help save soldiers' lives,' Pydynowski said.[60]

The tattoo application is done in less than three seconds, and with it, as with the *VeriChip*, every move of the future population of the NWO can be monitored and controlled. The tattoo may, in fact, contain personal data, medical records, bank accounts, and other personal information, as well as a GPS tracking device.

We all must understand, however, that the prophecies included in the *Holy Scriptures,* and in other religious texts, are not just revealing themselves naturally. There is a group of so-called *"believers"* from different faiths whom I usually refer to as *The Illuminati* who are facilitating their usage. They are acting secretly and behind the scenes to fulfill their aim to control the masses, without hiding the origins of their intention to the skilled eye. The interpretations *"messianic"* or *"apocalyptic"* are spreading, more than ever, on the net these days, thanks to a specific approach that simply reflects the original intentions of this

---

59   http://www.somarkinnovations.com/ ‡ Archived from the internet September 9, 2014.

60   http://www.livescience.com/1242-invisible-radio-tattoos-identify-soldiers.html ‡ Archived from the internet September 9, 2014.

Pope Francis: The Last Pope?

lobby, that follows a mix of Theosophy and politics, technology and Messianism, and toward the establishment of their supposed *Kingdom of God* on Earth. Remember, there are no coincidences!

Mentioned in his recent autobiography entitled *I Was Promised Paradise*, and published in Italy in January, 2013,[61] Mehmet Ali Agca, the Turkish assassin who I mentioned earlier, murdered a left-wing journalist named Abdi Ipekci (on February 1, 1979), and later shot and wounded Pope John Paul II (on May 13, 1981). Agca, still considered a figure of importance in the recent history of the Vatican, in his book says that even some sections of Islamic extremism would seek to *"hasten"* the fulfillment of the prophecies through armed struggle (such as the Grey Wolves and, in more recent times, ISIS). Plus, they employ the usage of Black Magic by summoning the *Jinn.*[62] Years ago, I was able to personally witness these secret practices when I was living in Oslo, Norway. They were performed in front of me by the son of one of the leaders of the Grey Wolves. In this case, they were preparing the ground for the return of the Mahdi—what the Islamists say will result in the final defeat of their enemies and the West. Agca recounts in his book:

> *Basically it's really as if the world finishes in favor of a new era. Go in mosques around the world. Listen to what they say about the return of the Mahdi. They all say the same thing: soon, very soon indeed, he is arriving. What does this mean? That a part of Islam is sharpening their weapons. The return of the Mahdi will bring bloodshed. If the Mahdi will not manifest himself their will (can) materialize him, and in short, the Islamic fundamentalists, will set on fire the whole Western world.*[63]

This is because, even in the days of Khomeini, it was believed that the condition for the return of the Mahdi was the decline of the West and, in particular, following the prophecies of Fátima, the end of the Church. Agca continues: *"I know that what I am about to say may make you smile a lot. But it is the truth, and many newspapers have given this news. In May 2011, twenty employees of Mahmoud Ahmadinejad have been arrested and charged with magic. In essence, the main collaborators of Ahmadinejad have been making for years Satanic practices."*[64] Agca concludes these incredible statements by giving a specific date and a warning: *"The 13th of May 2017 is a fruitful date to unleash hell, to give the definitive goodbye to the Western world,"*[65] as he mentions earlier in the same chapter, *"Islamic fanatics are preparing for the final battle. The 13th of May 2017,*

---

61   See. Mehmet Ali Agca, I Was Promised Paradise, (Milan: Chiarelettere, 2013).

62   **Jinn** or **djinn** are entities of the Islamic tradition, often considered part of the demonic realm because they have free will like humans, and unlike angels. They often choose to side with Iblis/Satan and are used for Black Magic.

63   Ali Agca,*Ibid.,* pp. 170-171.

64   *Ibid.*, p. 171.

65   *Ibid.*, p. 172.

and it is in fact, one hundred years after the apparition of Fátima."[66] During his 1985 trial, Agca made the statement that his assassination attempt was *"connected to the third secret of the Madonna of Fátima."* The apparition at Fátima first occurred on May 13, 1917, exactly 64 years before the attempted assassination of Saint John Paul II, on May 13, 1981. On Saturday, May 13, 2000, on the 83rd anniversary of the Fátima vision, the Roman Catholic Church, under the direction of the Bishop of Rome, revealed the contents of the third vision of Fátima to the world. The startling announcement was front page news all around the world. *The Los Angeles Times*, for instance, wrote that *"the third secret of Fátima had become one of the most intriguing mysteries of modern times."* According to Vatican sources, the vision described a bishop in white, agonizingly making his way to the Cross through a sea of corpses of Christian martyrs, suddenly cut down by a fusillade of bullets. Together with the Fátima revelation, the Vatican gave an interpretation that applied in part, but failed to address completely several major elements of the prophecy. Vatican officials concluded that the third Fátima prophecy applied to the past, especially to the attempted assassination in 1981 of Pope John Paul II in St. Peter's Square. The Vatican found compelling evidence to make this association during the subsequent trial of Mehmet Ali Agca, the Turkish gunman.

It was on the 13th day in May of 1917, and on the 13th of every month thereafter, until October of 1917, a period of five months, the visions appeared to Lucia and the other two school children with her. Pope John Paul's assassination attempt on the 13th of May in 1981 only added to the speculation concerning the prophecy, and with Lucia's own death on the 13th of February in 2005, it seemed to have sealed the symbolism, and insured to the faithful that God truly was its source.

The question that remains is whether or not Pope John Paul II was the end of it, but the prophecies insist that he was not. The Vatican, and especially Pope John Paul II, found the coincidence of the dates compelling, but they were completely awestruck by Mehmet Ali Agca's later trial announcement, because nobody knew the contents of the prophecy except for the Pope himself, and a very few of the highest Papal Cardinals. The obvious conclusion was that Agca must have been inspired to make that claim through supernatural means. It meant that the Holy Spirit had used the gunman to verify the truth of the Fátima prophecy. If any questions about the truth of the prophecies remained, they were swept away by Agca's comments. The incident guaranteed a permanent embrace of Lucia dos Santos' visions by the Catholic Church. All three visions were defined as true prophecy and Lucia's two cousins, partners to the vision, were beatified by the Pope. Lucia herself

---

66   *Ibid.,* p. 170.

could not be beatified at the same time because she was still alive.[67] But the question remains—can we really trust somebody like Agca? The previously mentioned Gioele Magadi also points his finger at the time of the attempted assassination, 17.17, stating that it is connected to the foundation of the first Grand Lodge of Freemasonry in 1717, and the real orchestrators of the event.

The first vision predicted the end of World War I and the coming of World War II. The second vision was an appeal to pray for the conversion of Russia, which occurred with the fall of the Soviet Union in 1992. The third vision, sealed by Lucia under orders that it could not be opened until 1960 apparently by the instruction of the vision of Mary, was never revealed. Not until now.

Agca's claim with respect to Fátima, and the fact that he said he did not act alone (many high officials say he was a paid gunman acting under orders of the Soviet Union and Communist Bulgaria) seem to tie the Fátima prophecies to the collapse of the Soviet Union, the second of the three aspects of the visions. Following the assassination attempt, the actions of Pope John Paul II played a central role in the collapse and the subsequent re-conversion of Russia, starting first with *Perestroika,* in 1984, and leading to the total collapse of Russian communism, in 1992. Those events, and the fact that the papal shooting coincided with the anniversary of the Fátima visions made a deep and personal impact on John Paul II. He felt that his life had been spared by Mary, the Virgin of Fátima, for the purpose of the prophecy, especially with respect to his role in the conversion of Russia. John Paul II realized that these visions came from the Holy Spirit, and were very important.

The facts surrounding the second vision speak for themselves and cannot be argued. However, the official Vatican's interpretation of the third vision seems to leave large vacancies. It does not, for instance, take into account the corpses of the martyrs that surround him as he is gunned down. Nor does it address the torturous process and singular character of his resolve to reach the Cross. The *"Bishop clothed in white,"* who is the Pope, *"makes his way with great effort toward the cross amid the corpses of those who were martyred. He, too, falls to the ground, apparently dead, under a burst of gunfire."* The fact that the vision states that the bishop also falls to the ground indicates that the sea of Christian bodies through which he is making his way were killed in the same time frame. The same day at most, or more likely within the same hour. A bloodbath seems to have occurred in the vision. Not in St. Peter's Square, but inside the basilica itself. Invaders have taken over the Vatican by force. They have murdered the Pope. This does not describe the shooting of John Paul II in 1981. The vision more likely points forward to something far more momentous, to something that has not yet occurred. It seems to describe the linchpin of the tribulation—the end of the 62 weeks in Daniel's vision—the

---

67   http://goodnewspirit.com/Fátima-prophecy.htm ‡ Archived from the internet September 9, 2014.

defining moment when the world passes from the millennium of Christian rule and reverts back to the reign of Satan. *"And after the sixty-two weeks an anointed one will be cut off." (Dn. 9:26).* The Fátima prophecy and its revelation shows that this terrible event has now drawn very close.[68]

THE VATICAN DEFENDS THE "GAY LOBBY" AND THE EARTH AND SKIES REBEL

During an interview given to the press by Pope Ratzinger on Thursday, September 22, 2011, on his papal flight to Germany, the Jesuit spokesman Father Lombardi addressed the growing scandal of sexual abuse on minors who, after disclosure in Ireland and the United States, said that such charges were also emerging at that time in Germany. He posed the following question before the many journalists present with the now *Pope Emeritus* Ratzinger: *"Holy Father, in recent years there has been an increase in people leaving the Church in Germany, in part because of the abuses committed against children by members of the clergy. What is your feeling about this phenomenon? And what would you say to those who want to leave the Church?"* At this point, Ratzinger, rather tired and visibly affected by this direct question, made the following statement: *"We distinguish perhaps above all, the specific motivation of those who feel scandalized by these crimes that have been revealed in recent times. I can understand that, in light of this information, especially when it comes to people nearby, one says: 'This is no longer my Church. The Church is now for me a force of humanization and demoralization. If representatives of the Church do the opposite, I can not live with this Church.'"*[69]

In this response we find in essence the reasons that led to the future resignation of Benedict XVI in 2013, as well as his many limitations against the true fight against pedophilia. The Pope was aware of what was happening in Germany, after all, he had himself been responsible once, as the Archbishop of Munich and Freising, for covering up the work of a pedophile priest in Bavaria called *"Priest H"* by the press. The online edition of the influential liberal newspaper of Monaco and Bavaria, the *Sieddeutsche Zeitung*[70] stated that *"Priest H"* was never punished by Ratzinger. The now *Pope Emeritus,*transferred the pedophile priest *here and there* to avoid public scrutiny, knowing very well what he was doing by leaving the priest unpun-

68   *Ibid.* (Emphasis added).

69   Archived from the internet originally on March 5, 2013 from the link in the English language: http://www.vatican.va/holy_father/benedict_xvi/speeches/2011/september/documents/hf_benxvi_spe_20110922_intervista-germania_it.html *Now present only in the Italian and German language.* ‡ Archived from the internet September 9, 2014: http://www.vatican.va/holy_father/benedict_xvi/speeches/2011/september/documents/hf_ben-xvi_spe_20110922_intervista-germania_it.html

70   www.sueddeutsche.de ‡ Archived from the internet July 28, 2014.

Pope Francis: The Last Pope?

ished. Ratzinger did nothing even after the story of Priest H was reported on several times, and Priest H was never defrocked. Another important German newspaper *DER SPIEGEL* revealed in an article from November, 2010, written by Conny Neuman and Peter Wensierski in the English language and published on their website, accused Ratzinger of incompetence and negligence, stating: *"Ratzinger did not give sufficient attention to the type of duties that were assigned to the alleged pedophile Priest H. Despite the massive allegations of abuse levied against the priest, the archdiocese led by Ratzinger allowed H to continue to be involved in church work with children and young people."*[71]

Thinking only of the reputation of the church, Ratzinger, as with many of his colleagues in the clergy, did nothing to prevent his priest, nicknamed by the press *"the Monster of Bavaria,"* from striking once again, in his predatory manor, an attack on another poor child. This time the victim was a boy who was only eleven years of age. The paper *Sieddeutsche Zeitung* recounts a terrifying story about this poor boy, who was apparently forced by *Don H* to have oral sex. This, of course, is only one of the many priests who were protected by Ratzinger during his career at the top of the Vatican hierarchy. God must be pretty upset with his *so-called servants* in these *End of Times*.

In the midst of all this evil, during his homily on the 31st of December, 2013, what Pope Francis said seems quite natural in this unprecedented scenario of decadence and destruction, *"The apostle John defines the present time in a precise way: the last hour has arrived."*[72] Confirming our worst fears, he added later, *"there will not be a new revelation, but a full manifestation of what Jesus has already revealed."*[73]

So yes, we are in the *"End of Times"* as predicted by the apostle John, but no, there won't be a new *"Revelation,"* implying that Jesus is not returning because he has already said everything that he needed to say, and completed his mission over 2,000 years ago. Sounds like a bit of a let down if you ask me. Jesus would definitely have a few things to say after 2,000 years of lies and diabolical compromises from his supposed Church. Of course, this is perfectly in line with the philosophy of the New World Order, and their Antichrist agenda in the hands of materialists and Satanists. Some of you will wonder who and what can stop all this evil?

Is God retiring like the Pope? Apparently not. In the beginning of March, 2013, my journalist friend Francesco Quartararo posted, on his website, a rather interesting article regarding a new interpretation of a certain event related

71   http://www.spiegel.de/international/germany/munich-abuse-case-archbishop-ratzinger-failed-to-deal-with-suspected-pedophile-priest-a-731683.html ‡ Archived from the internet September 9, 2014.

72   http://vaticaninsider.lastampa.it/vaticano/dettaglio-articolo/articolo/francesco-francis-francisco-30953/ ‡ Archived from the internet September 9, 2014.

73   *Ibid.*

to Ratzinger and the Vatican. This went almost unnoticed by the mass media, and which occurred soon after Ratzinger's shocking resignation in early 2013. Carlo Gustav Jung could have called it a very interesting case of *"synchronicity."* Quartararo, my long time collaborator and friend from Palermo, gave a *"strange"* and different perspective on this specific event, and I feel compelled to share with you. It involves the chaos theory, and was avoided by pure chance. It was a cataclysm in the Vatican that could have changed history forever, and would have been difficult to explain to the faithful masses. On the same day of the resignation of the German Pope, an incredibly synchronistic photo was taken of a lightning strike at the top of the Vatican. This apocalyptic photo was made by photographer Alessandro Di Meo (*Ansa*), who was able to capture the *exact moment* when the lightning struck down from the skies and hit the top of the Vatican dome. Obviously, this photo was considered an omen, and it made the rounds in all major newspapers in the world. The following is the fascinating story written by Francesco Quartararo:

It is the 15th of February, 2013, in Russia it is a peaceful sunny day, while in Rome, the 'Eternal City' is still in shock over the decision of Pope Ratzinger to resign. Above their heads, a meteorite is being monitored by NASA and the space agencies worldwide, because of its passing so close and below the altitude of satellites used for broadcasting and distribution of television signals. It was at a level considered safe enough to not arouse any safety concerns for the population. It happens, however, that some fragments fall upon the town of Chelyabinsk in Russia, with devastating effects. At the end of this ordeal there will be 1,200 people injured by the event, caused by fragments resulting in the explosion during contact with the upper part of the stratosphere. It had a rated power output comparable to a couple of nuclear bombs. It also happens that by better analyzing the data, it was found that if the fragments were precipitated with an angle slightly different, consistent with the entrance window possible with the initial speed of 17 km in a single second, on February 15, 2013 those meteorites would have actually fallen on Rome, bombing even the Vatican. A couple of pounds of meteorite already at a speed of 'only' 4.3 km would create panic, terror and destruction in the densely populated capital of Rome. If you think such a possibility is quite creepy, imagine the possibility if one of these fragments had hit the Vatican that day, killing the resigning Pope, causing absolute panic amongst one billion, three hundred million Catholic believers.

An apocalyptic scenario worthy of a movie, but a scenario far more feasible then you would think possible. What prevented such an accident? Maybe a 'miracle,' given the dramatic impact a meteorite on Rome could have had. If you want to be more practical and materialistic instead, without slipping into relativism or conspiracy theories, we must consider the inclination of the two meteorites, (yes, there were two meteorites that crashed, the other one only generated a swarm of 'shooting stars') the gravitational interaction between the two meteorites and the planet Earth, the temperature in the various layers of the atmosphere, the weather, the density of the main materials of meteorites, and the role played by greenhouse gases in the decay of meteoric debris, etc.

Renzo Baschera, the *"Prophecy Hunter"* we encountered earlier, writes in reference to the prophecies of Saint John Bosco: *"Rome, like Paris, will be destroyed. At this point, dozens of prophecies seem to agree. Destruction of the city of Rome, however, will not be so sudden and immediate. There will be certain 'signs' first. In fact, it is written: I will come to you four times. 'The first' sign will be given by an earthquake (but it will be a series of mini-earthquakes, which 'will run rampant on the Roman hills, as runaway goats')."*[74]

Joseph Ratzinger, in the words of the Cardinal of Palermo, would die exactly one year from the 10th of February, 2012, but he did not die, he resigned instead. Maybe something more powerful than the prayers of the faithful have changed the trajectory of those two meteorites directed on Rome, February 15, 2013. Lastly, it is worth mentioning that on the 3rd of March, 2013, a series of mini earthquakes did *indeed* take place in the Roman hills and in Castel Gandolfo where the *Pope Emeritus*, as I wrote earlier, went for a period after resigning. They were mild earthquakes, the epicenter of the main earthquake was of magnitude 2.5, in the place the Romans familiarly call, *the Castelli Romani.*[75] Certainly *Pope Emeritus*, well aware of the prophecies, must have had a few nightmares about it.

FIG. 33. *Lightning strikes the top of St. Peter's Basilica hours after Pope Benedict XVI announced his resignation. Photo by Alessandro Di Meo (ANSA).*

74   http://cosco-giuseppe.tripod.com/profezie/roma.htm ‡ Archived from the internet September 9, 2014.

75   http://roma.corriere.it/roma/notizie/cronaca/13_marzo_3/terremoto-lieve-scossa-castelli-roma-2123145191.shtml ‡ Archived from the internet September 9, 2014.

Chapter: VI
A "BLACK POPE" ON THE PAPAL THRONE

FRANCIS AND HIS ALLEGED ETHICS REVOLUTION IN THE VATICAN BANK

The resignation of Pope Benedict XVI was long meditated on and meticulously planned by Ratzinger, the former guardian of the faith, who for years before becoming Pope was the supreme leader of the Congregation for the Doctrine of the Faith. For the Catholic flock, his gesture initially caused fear and confusion among the faithful, and some people saw with the election of Bergoglio the arrival of a Jesuit as leader of the Church as the fulfillment of a dark prophecy. Others instead noticed the unprecedented shift towards an apparent transparency in the governance of the Vatican institutions, publicized in a flaunting way on several occasions by the Vatican media after Bergoglio's arrival. *"The pursuit of transparency is an indispensable objective, with even more reason for church-related institutions,"* said the former president of the IOR, Angelo Caloia, in a book that came out in 2013 entitled, *The Gospel According to Italians*. The book was written by F. Anfossi and A. M. Valli, and published by *Edizioni San Paolo,* one of the major Vatican publishers. [1] The Vatican propaganda machine was immediately put to work in a supposed attempt at transparency made by the Vatican after nominating

---

1 See. Francesco Anfossi, Aldo Maria Valli., Il Vangelo Secondo gli Italiani. Fede, potere, sesso. Quello che diciamo di credere e quello che invece crediamo. Vol. I, (Milan: Cinisello Balsamo, San Paolo Edizioni, 2013).

their first Jesuit to the throne of Peter. Pope Francis spoke often on the IOR, the infamous Vatican bank, and on the appointment of a group of Cardinals to *"harmonize"* the bank of scandals *"with the mission of the Universal Church"*— one of the stated missions of the New World Order.

The Church is moving in a direction that some of the flock cannot understand, and stands to become irrelevant to those who publicly already abandoned the faith because of the many scandals. Bergoglio publicly expressed himself on the matter from the beginning, and gained the media's attention by stating, *"The Church is in danger of turning into an NGO. And this is not the path."*[2]

Bergoglio repeated this concept more than once during his public appearances following his nomination, and in a homily made during the Mass in Santa Marta on the morning of Tuesday the 11th of June 2013, he stated that, *"St. Peter did not have a bank account, and when he had to pay taxes, the Lord sent him to the sea to catch a fish and find the coin in the fish, so he could pay."*[3] Even on this occasion he again repeated, *"The Church is not an NGO,"* and it *"arises from gratuitousness."* He later focused on the concept of a poor Church because, *"a rich Church is an aging Church."*[4] Such statements are good for a Church in desperate need of credibility, and it seems that on this point, Bergoglio continues the work undertaken by Ratzinger regarding transparency of Vatican financial institutions, a job often sabotaged and interrupted by Cardinal Bertone. Now put aside, at least at a public level, these actions are necessary to build new consensus from the believers and lay men regarding this delicate situation. Bertone could care less about what people might think of *The Bank of God*, or, as called by others, *The Bank of Satan*.

On April 4, 2013, the pontiff addressed the Vatican Bank by stating *"The IOR is necessary to a certain point."*[5] Later in his speech, a bit agitated, he concluded, *"Excuse me, what? When the Church wants to boast of it's quantity and creates organizations and offices, it becomes a bit bureaucratic, the Church loses its main substance."*[6] Then, a few months after this statement, Pope Francis instituted the Pontifical Commission's representative on the IOR to create a new body, chaired by another Salesian Cardinal Raffaele Farina, who is trying to promote, *"a better reconciliation of the same, with the mission of the universal Church and the Apostolic See, in the more general context of the reforms that should be car-*

---

2   http://www.ilfattoquotidiano.it/2013/04/24/papa-francesco-ior-necessario-ma-fino-a-certo-punto/574122/ ‡ Archived from the internet September 9, 2014.

3   http://www.repubblica.it/esteri/2013/06/11/news/papa_chiesa-pove-ra-60850385/ ‡ Archived from the internet September 9, 2014.

4   http://www.avvenire.it/Papa_Francesco/santmarta/Pagine/Chiesa-ricca-invec-chia-gratuità.aspx ‡ Archived from the internet September 9, 2014.

5   http://www.ilfattoquotidiano.it/2013/04/24/papa-francesco-ior-necessario-ma-fino-a-certo-punto/574122/ ‡ Archived from the internet September 9, 2014.

6   *Ibid.*

ried out by the institutions that give aid to the Apostolic See." This all sounds nice, including the intentions of Bergoglio's *"New Church,"* that sound truly great. But putting aside what Bergoglio has said, if you trust the Pope's actions and you believe in his propaganda, I am afraid you are in for a bitter disappointment. As Horacio Verbitsky, the already cited Argentinian author and journalist said, *"Don't trust Bergoglio, he is a great actor."[7]* It seems the Vatican is a perfect stage for his new acting role, and as Verbitsky wrote prophetically after Bergoglio's election: *"The friendly journalist will tell us about the way he travels on the bus or the underground,"* and the faithful, *"will listen to his homilies recited with the gestures of an actor, in which the parables from the Bible will coexist with a clear popular wording."[8]* This seems to be exactly what has been happening since his election. Verbitsky also stated his penchant for *"pardoning the exploiters, and preaching humbleness to the exploited."[9]* This is the style of the Argentinian actor turned Pope. Going back to the policy of transparency and the firm opposition of Bertone, the Cardinal in question has practically been forced to drop everything and leave, as the Jesuit Pope chose him as the perfect scapegoat for the situation. He made the shocking statement: *"If no one here in the Vatican defends me from who calls me corrupt, it is best to end it here."*

It would seem to be over for Bertone, or maybe not? Perhaps he is the perfect man for the job, as another Salesian is now the head of the commission presiding over matters relating to the IOR. His name is Cardinal Raffaele Farina, a confidant of His Holiness Pope Francis, a person who was consecrated Bishop by Bertone in 2006 and elevated to the position of Cardinal by Ratzinger soon after, in 2007.[10] Farina is accompanied on his mission by various characters, who are certainly not the lambs you would expect from persons working directly with Pope Francis. This commission of investigation has frightened even the now former Vatican Secretary of State Tarcisio Bertone, because it includes the young Francesca Immacolata Chaouqui, who tweeted against Bertone back in February 2012, writing: *"Bertone is corrupt! There seems to be secret archives and a company from Veneto involved."* It was Farina who was responsible for the Vatican Archives at the time, and the new Secretary of State, Pietro Parolin, was from the Veneto region. Is this all just a coincidence? Francesca Immacolata Chaouqui is not the only member of this commission to be fearful, perhaps naive, if we compare her with the ex-U.S. Ambassador to the Vatican, the dangerous Professor Mary Ann Glendon, a woman without scruples, very close to the Bush family and the Central Intelligence Agency, and this was said to have cooperated with the Vatican back in the days when

---

7   http://www.libreidee.org/2013/03/verbitsky-non-fidatevi-di-bergoglio-e-un-grande-attore/ ‡ Archived from the internet September 11, 2014.

8   *Ibid.*

9   *Ibid.*

10   http://it.wikipedia.org/wiki/Raffaele_Farina ‡ Archived from the internet September 11, 2014.

Pope Francis: The Last Pope?

George Bush Senior was the CIA director in the 1970s. *In the Epilogue I will include a complete list of the CIA's Chiefs of Section (CoS) within the Vatican from 1948 to 2009.* The present head of the CIA division in the Vatican is unknown, but it may still possibly be Glendon herself.

Glendon intensified her activity in intelligence during the time of Ronald Reagan, and alongside the then-CIA director William Casey. William Casey and his wife were followers of the controversial *Legionaries of Christ,* whose founder was the pedophile Marcial Maciel Degollado, and in 2013 Jason Berry wrote an article in *Newsweek* about the ties between Casey and Degollado. In the article he revealed that, *"Ronald Reagan's CIA director, William Casey, and his wife made a seven-figure donation for construction of a Legion building in Cheshire, Connecticut, and were memorialized by a plaque."*[11]

The same Mary Ann Glendon became an ardent follower of Father Marciel until his death, despite the heavy accusations of pedophilia made public in the last years of Marciel's life. Andrew Sullivan, who wrote for *The Daily Dish*, had these harsh words against Mary Ann Glendon in 2010, *"In some ways, Maciel's most disturbing enabler was Mary Ann Glendon, Harvard Law Professor and former ambassador to the Vatican. (Glendon) taught at Regina Apostolorum Athenaeum, the Legion's university in Rome, and advised in the planning that led to the order's first university in America, University of Sacramento, Calif. In a 2002 letter for the Legion website she scoffed at the allegations against Maciel and praised his 'radiant holiness' and 'the success of Regnum Christi (the order's lay wing) and the Legionaries of Christ in advancing the New Evangelization.' Maciel—whom John Paul II called an 'efficacious guide to youth'—ran what can only be called a corrupt cult, designed in part to protect his own long life of sexual abuse and misconduct, where members were ruthlessly pressured to raise and give money to the organization."*[12]

In addition to being a teacher at Harvard University, where she holds the esteemed title of the *Learned Hand Professor of Law* at Harvard Law School, Mary Ann Glendon also taught for many years at the University of the Legionaries in Rome, called the *Regina Apostolorum Athenaeum.* During her years of teaching in Rome she must have noticed what was going on regarding to Father Maciel, including scandals so outrageous that it lead Benedict XVI to act under increasing pressure from the media to finally define Maciel in a 2010 publication as a *"false prophet."*[13]

How could it be possible that Pope Francis would employ someone like Mary Ann Glendon in such a position of importance, especially in light of

11   http://www.newsweek.com/father-marcial-maciel-and-popes-he-stained-62811; ‡ Archived from the internet September11, 2014.

12   http://www.theatlantic.com/daily-dish/archive/2010/04/the-vaticans-watergate-follow-the-money/188415/ ‡ Archived from the internet September 11, 2014.

13   http://it.wikipedia.org/wiki/Marcial_Maciel_Degollado ‡ Archived from the internet September 11, 2014.

the fact that she was obviously following a false prophet? This appointment by Pope Francis, like many others, not only shows that nothing has really changed in the Vatican, but that Pope Francis is deliberately turning a blind eye on Father Maciel and the *"Legionary of Christ Affair,"* and the people relating to it. Some inside sources say this was because Father Maciel was really an agent of the Jesuits, as well as the CIA, as he admitted to his wife, and as was reported by *Newsweek* as follows: *"He gave her a house in Cuernavaca with financial support, visiting periodically, saying that he was a CIA agent and oil-company detective."*[14]

In the end, perhaps the moves by the pontificate were not so revolutionary after all. So what will change in the Pope Francis era? Probably nothing—apart from the great media frenzy and the constant show of Jesuit manipulation, and sadly confirming the words I cited earlier from Verbitsky, *"Don't trust Bergoglio, he is a great actor."*

To date, the only pope in the modern era who actually tried to change anything in the Vatican, who opposed the growing Masonic infiltration, and the satanic pedophile enemy, and who even wished to establish a new ethical Bank that could substitute the IOR, died after only 33 days into his pontificate. His Italian name was Albino Luciani, to become Pope John Paul I, and he was most likely killed. The Vatican has not investigated any claims of foul play in the death of Pope Luciani, and does not profess belief in any possible deceit. His reign is among the shortest in papal history, resulting in the unique "Year of Three Popes," the first to occur since 1605. Meanwhile, in 2014, Cardinal Bertone was substituted by Pietro Parolin as Secretary of State, and had unsuccessfully asked Pope Francis that he maintain control of the commission of Cardinals supervising the IOR, and that is now in the hands of Cardinal Farina. Cardinal Bertone ultimately moved to a penthouse in the luxurious *Palazzo San Carlo*, the size of almost 3,000 square feet, ten times larger than the present residence of the pope himself. This apparently upset Pope Francis, who feels helpless to do anything against one of the leaders of the powerful and feared *"Gay Lobby."* Bertone's luxurious birthday at the beginning of December, 2014, and consisting of a menu of truffle specialities and champagne that was served to 40 guests from the Gay Lobby and the Illuminati elite, apparently upset Pope Francis even more. And on the 22 of December, twenty days after Bertone's birthday, Francis delivered an unprecedented attack against his own cardinals, bishops and priests and accusing them of succumbing to greed, jealousy, hypocrisy, cowardice, and what he called the disease of spiritual Alzheimer's, that is, a *"progressive decline of spiritual faculties."* With this move the decline of the Catholic Church has now been acknowledged.

14   *Newsweek Ibid.*

FIG. 34. Pope John Paul I (Albino Luciani) and the then Cardinal Karol Józef Wojtyla, the future Pope John Paul II.

FINAL CONSIDERATIONS IN AN INTERVIEW WITH FERUCCIO PINOTTI

In the middle of 2013, a very interesting book was released by the Italian publisher *Piemme*. This is a very well-known publisher, founded in 1982, that joined the prestigious Mondadori Group owned by Berlusconi in 2003. In the past few years they have become the fifth largest Italian publishing house, with a 4.5 percent market share in Italy. I make this preface regarding the publisher simply because it was not so easy to publish the content of a book with the title *VATICAN FREEMASON*.[15] This book contains an entire chapter, and many other references in other sections, dedicated to revelations I have offered, and an interview I gave to one of the authors.

---

15   Giacomo Galeazzi, Ferruccio Pinotti, Vaticano Massone, (Milan: Piemme Editore, 2013).

The book in question was considered so dangerous that the publisher had to delay the release for several months while waiting for the initial Pope Francis frenzy to subside.

The book was an unprecedented project dedicated to the perilous subject of Freemasonry within the Vatican, and includes interesting documents and interviews with various Masonic Grand Masters. My friends and fellow journalists, Giacomo Galeazzi and Ferruccio Pinotti, are both well-known and established in Italy. One is a full-time Vaticanist for the daily newspaper *La Stampa*, and the other as an investigative journalist for the newspaper, *Il Corriere della Sera*, as well as an expert on Freemasonry. In the bestseller dedicated to Italian Freemasonry, *FRATELLI D'ITALIA*,[16] there is an interesting extract from the unedited version of the interview I gave to Ferruccio Pinotti a few days after the election of Pope Francis in March 2013, that is only partially included in the book *VATICAN FREEMASON*.[17]

Q. (Ferruccio Pinotti): *How do you evaluate the choice of Bergoglio as the new Pope? Is it a victory for Freemasonry?*

A. (Leo Zagami): *We had Mario Monti, a student of the Jesuits at the head of the Italian government recently, and we have Mario Draghi, another student of the Jesuits as the President of the European Central Bank, and at a European level we are governed by other students of the Jesuit lobby like Barroso and Van Rompuy. It seems obvious now that a Jesuit, who by the way is also named Mario, as is the full name of Jorge Mario Bergoglio, will become the first Jesuit Pope in this historical moment where you need a technical Pope in the Vatican to save what is still salvageable. Present in a Church irremediably damaged by scandals, both in terms of image and economically, as we have seen the scourge of pedophilia in the U.S. Catholic Church nearly leading to a collapse, as well as the decades of financial wheeling and dealing in which the IOR was to be used and abused by drug traffickers, terrorists and mobsters. With the resignation of Ratzinger, Freemasonry got what they wanted, however, and that's the final post-conciliar destruction of the sacredness of the papal figure, and now you switch to a character that immediately defines himself simply as the Bishop of Rome, not as Pope, from the start for a specific reason. Bergoglio is a shadowy figure, as stated to the writer and human rights activist Horacio Verbitsky by the brother of Orlando Yorio, one of the two Jesuits who disappeared for months during the dictatorship in Argentina. This way of acting in ambiguity is normal because of his membership in the Society of Jesus. They are the driving force of the Vatican security apparatus and intelligence with an archive in their central headquarters in Azpeitia, Spain, which is 'equal if not superior to that of the CIA.' This is what was written*

---

16   See. Ferruccio Pinotti Fratelli d'Italia, BUR Biblioteca Univ. Rizzoli, Milan, 2007.

17   Giacomo Galeazzi, Ferruccio Pinotti, *Ibid.*, pp. 307-317.

Pope Francis: The Last Pope?

by world intelligence expert Giuseppe Muratori some years ago in his Ency-
clopedia of Espionage published in 1993 by the Italian Parliament Editions.
The Jesuits with Bergoglio as their leader, have been called to save the Church
and certainly they choose a great actor for the occasion as Verbitsky also stated.

Q. *What kind of relation do the Jesuits have with the Freemasons in Argentina?*

A: *In the Jesuit College of Clermont in France, the Jesuits and the Stuarts lay*
the foundation of what will become the Templar degrees of the Ancient and
Accepted Scottish Rite. At the same time a certain Father Bonani SJ seems to
be the true author of the so-called Larmenius Charter, or Carta Transmissio-
nis, one of the documents at the base of modern neo-Templarism. The Jesuits
have therefore always been in a very close relationship to Freemasonry. Not
the British and Hanoverian side, but rather that of Jacobite origin linked to
the Catholic Stewarts that will place in France the foundations of the An-
cient Anglo-Scottish Freemasonry (constituted of Roman Catholics). This
fact would be later confirmed by both the historian of Freemasonry, Teder,
and by Henri Martin (in his Histoire de France) who wrote that in this con-
text 'were the monarchic losers, members of Ultramontane Catholicism that
propagated Freemasonry in France,' those who defended the Catholic dynasty
of the Stewarts against the Protestants. And from that moment they began
to establish the Ancient and Accepted Scottish Rite in the Latin countries, an
Order that still operates after almost three centuries in close contact with the
Jesuits, as evidenced in the significant Masonic conference organized in 2011
in Lisbon, which had as a special guest of honor the Jesuit Father Ferrer
Benimell, who was in Italy in 2002 to attend a conference organized by the
Grand Lodge of Italy (Palazzo Vitelleschi). Benimelli, a friend of Bergoglio,
defined as one of the greatest living experts in the history of Spanish and
Latin American Freemasonry, is the founder and president since 1983 of the
Centre for Studies on Spanish Masonry. He is considered a leading author-
ity on the subject also in South America. He is a Professor of Contemporary
History at the University of Zaragoza in Spain, and he writes, in a book pub-
lished in Italy in 1981, by Atanor Editions, the following words which leave
no doubt on the present apologetic position of the Jesuits on Freemasonry in
Argentina or any other country; 'Freemasonry of the Enlightenment—leav-
ing aside the deviations and errors that any widespread organization might
have—looks like a meeting, beyond political and religious divisions of the
moment, of men who believe in God, respect the moral nature and want to
know each other, help each other and work together, despite differences in
social rank, the diversity of religious faith and their membership in political
parties or religions more or less opposite. Undoubtedly, the Roman Church,
following the example of many European governments, pursued this associa-
tion in accordance with the legislation at the time, adding the civil and the
ecclesiastical penalties for conduct which at that time constituted suspicion of
heresy, and that in the present day the Church itself refers to as ecumenism.

Leo Lyon Zagami

Two centuries later the Church has overcome a situation which, thankfully, is now a thing of the past and today offers us many lessons as historians in search of understanding the unity among all men who form the Cathedral of the brotherhood of the Universe: Humanity.

Q. *How do you rate the allegations of Horacio Verbitsky that Bergoglio did not protect, but rather did the opposite with two of his priests, because they had left wing tendencies?*

A. *The accusations of Horacio Verbitsky are plausible due to the Jesuit ambiguity I just mentioned, and they are certainly true in regards to Bergoglio, who in this case did not to follow the long-standing tradition of the Jesuit left-wing. If you search Wikipedia you will read that it is the Jesuits that coined the term 'Compagno.'[18] Or go to the website of these Italian Jesuits, where you will see they were the ones laying the foundations of modern Communism with their so-called Jesuit reductions in South America and they say bluntly they were; 'directed by the missionaries, with some theocratic and communist organization.' Then you can view better the relationship of friendship and close cooperation between Fidel Castro who is by no coincidence a 33° of the Ancient and Accepted Scottish Rite of Freemasonry, and was a student of the Jesuits, and the former General of the Society of Jesus, Peter Hans Kolvenbach. In short, the Jesuits are not only left-wing but South America has always been their favorite lab, so they have a good relationship with the regimes of the left, a bit less with those of the right that from time to time would pop up on the South American scene instrumental to their manipulators in the United States of America. In the case of the Argentinian dictatorship, it was obviously linked to both the right wing of the P2 Lodge and the top controllers of the Pentagon and the CIA. Bergoglio reluctantly was forced by Ecclesiastical Masonry operating within the Church in Rome to act in a different way. He did this so he could protect the interests of the Vatican and the United States in that country. If one side made him unpopular with the Jesuits in Argentina and the family of the victims of the dictatorship, at the same time it prepared his way to scale the heights of power in the Vatican hierarchy to where he is today.*

Q. *Gelli and the P2 were very strong in Argentina, do you think they may have had contact with Bergoglio?*

A. *Of course the P2 and Bergoglio were in contact with each other, thanks to the direct intervention of the future Pope Francis with the member of the P2, Admiral Emilio Eduardo Massera. In the end the two Jesuits which have been discussed so much, were released, and in return the P2 member Massera was given an honorary award at the Jesuit University of Buenos Aires. Horacio Verbitsky recently disclosed other interesting documents which he then passed*

---

18 *Compagno* is the Italian version of "Comrade" a term frequently used by left-wing organizations around the globe.

on to the British newspaper Daily Mail. In particular, a memo from the Argentinian Ministry of Foreign Affairs from 1979 showing further collaborations between Bergoglio and the dictatorship after the sad incident that involved the Jesuits Orlando Yorio and Francisco Jalics. Obviously this 'strange' episode that undermines the credibility of the new pope should be seen through the lens of a typical operation between the intelligence services of the two allied countries, in this case those of the Vatican represented by Bergoglio with his two Jesuits believed to be possible 'traitors' and those of a foreign state. Argentina at that time was in the hands of a dictatorship whose members were Freemasons of the P2 Lodge of Licio Gelli, in turn, operated by the CIA and the top of the Vatican hierarchy. Let's not forget that Gelli to this day is a Grand Officer of the Order of St. Sylvester, Pope and a Grand Officer of the Order of the Holy Sepulcher of Jerusalem.

*FIG. 35. The late Licio Gelli (1919-2015) **Past Worshipful Master of the P2 Lodge** in a recent photo made in Gelli's residence in Villa Wanda, Arezzo, by Gerald Bruneau.*

FRANCIS ‡ THE "BLACK POPE" AND THE THIRD SECRET

Of all the visions and seers throughout the ages predicting the future of the Vatican, there are really only two prophecies deemed "apocryphal," and those include Saint Malachy, and the Nun of Dresden, who I have previously described in detail. Some believe these two prophecies have clear references to both Benedict XVI, and his successor Pope Francis. The two cycles also have similar prophetic visions regarding the end of the Church that should, according to some historians, terminate with Pope Francis. Both Malachy and the Nun of Dresden were deeply religious Christian clairvoyants who, by seemingly divine intervention, were told all of what to write.

*FIG. 36. On the left is Rev. Adolfo **Nicolás** Pachón SJ (b.1936) the present "Black Pope," and on the right is former Superior General Rev. Peter-Hans **Kolvenbach**, S.J. (b.1928). This photo was taken for a promotional press leaflet handed down to the press in 2009 that stated under this picture "The Era of the Two Generals."*

The "Prophecy of the Popes" consisted of 111 short phrases and doomsday coda in Latin, attributed to St. Malachy of Armagh, who lived in twelfth century Ireland. His coda was published several centuries later in 1595 by Arnold de Wyon, a Benedictian historian, as part of his book *Lignum Vitæ*. According to the traditional account, Malachy was summoned to Rome in 1139 by Pope Innocent II, and while he was there, he supposedly received a vision of all the future popes. The manuscript was then deposited in the Vatican Archives and forgotten about until its rediscovery in 1590, just in time for a papal conclave that was in session at the time, and just like today's revelations by the so-called *"Crow,"* it probably influenced the results. The list describes all the popes including "antipopes" such as Celestine II, who was elected in 1143, to the last one described as *"Petrus Romanus,"* who should end his pontificate with the destruction of Rome. It is here that the prophecy of Malachy seems to coincide with the vision of the *Third Secret of Fátima*, erroneously (according to some) identified with the 1981 assassination attempt made by Ali Agca against Pope

Pope Francis: The Last Pope?

John Paul II in St. Peter's Square, as amply demonstrated by the Catholic journalist Antonio Socci in his book, *Il Quarto Segreto di Fátima*. [19]

This misdirection becomes even more evident when we know who the three people involved in the official disclosure of *Third Secret of Fátima* made by the Catholic Church in the year 2000 were. Those three people are the now *Pope Emeritus* Joseph Ratzinger, the infamous Cardinal Tarcisio Bertone from the *"Gay Lobby,"* and Marcial Maciel Degollado, the biggest supporter of Cardinal Agelo Sodano. There was also Pope John Paul II, who insisted on Ali Agca's assassination attempt being the supposed secret, but also apparently sabotaged the original content. Can we truly believe the official version of the *Third Secret of Fátima* prepared and presented by these less-than-credible individuals, especially in comparison to an earlier version three times larger that appeared back in 1963 in the German magazine *Neues Europa?*

Let's start with who gave the first version to the press back in the early 1960s. Apparently it was Cardinal Alfredo Ottaviani (1890–1979), one of the custodians of the original secret, as he had the most influential position of power in the Vatican for many years, which included the *Secretariat of State* and also what used to be the *Santo Uffizio,* now known as the Congregation for the Doctrine of the Faith. Ottaviani gave his permission to *Neues Europa* for the publication of *"an extract"* known as a *"diplomatic document"* of the *Third Secret of Fátima* in 1963. This is the account of Father Luigi Villa, who died in November 2012, and who worked with Ottaviani for a long time. He revealed his involvement to collaborator Franco Adessa in 1996. [20] The revelations that were published in *Neues Europa* are called by some *"false secrets."* There is a lot of controversy and probably disinformation surrounding them, therefore I will quote at length the two articles within the German review regarding the subject that were made public in 1963. The text of this *"extract"* was preceded by the following introduction from the editor, Louis Emrich: *"I have done everything possible to procure for myself the original text of the third message of Fátima, but all my efforts remained futile. The Vatican has made all the arrangements for this document to remain a papal secret until a new order. However, today I am in a position to communicate to readers of Neues Europa and to all countries an extract of the content of the Third Secret, in the form made available as inside information in the diplomatic circles of Washington, London and Moscow."*

The editor then claimed that the *"extract"* was read by President Kennedy, Great Britain's Prime Minister MacMillan, and Soviet leader Khrushchev, and led to the signing of the Anglo-American-Russian accord in Moscow. He concluded by stating that *"although this document is not the original text of the message of Fátima, such as it was revealed on October 13, 1917, by the Mother of God to the*

19   Antonio Socci, *Il Quarto Segreto di Fátima*, BUR Biblioteca Univ. Rizzoli, Milan, 2008.

20   Article in Chiesa viva - Year XLIII - n° 462 - July-August 2013.

little seer Lucy, essential points of the original are nevertheless found there."²¹ Here is the *"extract"* of the Third Secret of Fátima, as it was published by *Neues Europa*:

> It was the thirteenth of October, 1917. On that day, the Holy Virgin appeared for the last time to the little visionaries, Jacinta, Francisco, and Lucy, at the end of a series of six apparitions in all. After the manifestation of the miracle of the sun at Fátima, the Mother of God revealed a special secret message to Lucy, in which She particularly stated:

> Don't worry, dear child. I am the Mother of God speaking to you and begging you to proclaim in My name the following message to the entire world. In doing this, you will meet great hostility. But be steadfast in the Faith and you will overcome this hostility. Listen, and note well what I say to you: Men must become better. They must implore the remission of the sins which they have committed, and will continue to commit. You ask Me for a miraculous sign so that all may understand the words in which, through you, I address mankind. This miracle which you have just seen was the great miracle of the sun! Everyone has seen it believers and unbelievers, country and city dwellers, scholars and journalists, laymen and priests.

> And now, announce this in My name:

> A great punishment shall come to all mankind, not today as yet, nor even tomorrow, but in the second half of the 20ᵗʰ Century. What I have already made known at La Salette through the children Melanie and Maximin, I repeat today before you. Mankind has not developed as God expected. Mankind has gone astray and has trampled underfoot the gifts which were given it. There is no order in anything. Even in the highest positions, it is Satan who governs and decides how affairs are to be conducted. He will even know how to find his way to the highest positions in the Church. He will succeed in sowing confusion in the minds of the great scientists who invent arms, with which half of humanity can be destroyed in a few minutes. If mankind does not refrain from wrongdoing and be converted, I shall be forced to let fall My Son's arm.

> If those at the top, in the world and in the Church, do not oppose these ways, it is I who shall do so, and I shall pray God My Father to visit His justice on mankind. There will also come a time of the hardest trials for the Church. Cardinals will be against Cardinals and bishops against bishops. Satan will put himself in their midst. In Rome, also, there will be big changes. What is rotten will fall, and what will fall must not be maintained. The Church will be darkened and the world plunged into confusion. God will punish men still more powerfully and harshly than He did by means of the Flood, and the great and powerful will perish just as much as the small and the weak. The greatest World War will happen in the second half of the 20ᵗʰ Century. Then fire and smoke will fall

21   Article in *Neues Europa*, bimonthly review of Stuttgart, No. 20, October 15, 1963, p. 5.

from the sky, and the waters of the oceans will be turned to steam, hurling their foam towards the sky; and all that is standing will be cast down. Millions and millions of men will lose their lives from one hour to the next, and those who remain living will envy those who are dead. There will be tribulation as far as the eye can see, and misery all over the earth and desolation in every country. The time is continually approaching, the abyss is growing wider, and there is no end in sight. The good will die with the wicked, the big with the small, the princes of the Church with their subjects. Satan's henchmen will then be the only sovereigns on earth. This will be a time which neither king nor emperor, Cardinal nor bishop expects, but it will come, nevertheless, in accordance with My Fathers plan to punish and take vengeance. Later, however, when those who survive all this are still alive, God and His glory will once more be invoked, and He will once more be served as He was, not so long ago, when the world had not yet become corrupted. I call on all true imitators of My Son, Jesus Christ, all true Christians and apostles of the latter days! The time of times is coming and the end of everything, if mankind is not converted, and if this conversion does not come from above, from the leaders of the world and the leaders of the Church. But woe! Woe if this conversion does not come about, and if all remains as it is, nay, if all becomes even worse! Go, My child and proclaim this! I shall always remain by your side to help you.[22]

Louis Emrich concludes the article, stating as mentioned earlier: *"I add once more that this is not the text of the original message such as the Mother of God revealed it on October 13, 1917, to the little seer Lucy, now a Carmelitè (nun), **but as an extract of the third message of Fátima such as it is circulating this moment in diplomatic circles.** I am assured that the authentic text of the message is even harsher and more overwhelming than the extract related above. However, it is not inevitable in its conclusions, because it places the conversion of humanity before its perdition. How will humanity decide? This question, before just as after, remains open."*[23]

On November 1, 1963, *Neues Europa* added this additional information regarding the Secret of Fátima, specifying there is also an even bigger secret that cannot be revealed in the extract:

In the last edition of Neues Europa, we stated formally that the text we published there of the Third Message of Fátima constituted only an extract of that which is known in diplomatic circles. The most important part, the quintessence of the revelations of the Mother of God, was unavailable to us. In this case it concerns words of the Holy Virgin predicting events which will take place in Rome and which will happen to the Vatican and the papacy at the dawn of D-Day, when humanity will be delivered to the divine chastisement. The passage related to it, and which forms the basis and conclusion of the

22   http://www.Fátima.org/thirdsecret/neueseuropa.asp ‡ Archived from the internet September 12, 2014.

23   *Ibid.* Emphasis ours.

third prediction of Fátima, was integrally detached from it and remains a state secret of the Vatican, until a new order is given. We know, however, what is said in the passage in question. It is related to the future of the Holy See and all the institutions attached to it. All the Vatican circles which were solicited to reveal the authentic text of this passage have categorically refused to make any kind of pronouncement on this subject. This intransigent attitude of Vatican diplomacy is the result of formal instructions emanating from Pope Paul VI, who decided that neither the wording of the third message of Fátima nor its principal part would be made accessible, for the moment, to public knowledge. Such a papal prohibition can only increase in a very considerable proportion the interest attributed, up to the present, to the affair of Fátima.

At what period will the Pope judge it opportune to lift this prohibition? Nobody knows.

Theoretically this restriction can cease tomorrow, but it could equally well remain in force for a more or less long period of time. The political situation at the world level will decide, according to its favorable or unfavorable evolution. But here and now it is certain that the Third Message of Fátima will be communicated in full and without any omission to the entire world, when the needs and the seriousness of the hour demand it. –Dr. Angel S., Rome[24]

With such terms as, *"Dawn of D-Day, when humanity will be delivered to the divine chastisement,"* there is an immediate similarity with the scenario of martyrdom and destruction of Rome, also described by Malachy's final words in his 111th prophesy dedicated to the Last Pope, where he states: *"In the final persecution of the Holy Roman Church there will reign Petrus Romanus, who will feed his flock amid many tribulations; after which the seven-hilled city will be destroyed and the dreadful Judge will judge the people."* It is also striking that at least one Pope had a similar mystical vision; in 1909, while granting an audience ... Pope Pius X leaned back and closed his eyes. Suddenly he "awoke" and cried out:*"What I see is terrifying. Will it be myself? Will it be my successor? What is certain is that the pope will quit Rome, and in leaving the Vatican, he will have to walk over the dead bodies of his priests."*[25]

Just prior to his death on August 20, 1914, Pope Pius X had another vision: *"I have seen one of my successors, of the same name, who was fleeing over the bodies of his brethren. He will take refuge in some hiding place; but after a brief respite he will die a cruel death. Respect for God has disappeared from human hearts. They wish to efface even God's memory. This perversity is nothing less than the*

---

24   Article in http://www.catholicvoice.co.uk/Fátima3/ch3-2.htm#notes , *Emphasis ours.* ‡ Archived from the internet on September 12, 2014 and no longer online.

25   http://www.worldprophecies.net/Pope_Pius_X_Prophecy.htm ‡ Archived from the internet September 12, 2014.

Pope Francis: The Last Pope?

beginning of the last days of the world."[26]

Strangely enough, such a doomsday scenario prophecy made its way to the mainstream Italian media just before the Conclave that elected Bergoglio. On the 9th of March 2013, just three days before the start of the Conclave, Galeazzi wrote for the newspaper, *La Stampa; "The Prophecy of the Popes by Malachy lists 112 short phrases in Latin that purport to describe all the popes from Pope Celestine II (elected in 1143) to a Pope yet to come, described in the prophecy as 'Peter the Roman,' whose pontificate will end with the destruction of Rome and the last judgment. According to the list, the last Pope should arrive after the one called "de gloria olivae," a Pontiff who, following the chronology, should be Benedict XVI. But a lost prophecy says that between Benedict XVI and the last Pope there would be another one, a 'caput nigrum,' a dark-skinned Pope."*[27]

So where is the *"caput nigrum"* of the 112th lost prophecy, and not to be confused with the doomsday coda? Why are serious Vaticanist's taking this hypothesis into consideration, as it is not even mentioned in the 111 prophecies attributed to St. Malachy? The answer is in the book *"La Profezia Dell'Ultimo Papa,"* a highly influential novel written by Schmeig Maria Olaf, and published by *Edizioni Fazi* in 2001. Beginning in 1992, the author spent nearly a decade researching in Rome, until the book's publication.[28] He made complex studies in search of the truth about Malachy's prophecies so he could better include them in the context of his fictional novel. Unfortunately, the relevant discoveries he apparently made at a historical level were never indicated in his book with the necessary details to follow up on his studies. The only thing I can say is that there is a long standing oral tradition in Rome regarding the arrival, at some point in history, of a *"Black"* Pope before the end of the Church. The tradition is so ingrained in the consciousness of the Romans that some people gathered in the square for the election of what would become Pope John Paul II, shouting *"the Black Pope"* when they heard the name of a foreigner, Cardinal Wojtyla,[29] nominated from the balcony in St. Peters Square. Regarding instead Nostradamus' reference to *"the Black Pope,"* he made predictions on the legacy of various popes. There is only one reference to a Black Pope by Nostradamus, which seems still a bit far-fetched and difficult to interpret, and is found in *C6:Q25,* where he states:

> *Through adverse Mars will the monarchy of the great fisherman be in ruinous trouble: The young red black one will seize the hierarchy, The traitors will act on a day of drizzle.*

---

26   *Ibid., Pope Pius X Prophecy.*

27   http://vaticaninsider.lastampa.it/en/the-vatican/detail/articolo/conclave-23008/ ‡ Archived from the internet September 12, 2014.

28   Schmeig Maria Olaf, *La Profezia Dell'Ultimo Papa* (Rome: Edizioni Fazi, 2001).

29   http://it.nostradamus.wikia.com/wiki/Profezia_perduta_sul_Papa_nero / ‡ Archived from the internet September 12, 2014.

Leo Lyon Zagami

Of course, *"the monarchy of the great fisherman,"* refers to the Vatican and having Mars adverse is not considered a good thing. In Natal Astrology, Mars plays a very prominent role, governing as it does the first and eighth signs of the zodiac, Aries and Scorpio. In the physical world Mars causes accidents, fevers, and violence. One is left wondering if the date May 13th, 2017, referred to as the *"day of drizzle"* as predicted by Ali Agca, may become the most significant day in global history?

THE BLACK POPE ‡ CROWLEY
AND THE DECLINE OF CATHOLIC MORALITY

Just before the election of Pope Francis, one of the main agents of Jesuit intelligence, the sociologist and occultist named Massimo Introvigne, who is also the OSCE representative against the discrimination of Christians, explained to Galeazzi in *La Stampa* that the numbers, *"are in favour of the Black Pope because if the Church grows, it is due especially to Africa, where Christians have surpassed Muslims."* Indeed, a *"caput nigrum"* for the Church.[30] Things went differently, because of course there was no *"Black Pope"* in the traditional sense, as it has been rumored for many years in the conspiracy circles. The new pope is instead a Jesuit, someone most people associate with the term *"Black Pope."* The Provost General of the Society of Jesus, or the General of the Jesuits as he is universally known, already goes also by the nickname *"Black Pope."* Currently this office belongs to Father Adolfo *Nicolás* Pachón (b.1936), who is close to resigning. He followed another resigning General, Father Peter Hans *Kolvenbach* (b.1928). In a recent letter published by Father Adolfo Nicolás in 2008, the twenty-ninth successor of St. Ignatius of Loyola as the head of the Society of Jesus, originally addressed his letter to seventeen Jesuits scattered in 112 countries around the world. The current *"Black Pope"* announced the long path to the end of which, *"in the last months of 2016,"* Father Nicolás will be presented at the Thirty-Sixth Congregation of the Jesuits as the resigning General, only the second in history to abdicate, and they will be called to elect a new Father General. Basically like his predecessor, Nicolás is just following the trend of the moment in the Vatican, which is resigning. I can actually state with certainty that this new trend was generated first in the Jesuit community, and only later did Pope Ratzinger pick up on the idea, which was started by the Jesuits in 2008. No wonder Pope Francis, a Jesuit, is also speaking of his own resignation. Resigning has become the latest plague to affect the Church, as I stated earlier, because it destroys the sacrality of the Papal office in favor of the materialist view promoted by the New World Order. Going back to the aforementioned Massimo Introvigne, a key figure I investigated in detail in volume one of my trilogy, *Confessions of an Illuminati,*[31]

---

30   *Ibid.*, article, *La Stampa.*

31   Leo Lyon Zagami, Confessions of an Illuminati (Vol. I, II, III), CCC Publishing, San Francisco 2016-2018.

in addition to his direct link to the Jesuits, he is also part of French Freema-sonry, Martinism, and even holds an honorary degree in the infamous O.T.O. (Ordo Templi Orientis). Irregardless if the O.T.O. is a relatively small order of fewer than 4,000 registered members worldwide, it has had a huge impact on contemporary Masonic culture, and a very negative influence on the Catholic world, especially the American Catholic Church in particular. So how did this happen? It happened thanks to the expansion in the 1960s of the perverse ide-ology of one of its greatest exponents, Aleister Crowley (1875 - 1947), known also as *"The Great Beast 666."* Such accusations were nothing new, as they were made years ago by Michael S. Rose, considered one of the leading Ameri-can experts in the contemporary Catholic world. In his book, *Goodbye, Good Men: How Liberals Brought Corruption into the Catholic Church,* [32] he devoted the majority of his research into the subject of homosexuality in the seminaries, and the growing phenomenon of child pedophilia in the Catholic Church. It is interesting that this book was released just before the first wave of scan-dals in the Roman Catholic Church broke out on a widespread public level. Some say Rose's book appears prophetic, as he documented the systematic rejection of pious, orthodox seminary applicants in many dioceses, and the encouragement of questionable attitudes and agendas instead. Rose argues that the root of this problem was the growing popularity of Crowley's work in the 1960s. Some of the rebel seminars were nicknamed *"Pink Palaces,"* in particular, because they facilitated the plague of pedophilia in the U.S. Catho-lic Church. The seminarists discovered the deviant teachings of the satanist Aleister Crowley, especially those of his Gnostic Catholic Church, that lead in the following decades to an even greater moral decline.

Ultimately, given the immense sums to be paid as compensation to the vic-tims, such a vision change would manifest in scandals and economic disaster for the Vatican. In 1995, Archbishop Elden Curtiss of Omaha, Nebraska, raised eyebrows throughout the Catholic Church by writing and publicly stat-ing that the so-called vocations crisis and priest shortage were *"artificial and contrived."* The Archbishop's words came as a shock to many lay Catholics, confirmed the suspicions of many others, and provoked outrage and hostil-ity among Catholic progressives. Michael Rose took the Archbishop's state-ment as his starting point for *Goodbye, Good Men*, in which he describes and chronicles the reasons behind the drastic decline in the number of young men entering Catholic seminaries in the 1970s and 1980s. Reverend Robert J. Jo-hansen, an American Catholic priest and book reviewer, wrote in the May, 2002 printed edition of *Culture Wars* magazine:

> *Fidelity to the Church, its teaching and discipline, would seem to most people, Catholic or otherwise, to be a* sine qua non *for Catholic priests. But in* Good-

---

32   See. Michael S. Rose, Goodbye, Good Men: How Liberals Brought Corruption into the Catholic Church, (Washington DC: Regnery Publishing, 2002).

Leo Lyon Zagami

bye, Good Men *Rose describes an environment in many Catholic seminaries during the 70's and 80's that encouraged dissent and disobedience, as well as moral and doctrinal laxity. In these seminaries, Rose writes, those responsible for recruitment and admissions actively sought out men who supported the 'progressive' or liberal Catholic agenda: abolition of priestly celibacy, ordination of women, acceptance of the gay lifestyle, and liturgical experimentation. Those few men with more traditional views who got into these seminaries were subjected to harassment and attempts at re-indoctrination. Rose describes an atmosphere in which expressions of reverence such as genuflection or kneeling were derided, and traditional devotions such as the rosary received scorn and hostility.* Goodbye, Good Men *has twelve chapters, each of which details some aspect of the vocations crisis. In the first three chapters, Rose shows how some seminaries and vocation directors (the person in a diocese or religious community responsible for the recruitment of candidates) actively attempted to screen out candidates who voiced loyalty to the teachings and discipline of the Church, or who showed an attachment to traditional expressions of piety such as the rosary or Eucharistic adoration. In the fourth and perhaps most disturbing chapter, Rose describes a homosexual 'subculture' which came to dominate some seminaries in the 70's and 80's. The middle chapters of the book describe the denigration and deconstruction of Catholic doctrine, liturgy, and devotion which subsisted in some seminaries during the same period. Other chapters detail the misuse of psychology in the seminary admissions and formation process, allegations of whitewashing of seminary problems by the American hierarchy, and how seminary admissions and formation were taken over by people with a 'death wish' for the priesthood. The book concludes with an examination of the Church's standards for seminary life, and a look at some dioceses which are experiencing success in fostering priestly vocations.* Goodbye, Good Men *is not easy reading. Rose's portrayal of vocational and seminary abuses could lead the reader to the conclusion that American Catholics have, by and large, been deliberately deprived of priests by men and women whose agenda was 'reshaping' and 're-imaging' the Church. In Rose's view, there hasn't been a shortage of vocations, there has been a shortage of what the progressive Catholics in power desired as the 'right kind' of vocations: those supportive of the progressive agenda of women's ordination, married clergy, and the like. Rose's contention is that many men who had genuine vocations were deliberately screened out of the priesthood because the liberal Catholics in control of the process found them unsupportive of their agenda. Those who read* Goodbye, Good Men *will come away with an appreciation of the prophetic nature of Archbishop Elden Curtiss' claim that the vocations shortage is 'artificial and contrived.'* Adding in the end, after a very long and in-depth analysis, his final thought and criticism on the controversial publication Goodbye, Good Men *is, in many ways, an unfortunate book. It is unfortunate because the story of the problems in American seminaries needed to be told, but it needed to be told with scrupulous concern for accuracy and truth.*

Pope Francis: The Last Pope?

It needed to be told in such a way as to elicit more than righteous indignation from the faithful. It also needed to be told with more nuance and penetration. It is also unfortunate because Rose's failure to make distinctions will actually distract attention from the real remaining problems in American seminaries. Rose's credibility problems and his relative lack of analysis do little to shed light on what may be done to strengthen our seminary system. Only in the last two chapters does he have anything to say about what factors come together to make a good seminary. Goodbye, Good Men *may create a great deal of controversy, but I fear that ultimately it will do little to serve the good.*[33]

Uwe Siemon-Netto, a Lutheran layman and non-ordained theologian, and the now-former religion editor of *United Press International*, reviewed Michael Rose's work for *UPI* on September 10th, 2003, in a very different light from Rev. Johansen. Besides being a more positive book review, his article upset the people in charge of the *Ordo Templi Orientis*, touching on those lesser-known aspects of Crowley's responsibility in this infamous affair:

With the $85 million settlement for the victims of sexual abuse in the Catholic Archdiocese of Boston, a singularly revolting chapter in the Church's 2,000-year history is drawing to a close. It is all the more disgusting as perverted men ordained to represent Christ at the altar took advantage of the secular society's 1960s dementia to act out their fantasies—chiefly on adolescents. Equally revolting was the clubby mindset of their overseers, who more often than not simply reassigned offending priests rather than handing them over to secular authorities for trial and punishment. But that's just stating the obvious. Fairness demands that one looks for the roots of this massive disaster—a disaster, by the way, not just for Roman Catholicism but Christianity on the whole. These roots were not 'Christian' by any stretch of the imagination. In fact they were distinctly anti-Christian, indeed Satanic, if one analyzes the message of the 1960s from a theological and historical perspective. It was in the '60s that some Catholic seminaries, especially those in dioceses headed by liberal bishops, earned nicknames such as 'Pink Palace' because they gave shelter to fiends while rejecting faithful young men of orthodox persuasion. All this is convincingly documented in Michael S. Rose's bestseller Goodbye, Good Men. *But all this did not occur in a vacuum. It occurred in an era whose motto was 'Do what thou wilt shall be the whole of the law.' This axiom poisoned the Church as it did other institutions. It is worth noting who authored this maxim. It was the British writer and warlock Aleister Crowley, the self-named 'Beast 666,' whom Somerset Maugham described as the most evil man he has ever met. Crowley died in 1947. But strangely, his anti-Christian worldview, his advocacy of the most appalling forms of sexual behavior, his relentless, though elegantly penned appeal to selfishness spread two decades after his death. Check the Internet, and you will find that Crowley is still*

---

33   http://www.culturewars.com/2002/may02_ggm.html ‡ Archived from the internet September 12, 2014. Emphasis ours.

alive—with the Google search engine producing 84,000 mentions of his name. Click on, if you can bear it, and you are swiftly linked to websites you do not want to know about—the sites of the Church of Satan, of sadomasochistic, occult, atheistic and other groups which are still flourishing. The good news is that the spirit of Crowleyism, which presented itself as an alternative religion, no longer plagues American Catholic seminaries, many of which are churning out an entirely new species of strong, manly, committed clergymen—heroes in the priesthood—as Michael S. Rose reports in his newest book, Priest *(Manchester: Sophia Institute Press, 2003, 185 pp., $14.95). The priestly crimes of the 20th century will of course remain a huge blot on Catholicism's history forever, just like the Inquisition. But like the Inquisition, it was overcome, and this strengthened the church. For this Catholics and other Christians owe gratitude to the victims, who brought the scandal to the open. As this tragedy unfolded, all kinds of advice were given to the church, including the nostrum that Rome should open the ministry to married men; that would keep the depraved out. As a Protestant, this columnist obviously favors married pastors. In the past, the Protestant parsonage did much to shape the cultures of Europe and North America. But the sorry behavior of many of today's ministers makes it clear that the right to marry is no bulwark against sexual misconduct. Pastors break their marriage promises, leave their children, and wind up in the arms of other women—or men, and then expect to be consecrated bishop, calling their new relationships 'sacramental.' That's Crowley talk; this is how he described his behavior. For the Catholic Church, a settlement of $85 million is a terrible price to pay for the Crowleyism that had crept into its seminaries and parsonages. But at least it has now put an end to this aberration. Meanwhile, in some mainline Protestant denominations Crowleyism is alive and well—and celebrated as a virtue, called 'tolerance,' while these church bodies continue to shrink. It is amazing how evil, blindness and madness have evolved into an alternative trinity.*[34]

Perhaps Uwe Siemon-Netto's statement about the disappearance of *"the Spirit of Crowleyism"* from the seminaries in support of Michael S. Rose's position in his newest book, *Priest*[35] is a positive statement, albeit unrealistic, to say the least. It is no coincidence that in Pope Francis' episcopal genealogy we find Cardinal Mariano Rampolla del Tindaro (1843-1913).[36] He is the Cardinal and Freemason that, because of his membership in the *Ordo Templi Orientis* and Freemasonry, was prevented from becoming Pope at the 1903 Conclave. The times were not yet as mature as they are now for such a move,

---

34 http://www.upi.com/Odd_News/2003/09/10/Commentary-Aleister-Crowleys-legacy/UPI-39961063218162/ ‡ Archived from the internet September 12, 2014. Emphasis ours.

35 See. Michael S. Rose, Priest: Portraits of Ten Good Men Serving the Church Today and Striving to Serve Him Faithfully, (Bedford, NH: Sophia Institute Press, 2003).

36 *Cf.* also http://www.catholic-hierarchy.org/bishop/bbergj.html ‡ Archived from the internet September 12, 2014.

Pope Francis: The Last Pope?

that's for sure. Craig Heimbichner, writing in the August 2003 issue of *Catholic Family News*, states that Monsignor Jouin is said to have intervened personally with Emperor Franz Joseph to ask for the *Jus exclusivae* to be invoked, having procured some evidence that Cardinal Rampolla had at least a close affinity with the Freemasons.[37]

On behalf of the O.T.O. itself, in the November 1999 newsletter for *Thelema Lodge* in Berkeley, California, the organization acknowledges that Msgr. Jouin accused Cardinal Rampolla of belonging to the OTO.[38] The Dean of the former *College of Hard NOX*, of the now-defunct O.T.O. Thelema Lodge, disputes the accusation made by Msgr. Jouin.[39] He is contradicted, however, by the independent O.T.O. archivist, Peter-Robert König[40] who is, by the way, also a friend and close collaborator of Massimo Introvigne. Of interest is the first order of business of Pope Pius X, elected after Franz Josef vetoed Rampolla and *"abolished the veto of heads of state, declaring that anyone who dared introduce a civil veto in the conclave would suffer automatic excommunication."*[41] Further, Pius X instituted an oath forbidding future conclave attendees from transmitting a veto by a secular monarch to the conclave so that no one could ever stop again a Freemason or a member of the Ordo Templi Orientis or any other sect in becoming the new pope. Therefore, Rampolla was held in the highest regard by Aleister Crowley, as Rampolla was a member of the Ordo Templi Orientis several years before Aleister Crowley took control of the Order. Crowley introduced the blasphemous *'Gnostic Mass'* of the OTO *Ecclesia Gnostica Catholica*, or the "Gnostic Catholic Church," shortly before Cardinal Rampolla's death in 1913. And later, included him among the Saints of his heretical and Neo Libertine Church, the official Church of today's *Ordo Templi Orientis*[42] that now rejoices in secret when acknowledging the general ignorance surrounding the subject. Pope Francis was elected Pope on whose Apostolic succession depends on a Freemason who belongs to a Satanic Order, who never reached the Papal throne, perhaps for this reason, but now has without a doubt found a worthy successor in Bergoglio, *the first Jesuit Pope.*

37   See. "Pope Saint Pius X" in From the Housetops, No. 13, Fall, 1976, St. Benedict Center, Richmond, New Hampshire.

38   See. Theodor Reuss and Aleister Crowley, edited by Peter Koenig, O.T.O. Rituals and Sex Magick (London: Pentacle Enterprises pp. 79-107).

39   http://en.wikipedia.org/wiki/Mariano_Rampolla ‡ Archived from the internet September 12, 2014.

40   http://www.pararreligion.ch/books/oto.htm ‡ Archived from the internet September 12, 2014.

41   http://en.wikipedia.org/wiki/Papal_conclave,_1903 ‡ Archived from the internet September 12, 2014.

42   http://en.wikipedia.org/wiki/Ecclesia_Gnostica_Catholica ‡ Archived from the internet September 12, 2014.

Leo Lyon Zagami

THE MYSTERIOUS DEATH OF WILLIAM H. KENNEDY AND LUCIFER'S LODGE

William H. Kennedy, also known as "Teddy," passed away suddenly at home in the month of August, 2013 at the age of 48. His death was never really investigated, and when approached about it, his family seemed quite scared to stir things up, and therefore no attention whatsoever was given to his passing by the media. Teddy was a controversial life-long Catholic writer and radio host, and he was the author of the now out-of-print and highly collectable books: *Satanic Crime—A Threat in the New Millennium,* and the even more controversial title *Lucifer's Lodge: Satanic Ritual Abuse in the Catholic Church.* He was a regular guest on Dr. Stan Monteith's nationally syndicated radio show.

He was found dead on August 14th, 2013, but may actually have died on Tuesday August 13th, 2013, and as some of you may know, the death tarot card resides at number 13. This date indicates the possibility of an occult murder. If he was indeed dead on the 13th, his murder would have occurred exactly one week after recording an important interview about Pope Francis and the Vatican bank with Dr. Stan Monteith, on August 6th 2013. In addition to this, some clear statements made in his previous radio interviews, which are still available on the internet, speak of having managed to avoid his own contract killing by the mob once before, and that nefarious parties were apparently interested in murdering him because of his investigations. There was no indication of prior illnesses given in regards to William Kennedy health, but he wrote books exposing Satanism, and hosted a radio program that for a period delved into esoteric and controversial topics. The late Dr. Stan Monteith, who also recently passed away in September 2014, mentioned Kennedy's passing briefly at the end of one of his famous shows soon after William's death, but Monteith only said that William Kennedy had been a regular guest on his show, and that he was recently found dead in his home. Strangely, nothing more was stated or speculated by the always investigative mind of Monteith, who was probably too shocked by the bad news to follow up on the story with bias. In the so-called "conspiracy world," no one has dug further into this highly suspicious death. For one reason or another, no one has dared to adequately look into it.

William H. Kennedy closed his pioneering investigation into the sexual abuse crisis in the Roman Catholic Church with the following statement: *"Malachi Martin was correct in his assertion that Lucifer's Lodge exists within the Church of Rome. Unfortunately, there are no quick answers as to how to deal with this horrible state of affairs. Lucifer's Lodge is an ongoing problem. It is still in operation and should be of major concern to people of goodwill everywhere."*

After reading this passage one searches for a word: "Shocking" perhaps? If only *I* were shocked. Things that I was not prepared to believe of priests

Pope Francis: The Last Pope?

have turned out to be true over and again since I was a child, and the time to be shocked has passed since reading the previously mentioned *Goodbye, Good Men* and other similar books published in my native Italy, like *Gone with the Wind in the Vatican,* a controversial book that came out in 1999 about nepotism, homosexual scandals, corruption, and "clientism" within the Vatican City, and written under the pseudonym *I Millenari,* or "The Millenarians."

Some accounts of priestly sexual abuse he used to illustrate his story are now all too familiar, and the findings in the William H. Kennedy books are fully confirmed by my own research and the never-ending scandals that have rocked the Catholic Church over the last several years.

Halfway through reading his books, like others before me, I checked into some of the sources for his research and found them to be 100% credible. He does use a few marginal sources, which I would like to check further, but the fact that he was connected to Fr. Malachi Martin, Fr. Al Kunz, and Fr. Charles Fiore, made his information truly ground-breaking and credible at the time, as I hope mine is now. This priestly trio became aware that something was seriously wrong in the U.S. Catholic priesthood, and began collecting data and evidence to expose the evil-doers. William Kennedy came a bit later to join in the investigation, making it a foursome.

What is sad today is that all of them, including Kennedy, are strangely dead. Fr. Kunz's death in 1998 was sudden and bloody, and the crime has never been solved. Kunz's parishioners witnessed a man who looked like the very essence of evil sneering from a back pew at Kunz during Mass shortly before he died. However, no leads have turned up in the following investigations as written by Kennedy himself. No one has been arrested in the case either. But when reviewing the situation just before the murder, some strange facts emerge.

After Kunz died, Malachi Martin—who had endured years of cardiac problems—saw his health deteriorate further until his passing in July, 1999. Father Charles Fiore likewise suffered ill-health just after the murder, and Kunz's passing may have adversely affected him physically.

They were all unable to assist William H. Kennedy in the 2002 exposure of the priest pedophile ring that gained traction like never before after the previously mentioned *Boston Globe* article came out, which lead to other cases receiving significant media and public attention throughout the world.

Father Fiore was still around, but left this world in March 2003, not long after speaking on the telephone with William H. Kennedy. Apparently the conversation revolved around the request that Kennedy look closely into the Kunz murder, especially after he defended Malachi Martin against critics on the syndicated talk show *A Closer Look* (ACL) hosted by Michael Corbin.

The directly involved pedophiles Archbishop Weakland and Cardinal Mahoney attended a symposium at Notre Dame in December, 2001. That is the last time they would meet again as reigning prelates in the Roman Catholic Church. Kennedy wrote that *"Martin, Fiore, and Kunz were to be vindicated in their efforts to expose the pervert cult that had stolen the church from the faithful."*

And indeed, in May 2002, the BBC reported that a new lawsuit was filed against the head of the largest Roman Catholic diocese in the United States by four men who said that a priest sexually molested them when they were boys. The men accused the Archbishop of Los Angeles, Roger Mahoney, of conspiring to commit fraud and obstruct justice by covering up the activities of the pervert priest, Father Michael Baker. They also alleged that the Los Angeles Archdiocese and the church acted as a "criminal enterprise" in covering up the abuse. William H. Kennedy knew this was to be only the beginning of the present decline of the Catholic Church, and wrote in his *Lucifer's Lodge* that *"This was only the latest blow to the Roman Catholic Church, which had already been engulfed in countless scandals over sexual abuse of children by its priests."*

So let me attempt to summarize for you the main points of my investigation in the mysterious death of the 48-year-old William H. Kennedy, whose death was never fully explained. In brief, everything started with Fr. Kunz's death in 1998, then Fr. Fiore's, as well as Fr. Martin's, health declined immediately after the murder. Within 16 months Fr. Martin was dead, and Fr. Fiore was not well enough to continue their on-going investigation. Interestingly enough, Kennedy stated that a mutilated calf was also found on the morning that Fr. Kunz's body was discovered, and that such finding was the calling card or signature of Satanists, just like the possible date of his own death.

A person describing himself as a life-long friend named "Steve" stated on Facebook, in response to a post regarding the death of William H Kennedy:

I am a lifelong friend of William (Ted) Kennedy, and can offer a little information about his passing. His death is indeed sudden and mysterious. Ted was in good health. He had not received any death threats per se, but he certainly had enemies who had threatened him with physical violence. Ted regarded these people as cranks and thought all people should live their lives as if they might be hit by a bus at anytime. He was no shrinking violet regarding his scholarship. I was skeptical about what he and Father Malachi discussed, but the whole thing erupted in front of me in the pages of the Boston Globe (which is no conspiracy rag). Although 'liberal' at the editorial level, the Globe definitely primarily expresses the concerns of the Boston Brahmin 'old money' class. So, when they printed confirmation of the events the Archdiocese could no longer deny, then Ted's work was vindicated. There is no longer any question of the reality of widespread pedophilia and satanic ritual abuse in the Church which was managed, in the United States, by Bernard Law, Cardinal of Boston. This didn't make any friends for Ted and he was also a well-known attendee at the weekly protests by the faithful outside the Cathedral and Chancellery.

In his public statement, the same person close to William H. Kennedy made another note of interest:

> Also, one thing Ted never advertised is that he shared the Kennedy name with the Kennedy's of Hyannisport, MA. He was cousin to John F., Robert F., and his nick-namesake (was from) Edward M. 'Teddy' Kennedy. He also had immediate family prominent in politics at the local and state level. I cannot attest to any intrigue or mystery surrounding that fact, but everyone knows of the tragedy and other unresolved questions surrounding the Kennedy family.
>
> Lastly, Ted's scholarship is what may have gotten him in trouble. I am by no means saying there was any wrongdoing surrounding his death. Nobody knows the cause at this time. What I am trying to say is that although his work seemed preposterous and outlandish at first blush, it was always borne out with excellent research and facts. Authors who had sold many more books, such as Brad and Sherri Steiger, would defer to Ted. I personally watched him meticulously compile the sources for Lucifer's Lodge and, until the scandal broke, had dismissed my good friend as a kook. He was no kook. He knew about the operation of dark forces in the world and was never afraid to confront them.

So on closing this personal tribute to his courageous work, I remind myself to try to avoid such a tragic ending. I also discovered that Kennedy was not your ordinary Catholic or your ordinary researcher, but a relative of the powerful, yet cursed, Kennedy family. Maybe his work and his research will now be evaluated again under a different light.

THE MASONIC ENDORSEMENT OF POPE FRANCIS

More and more documents that show different Masonic luminaries praising and supporting Pope Francis are becoming public knowledge since his election. Recently, the official salute of Argentine Freemasonry became accessible on the Internet. After praising Bergoglio, the Grand Master of the Lodge of Argentina expresses its pride in having a *"co-patriot"* elected Pope. His letter was documented on the websites of both *Actualidad Masónica* and *Impulso Baires*, which received the scoop. This is the article *"Pope Francis and the Freemasons"* that appeared on *Actualidad Masónica* on March 20, 2013, published by the editor in the following form:

> Last March 13th, the members of the College of Cardinals who were gathered in Vatican City elected the Argentine Jorge Mario Bergoglio as the new Pope of the Catholic Church. Bergoglio, who took the name of Francis after his election, is the first South American to occupy this office; he was Archbishop of Buenos Aires before his election. The naming of the new pontiff motivated a communiqué by the Grand Lodge of Argentina, which was diffused by Impulso Baires on the same day of Pope Francis' election.

Its text follows: 'A man of austere life consecrated to his devotions, the designation of the new pontiff of the Catholic Church supposes a great recognition of the Argentine Nation. In Argentine Freemasonry, based on the principles of tolerance, profound respect for personal convictions, liberty, equality and fraternity, the brothers who profess or adhere to this religious faith stand together with others who belong to other creeds, are agnostics or lack any faith. In the name of all, the Grand Lodge of Argentina greets our co-patriot a Cardinal who just received such a high world distinction.' –Angel Jorge Clavero, Grand Master

Another article that appeared in *Impulso Baires* on March 13, 2013 is entitled, ***In a communiqué the Grand Lodge of Argentine Freemasonry salutes the naming of the new Pope Francis I,*** and reads as follows: *"Federal capital—The Grand Lodge of Free and Accepted Masons, an institution rooted in our country since 1857, salutes the naming of our co-patriot Cardinal Jorge Bergoglio as Pope Francis I, said a communiqué sent to the editor of* Impulso Bares: *'A man of austere life consecrated to his devotions, the designation of the new pontiff of the Catholic Church supposes a great recognition of the Argentine Nation. In the Argentine Freemasonry, based on the principles of tolerance, profound respect for personal convictions, liberty, equality and fraternity, the brothers who profess or adhere to this religious faith stand together with others who belong to other creeds, are agnostics or lack any faith. In the name of all, the Grand Lodge of Argentina greets our co-patriot Cardinal who just received such a high world distinction.'" –Angel Jorge Clavero, Grand Master, who signed at the end of the document."*[43]

The day after the election of Pope Francis I, the Grand Orient of Italy (GOI), which as I mentioned earlier is the main form of what is considered "regular" Freemasonry in Italy, issued a formal communication praising Bergoglio for the first egalitarian measures he took on the day of his election. The document also made public the Masonic expectations of Italian Freemasonry that the new Pope shall lead the Church on the democratic path desired by Freemasonry. This announcement by the now former Grand Master Gustavo Raffi was published as follows on the official GOI website on March 14, 2013:

> *With Pope Francis, nothing will be more as it was before. It is a clear choice of fraternity for a Church of dialogue, which is not contaminated by the logic and temptations of temporal power.*

> *A man of the poor far away from the Curia. Fraternity and the desire to dialogue were his first concrete words. Perhaps nothing in the Church will be as it was before. Our hope is that the pontificate of Francis, the Pope who 'comes from the end of the world' can mark the return to the Church—Word instead of the Church—Institution, promoting an open dialogue with the contemporary world, with believers and non-believers, following the springtime of Vatican II.*

---

43   http://www.traditioninaction.org/ProgressivistDoc/A_169_Arg-Mason.html
‡ Archived from the internet September 14, 2014.

Pope Francis: The Last Pope?

The Jesuit who is close to the least ones of history, has the great opportunity to show the world the face of a Church that must recover the announcement of a new humanity, not the weight of an institution that closes itself off in defense of its own privileges. Bergoglio knows real life and will remember the lesson of one of his favorite theologians, Romano Guardini, for whom the truth of love cannot be stopped. –Grand Master Raffi, Grand Master of the Grand Orient of Italy, at the beginning of the pontificate of Francis

Praise was also made by another high-ranking Freemason: *"The simple cross he wore on his white cassock,"* concludes the Grand Master of Palazzo Giustiniani, *"lets us hope that a Church of the people will re-discover its capacity to dialogue with all men of good will and with Freemasonry, which, as the experience of Latin America teaches us, works for the good and progress of humanity, as shown by Bolivar, Allende and José Martí, to name only a few. This is the 'white smoke' that we expect from the Church of our times."*[44]

In June 2014, the newly elected Grand Master Stefano Bisi made an even more bold statement on this subject: *"I would like to know what Pope Francis thinks of Freemasonry,"* adding during this public conference held in Rome and organized by the library service of this Masonic Obedience: *"I am deeply convinced that in the field of human rights and freedom there will be fruitful contacts between the Catholic Church who is definitely a believer. I think it's time to unite rather than divide and I'm sure we can find a valuable point of encounter and dialogue. The breach of Porta Pia in 1870 should be updated. September 20 must be remembered for another breakthrough, a breakthrough that could serve to break down the walls that separate different worlds who want to meet. There is strong need for connections. This was also the message of the Second Vatican Council."* Unfortunately, the Second Vatican Council referred to by the Grand Master Stefano Bisi is the one that has gradually handed over the Catholic Church to the worst Italian and International Masonic Lobby, and there is nothing "regular" about it. It lives and strives thanks to the silence of too many Freemasons. Interestingly enough, the notorious Vatican Journalist Msgr. Mario Pieracci went public at one point stating that Bergoglio will become, *"the punisher of Freemasonry in the Vatican."* Mons. Pieracci, an old acquaintance of mine, made such a statement on the Italian state television network, *RAI UNO* in broad daylight, shocking, perhaps deliberately, his viewers so he could reassure them of the self-righteous nature of this Pope. For others, however, it is the same Bergoglio, a Freemason, or at least somebody who supports their monolithic goals. The traditional and international Catholic blog *RORATE CAELI* asked their cherished friend Marcelo González, of *Panorama Católico Internacional*, who knows the Church of Argentina like the back of his hand, to send them a

---

44   http://www.grandeoriente.it/eventinewsgoi/2014/06/chiesa-e-massoneria-il-gran-maestro-bisi-mi-piacerebbe-sapere-cosa-pensa-papa-francesco-dei-liberi-mura-tori.aspx ‡ Archived from the internet September 14, 2014.

report on Pope Francis after his election. What he said in return is worth reading. It is one of the strongest criticisms to date Bergoglio has received from the Catholic media. It reads as follows:

> *Of all the unthinkable candidates, Jorge Mario Bergoglio is perhaps the worst. Not because he openly professes doctrines against the faith and morals, but because, judging from his work as Archbishop of Buenos Aires, faith and morals seem to have been irrelevant to him. A sworn enemy of the Traditional Mass, he has only allowed imitations of it in the hands of declared enemies of the ancient liturgy. He has persecuted every single priest who made an effort to wear a cassock, preach with firmness, or that was simply interested in Summorum Pontificum. Famous for his inconsistency (at times, for the unintelligibility of his addresses and homilies), accustomed to the use of coarse, demagogical, and ambiguous expressions, it cannot be said that his magisterium is heterodox, but rather non-existent for how confusing it is. His entourage in the Buenos Aires Curia, with the exception of a few clerics, has not been characterized by the virtue of their actions. Several are under grave suspicion of moral misbehavior. He has not missed any occasion for holding acts in which he lent his Cathedral to Protestants, Muslims, Jews, and even to partisan groups in the name of an impossible and unnecessary interreligious dialogue. He is famous for his meetings with Protestants in the Luna Park arena where, together with a preacher of the Pontifical House, Raniero Cantalamessa, he was 'blessed' by Protestant ministers in a common act of worship in which he, in practice, accepted the validity of the 'powers' of the TV-pastors. This election is incomprehensible: he is not a polyglot, he has no Curial experience, he does not shine for his sanctity, he is loose in doctrine and liturgy, he has not fought against abortion and only very weakly against homosexual 'marriage' (approved with practically no opposition from the episcopate), he has no manners to honor the Pontifical Throne. He has never fought for anything else than to remain in positions of power. It really cannot be what Benedict wanted for the Church. And he does not seem to have any of the conditions required to continue his work. May God help His Church. One can never dismiss, as humanly hard as it may seem, the possibility of a conversion ... and, nonetheless the future terrifies us. [45]*

So why are traditional Catholic's confused and terrified by his election? A mere four months before his election as "Pope" of the modernist Vatican II Church, Jorge Mario Bergoglio, then known as Cardinal Bergoglio, collaborated with the Jewish-Masonic *B'nai B'rith* lodge to celebrate a *"Kristallnacht,"* or Holocaust memorial, in his Catholic cathedral of Buenos Aires, Argentina. The two main speakers of the event were Bergoglio himself and his friend Rabbi Alejandro Avruj of the Fundacion Judaica of Buenos Aires. Representatives of various non-Catholic religions also took official part

---

45   http://rorate-caeli.blogspot.com/2013/03/the-horror-buenos-aires-journalist.html
      ‡ Archived from the internet September 14, 2014. Emphasis ours.

Pope Francis: The Last Pope?

in the event. This shows that the new religious head of the Vatican II is yet another apostate, and therefore is incapable of being a true Pope, just as is any non-Catholic. Take it on faith from Pope Pius XII, excerpted from *Encyclical Mystici Corporis* par. 23: *"For not every sin, however grave it may be, is such as of its own nature to sever a man from the Body of the Church, as does schism or heresy or apostasy."*

This is what the *Catholic Encyclopedia* states in the *"Papal Elections"* section: *"Of course, the election (as Pope) of a heretic, schismatic, or female would be null and void."*[46] His participation in interfaith ceremonies also diminish his legitimacy, according to a popular blog site: *"The commemoration of the Jewish Lodge, officially even called a 'commemorative liturgy,' took place in the Cathedral of Buenos Aires, (and) the then Cardinal Jorge Mario Bergoglio participated actively."* The blogger continued, *"Under Archbishop Bergoglio it became customary in the Archdiocese of Buenos Aires since 1994 that B'nai B'rith performs its annual memorial service held for the Jewish victims of Nazism in Argentina's Catholic churches."* Lastly, it observed, *"The official program book with the symbol of B'nai B'rith and the coat of arms of the Archdiocese of Buenos Aires is called an 'Inter-religious Liturgy.'"*[47] Another reason to be worried about the Francis Papacy, apart from his interfaith dialogues, are projects long supported by USA intelligence services, as classified documents in my possession continue to prove. In regards to the homosexual issue, Pope Francis made some surprising remarks in the summer of 2013 in response to a question about an alleged *"Gay Lobby"* in the Vatican.

His response on the subject: *"When I meet a gay person, I have to distinguish between their being gay and being part of a lobby. If they accept the Lord and have goodwill, who am I to judge them? They shouldn't be marginalized. The tendency is not the problem."* He added: *"They're our brothers."*[48]

One year later the Patriarchate of the Byzantine Catholic Patriarchate, whose members are priests of the Ukrainian Orthodox Greek Catholic Church, formally of the Ukrainian Greek Catholic Church recognized by the Holy See, operating out of the city of Lviv in western Ukraine, launched their *"anathema"* against Pope Francis who was addressed as the *Bishop of Rome*. In the New Testament, the word *"anathema"* is used to signify a curse and forced expulsion of someone from the Christian community.[49]

46   http://www.novusordowatch.org/wire/bergoglio-jewish-liturgy.htm ‡ Archived from the internet September 14, 2014. Emphasis ours.

47   http://pagina-catolica.blogspot.com.ar/2012/11/fue-profanada-la-catedral-de-buenos.html ‡ Archived from the internet September 14, 2014.

48   http://www.nytimes.com/2013/07/30/opinion/a-papal-surprise-humility.html?_r=0 ‡ Archived from the internet September 14, 2014.

49   http://en.wikipedia.org/wiki/Anathema ‡ Archived from the internet September 14, 2014.

The reason for such a *curse* is described in a video statement by Archbishop Elias Dohnal[50] who was selected as the first Patriarch of this new schismatic body of the Catholic Church. Delivered on the 2nd of August 2014, the date of Saint Elia, the following extract sums up the content of the *"anathema"* against Pope Francis: *"He promotes the immoral mentality of homosexuality that is contrary to the essence of the Gospels and destroys every moral value,"* and stated that with this act, *"Bergoglio is excluded by the invisible Body of Christ and he is occupying illegally his office in the visible organization."* Adding that, *"with his acts he is approving syncretism and paganism."*[51]

The present Grand Master of the Grande Oriente Democratico, the already cited Gioele Magaldi, whose title is the Past Worshipful Master of the prestigious Roman lodge of the Grand Orient of Italy, Har Tzion Montesion 705, revealed on his web site after the election of Bergoglio, that Pope Francis will be *"an innovative and progressive Pope, sustaining this are some Brothers close to the Grande Oriente Democratico, that assure they have contributed in some way, indirectly, also within the Conclave, through some fraternal friends, to the election of a man that will be able to regenerate the Catholic Church and help human society in his complexity."*[52] The fact that Magaldi revealed *"some Brothers,"* a term used to define Freemasons, had actively *"contributed"* to the election of a Pope, should make us meditate on the future of this Church, a church that is increasingly in line with the synchronistic view promoted by the New World Order, and not with their Christian roots.

On June 22, 2014, the *New York Times* reported that *Ekspres,* a Lviv-based newspaper, conducted a lengthy investigation of Patriarch Dohnal's church and concluded that it had discovered an important clue to the group's supposed pro-Moscow allegiances, and advocacy on the side of Moscow during the 2014 pro-European anti-Moscow revolution in Ukraine: *"Before the 1989 collapse of Communism in his homeland, then still Czechoslovakia, Mr. Dohnal worked as an informer for Soviet Intelligence. The newspaper published what it said to be a document from former Czechoslovak archives that identified him as a mole for Soviet intelligence with the code name 'Tonek.'"*[53] It was Dohnal's church that,

---

50   http://www.attivo.tv/player/news-e-informazione/dichiarazioni-shock-su-papa-francesco-bergoglio-guardate-e-diffondete-il-video.html ‡ Archived from the internet September 14, 2014.

51   http://www.ioamolitalia.it/video/il-patriarca-del-patriarcato-cattolico-bizantino-condanna-di-apostasia-papa-bergoglio-perche--promuove-l-omosessualita.html ‡ Archived from the internet September 14, 2014.

52   http://www.grandeoriente-democratico.com/Grande_Oriente_Democratico_saluta_il_nuovo_Papa_Francesco.html ‡ Archived from the internet September 14, 2014.

53   http://www.nytimes.com/2014/06/22/world/europe/ukrainian-church-faces-obscure-pro-russia-revolt-in-its-own-ranks.html?_r=0 ‡ Archived from the internet September 14, 2014.

Pope Francis: The Last Pope?

in December 2013, issued an appeal to Mr. Putin to intervene militarily to restore order and defeat what it scorned as *"Euro-sodomitic occupation by Brussels, programmed by U.S. agents."* It was also Patriarch Elias Dohnal who condemned Patriarch Kyrill of the Russian Orthodox Church for *"apostasy,"* when Kyrill accepted membership into the NWO-inspired "Council of Religious Leaders," held on May 30-31, 2012. The *"apostasy"* accusation was made after Kyrill attended the IV Congress of Leaders of World and Traditional Religions in Astana, the capital city of Kazakhstan. [54]

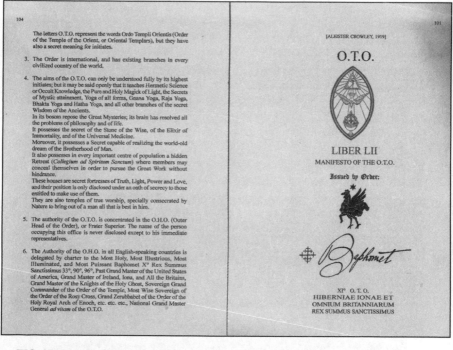

FIG. 37. Images of original documents belonging to the Ordo Templi Orientis published by Aleister Crowley in 1919, featured in the book OTO Rituals and Sex Magick *written by Theodor Reuss and Aleister Crowey, and edited by P. R.-König for Pentacle Enterprises in 1999.*

---

54   http://www.youtube.com/watch?v=hTLFDbSslJs ‡ Archived from the internet September 14, 2014.

102

LIBER LII
MANIFESTO OF THE O.T.O.

PEACE, TOLERANCE, TRUTH; SALUTATION ON ALL POINTS OF
THE TRIANGLE; RESPECT TO THE ORDER. TO ALL WHOM
IT MAY CONCERN: GREETING AND HEALTH.

Do what thou wilt shall be the whole of the Law.

1. The O.T.O. is a body of initiates in whose hands are concentrated
the wisdom and the knowledge of the following bodies:
    1. The Gnostic Catholic Church.
    2. The Order of the Knights of the Holy Ghost.
    3. The Order of the Illuminati.
    4. The Order of the Temple (Knights Templar).
    5. The Order of the Knights of St. John.
    6. The Order of the Knights of Malta.
    7. The Order of the Knights of the Holy Sepulchre.
    8. The Hidden Church of the Holy Graal.
    9. The Hermetic Brotherhood of Light.
    10. The Holy Order of Rose Croix of Heredom.
    11. The Order of the Holy Royal Arch of Enoch.
    12. The Antient and Primitive Rite of Masonry (33°).
    13. The Rite of Memphis (97°).
    14. The Rite of Mizraim (90°).
    15. The Ancient and Accepted Scottish Rite of Masonry (33°).
    16. The Swedenborgian Rite of Masonry.
    17. The Order of the Martinists.
    18. The Order of the Sat Bhai, and many other orders of equal
    merit, if of less fame.
It does not include the A∴A∴, with which august body it is,
however, in close alliance.
It does not in any way infringe the just privileges of duly authorized
Masonic Bodies.

2. The dispersion of the original secret wisdom having led to confusion,
it was determined by the Chiefs of all these Orders to recombine
and centralize their activities, even as white light, divided in a prism,
may be recomposed.
It embodies the whole of the secret knowledge of all Oriental Orders;
and its chiefs are initiates of the highest rank, and recognized as
such by all capable of such recognition in every country in the world.
In more remote times, the constituent originating assemblies of the
O.T.O. included such men as:

103

Fohi	Hippolytus
Laotze	Merlin
Siddartha	Arthur
Krishna	Titurel
Tahuti	Amfortas
Ankh-f-n-khonsu	Percivale
Herakles	Mosheh
Orpheus	Odysseus
Vergilius	Mohammed
Catullus	Hermes
Martialis	Pan
Apollonius Tyanæus	Dante
Simon Magus	Carolus Magnus
Manes	William of Schyren
Basilides	Frederick of Hohenstaufen
Valentinus	Roger Bacon
Bardesanes	Jacobus Burgundus Molensis
King Wu	Ko Hsuen
Christian Rosenkreutz	Osiris
Ulrich von Hutten	Melchizedek
Paracelsus	Khem
Michael Maier	Menthu
Jakob Boehme	Johannes Dee
Francis Bacon	Sir Edward Kelly
Andréa	Thos. Vaughan
Robertus de Fluctibus	Elias Ashmole
Chau	Comte de Chazal
Saturnus	Sigismund Bacstrom
Dionysus	Molinos

And recently:

Wolfgang von Goethe	Friedrich Nietzsche
Sir Richard Payne Knight	Hargrave Jennings
Sir Richard Francis Burton	Karl Kellner
Forlong Dux	Eliphas Lévi
Ludovicus Rex Bavariæ	Franz Hartmann
Richard Wagner	Cardinal Rampolla
Ludwig von Fischer	Papus (Dr. Encausse)

The names of women members are never divulged.
It is not lawful here to disclose the name of any living chief.
It was Karl Kellner who revived the exoteric organization of the
O.T.O. and initiated the plan now happily complete of bringing all
occult bodies again under one governance.

*FIG. 38. On the right page, clearly amongst the members of the O.T.O., appears the name of **Cardinal Rampolla**, second from last. (Theodor Reuss and Alister Crowley OTO Rituals and Sex Magick, op.cit. p. 103)*

FIG. 39. Leo Lyon Zagami and Monsignor Mario Pieracci in the summer of 2008.

Fig. 40. Patriarch Elijah Anthony Dohnal OSBMr (b. 1946) elected as first Patriarch of the Byzantine Catholic Patriarchate by the Bishops' Synod of the Ukrainian Orthodox Greek Catholic Church in an extraordinary assembly on 5 April 2011. In a YouTube video, Patriarch Dohnal made the charge of "anathema," levied against Pope Francis.

Leo Lyon Zagami

```
DEPT FOR G, S/P, S/GPI, AND S/SRMC


E.O. 12958: DECL: 12/18/2019
TAGS: PREL, PHUM, KIRF, SOCI, SCUL, VT
SUBJECT: AN INVENTORY OF THE VATICAN'S INTERFAITH DIALOGUES


REF: A. 08 VATICAN 87
B. VATICAN 124
C. 08 USUN 1126
D. VATICAN 106
E. VATICAN 122
F. VATICAN 100
G. VATICAN 126


VATICAN 00000134 001.2 OF 003


CLASSIFIED BY: Julieta Valls Noyes, DCM, EXEC, State.
REASON: 1.4 (b)
1. (SBU) Summary: The Vatican is a leader or partner in many
inter-religious dialogues, primarily with the "Abrahamic"
religions - Islam, Judaism, and of course, other Christians.
Vatican leaders are also beginning to reach out to Asian
faiths.
This cable describes the Vatican's primary, organized
dialogues. Septels: A) analyze why the Vatican pursues
interfaith dialogue, and B) propose USG-Holy See
collaboration
in support of such discussions. End Summary.
```

FIG. 41. Previously classified document regarding the inter-religious dialogue subject, sent by the U.S. Embassy in the Vatican to Washington DC, on the 27th of January 2009.

EPILOGUE

by the Author

The permanent headquarters for the Congress of World Religions is located in the city of Astana, Kazakhstan, a former Soviet Union nation in Central Asia.[1] The religious campus features a classic Egyptian pyramid, loaded with ancient Sumerian, Egyptian, Illuminati and other occult symbolism throughout. CNN.com called Astana the "weirdest" capital city in the world. The logotype for the Congress of World Religions depicts uncanny similarities to the logotype of a New Age guru, perhaps portraying *"Maitreya,"* the False Messiah whom I suspect will play a role in presenting any new global religion to the world masses in line with what I have demonstrated in regards to the *Vatican 2* project in Palestrina. The Vatican backing of a new *"Universal"* religion where the term *"Holy Spirit"* is used, or more appropriately abused, as a unifying force for this endeavor, and attributing to the Holy Spirit that which is clearly not the work of the Holy Spirit.

The resemblance of Maitreya's logo is practically identical to the logo which represents the Congress of World Religions.[2] This apparent logo connection between the Congress of World Religions and Maitreya is just one of many mysteries surrounding Astana that bear further investigation. For those who have not yet noticed, the word "Astana" is a plausible anagram for the word "SATAN."[3] Lest we not forget, during the *Fátima 2000 Congress* in the 1990s, the now former archbishop Emmanuel Milingo made the shocking accusation that there are *"Satanists in the Vatican."*

As presented earlier, in the coming years, the subcutaneous injection of a microchip will be introduced to us as a wonderful and necessary device, making it appear perfectly acceptable without a second thought. But never forget this: If you let them implant that evil in your body, you will lose your freedom. Both your privacy and your life, in both the material and the spiri-

---

1   http://www.religions-congress.org/content/view/342/60/lang,english/
     ‡ Archived from the internet September 14, 2014.

2   See. http://333crucible.wordpress.com/maitreyas-logotype/ then compare with the logo that appears in the video clip on the Congress of World Religions web page.

3   http://biblicaltimes.wordpress.com/2010/11/26/astana-kazakhstan2012/
     ‡ Archived from the internet September 14, 2014.

tual sense. All this comes together, as described, for a distinct purpose. There is a potent Doomsday scenario that deeply involves the Vatican, and some say the main protagonist may be *the Last Pope*. Also bear in mind that within this context are the growing tensions at a geopolitical level, described clearly by Pope Francis since the summer of 2014, and suggesting that the *Third World War* has already begun, with the possible Islamization of the Vatican hierarchy. This all seems to fit in with the words of the New Testament from Matthew 24: *"For many will come in my name, claiming, 'I am the Messiah,' and will deceive many. You will hear of wars and rumors of wars, but see to it that you are not alarmed. Such things must happen, but the end is still to come. Nation will rise against nation, and kingdom against kingdom. There will be famines and earthquakes in various places."*[4]

It is hard not to wake up every morning and see history repeating itself. After one hundred years since World War I, many nations seem to be on the brink of the biggest conflict in history, with the stakes higher than ever before. A 21st century world war would bring nation to *"rise against nation"* for the last time, this due to new technology ... the use of nuclear or biological weaponry ... that doesn't leave much room for survival. Pope Francis urged the world on September the 13th, 2014, to shed its apathy in the face of what he characterizes as a third world war, intoning *"war is madness"* while standing at the foot of a grandiose monument devoted to soldiers killed in World War I.[5]

To demonstrate further the Vatican hypocrisy, the Holy See has appointed the German lawyer Ernst von Freyberg, a high-ranking member of the Sovereign Military Order of Malta, to be a weapons dealer and president of the *Voss Schiffswerft und Maschinenfabrik*, a company from Hamburg active in the creation of warships.[6] Ernst von Freyberg had been the president of the Vatican bank for a period that lasted until July, 2014. It was announced that Freyberg was replaced by Jean-Baptiste de Franssu to head the Institute for Works of Religion. This shows once again the hypocrisy of the Pope and the Vatican institutions that, along with the *"Gay Lobby"* affair, bring to mind another passage of the Gospel According to Matthew: *"Let the little children come to me, and do not hinder them, for the kingdom of heaven belongs to such as these."*[7]

4   New International Version (NIV)

5   http://www.huffingtonpost.com/2014/09/13/pope-francis-world-war-
     3_n_5815046.html ‡ Archived from the internet September 14, 2014.

6   http://www.saverianibrescia.com/missione_oggi_stampa.php?centro_
     missionario=archivio_rivista&rivista=2013-03&id_r=141&sezione=lettere_in_
     redazione&articolo=rammarico_e_disagio_per_la_nomina_del_nuovo_presi-
     dente_dello_ior_lenciclica_della_dignit_umana&id_a=5185 ‡ Archived from the
     internet September 14, 2014.

7   Matthew 19:14, New International Version.

Pope Francis: The Last Pope?

I wrote this book to bring awareness to what is happening at the highest levels of the Catholic Church hierarchy. Whether you consider yourself a Christian, a Muslim, a Jew, a Buddhist or anything else, these matters of faith pertain to your world and your relationship with your Higher Self, or whatever you consider to be God. Above all the dogmas and religions that have been abused by humanity since ancient times, there is a higher calling of personal spirituality. Let this be your guiding light. We need to know what is true and what is false concerning allegations made in relation to supposed prophecies or conspiracy theories. This information will make you, as a human being, aware of truth beyond all divisions. One day mankind will leave this primitive stage of understanding to embrace something truly universal, and I can assure you, it will not be the fruit of sin and perversion manipulated by the hypocritical New World Order or their Congress of World Religions.

Patriarch Kirill of Moscow and Russian President Vladimir Putin seem to understand that in this tumultuous endgame, before *"the Beast"* springs his trap for the rest of humanity, that perhaps they can act in opposition to the tragic manipulation by the world powers-that-be. Let's see if in this period of *"Tribulation"* and *"Revelation,"* which is set to end in 2020, humanity can manifest the real Kingdom of God and righteousness, instead of the looming Orwellian dictatorship led by the globalist Bilderberg Club, and the evil plan that we have begun to expose. The fate of our planet and civilization, with every passing day, seems to be teetering on a perilous "razor's edge." On one side, there is our worst dystopian nightmare. On the other, the promise of a Golden Age.

Before closing, I would like to thank all those people who collaborated in the realization of my first book into the English language, in particular my wife Christy, my publisher and editor Brad Olsen at CCC Publishing in San Francisco, and my long-time friend and collaborator, Historian Luciano Fortunato Sciandra, for the inside information he kindly made available to me. My newly-released *"Confessions of an Illuminati"* trilogy will clear up any other questions you may have pertaining to these hidden and sometimes disturbing subjects.

FIAT LUX ... The Author

FIG. 42. *The delegation of IV Congress of Leaders of World and Traditional Religions, which was held May 30-31, 2012, in Astana, Kazakhstan.*

FIG. 43. *The Palace of Peace and Reconciliation, also called the Pyramid of Peace, rises high above Astana, located in the northern part of the country. Photo by G. Zaphar from http://www.panoramio.com/photo/20732440*

The Italian press coverage of Fatima 2000 especially focused on Archbishop Milingo' speech. The largest Rome daily, Il Messaggero gave front page headlines to Archbisho Milingo's startling accusation that satanists are working in the Vatican. Various othe newspapers also featured this revelation of Archbishop Milingo. Because it was a shocking and amazing, the Archbishop called a press conference a few days later an reconfirmed his accusations that satanists are active today in the Vatican. See Englis anslation of excerpts on page 19.

Father Gruner listens while His Grace, Archbishop Milingo, speaks to the Bishops and delegates about exorcisms, and the existence of satanic worship that is taking place right inside the Vatican.

FIG. 44. Images regarding former archbishop Milingo's participation at the Fátima 2000 Congress when he accused high members of the hierarchy in Rome of practicing Satanism. Italian and newspaper cutouts from Il Messagero and other major daily papers that reported this stunning news.

Leo Lyon Zagami

Archbishop Milingo: "Satanists in the Vatican"

Excerpts of press clippings on page 90...

Are there men of the curia who are followers of satan? "Certainly there are priests and bishops. I stop at this level of ecclesiastical hierarchy - (Archbishop Milingo) said - because I am an archbishop, higher than this I cannot go." "In December of 1975 - the special delegate of the Pontifical council for the pastoral care of migrants has said - Paul VI said that the smoke of satan had entered into the Vatican." "He has entered - he commented - but I have not heard that anyone has seen him leave. We must pray so that he will go away." (Il Tempo 11/27/96)

The Archbishop Emeritus of Lusaka (Archbishop Milingo), presently working at the Secretariat of the Holy See for Immigrants is certainly convinced that inside the leonine walls (the Vatican) that there are among the beaucrats of the Roman Curia present today and active some followers of evil forces. The unexpected revelations of satanism has been confirmed by Malachi Martin, the ex-Secretary of Cardinal Augustine Bea. Martin was reached in Manhatten by the magazine The Fatima Crusader. According to Martin, "the prince of darkness has had and continues to have his surogates in the court of St. Peter in Rome". The Fatima Crusader is a magazine for a Fatima movement which is active in both Americas. The North American magazine organizes periodically regional and national conferences for the study of the message of the Madonna given in 1917 to three shepherd children to the Church and humanity. Msgr. Milingo accused parts of the Vatican bureaucracy of having succumbed to the devil, while speaking yesterday at the world congress dedicated to "Fatima 2000, World Peace and the Immaculate Heart of Mary." (Il Messaggero 11/24/96)

Satan in the Vatican? When the last explosive declaration of Msgr. Milingo appeared a few days ago in the pages of the newspapers, the effervescent bishop-the African healer, had to be called to order for words which were so compromising. Inperturbably, the ex- Archbishop of Lusaka has called a press conference and ... has confirmed everything. While declaring at the same time to not want to attack the curia but calling in support to his position, none other than a Pope, "Already in 1975, in December, Paul VI said that the smoke of satan had entered into the rooms of the Vatican" and he added with a pause for effect, "no one since that time has ever said that he has exited from there." (La Nazione 11/27/96)

FIG. 45. *Excerpts from Italian newspaper articles regarding Milingo's statements at the The Fátima 2000 Congress that took place in the mid-1990's, sponsored by publisher Father Nicholas Gruner.*

FIG. 46. Cav. Luciano Fortunato Sciandra, Member of the Equestrian Order of the Holy Sepulchre of Jerusalem and the Pontifical Equestrian Order of St. Sylvester Pope and Martyr, shows his library collection to the author.

FIG. 47. Cav. Luciano Fortunato Sciandra as Grand Master of the Ordo Nova Militia Templi (Militia Spiritus Sancti, Rosae+ Crucis et Graal) during a official meeting of various Knighthoods with the author present as Grand Master of the Ordo illuminatorum Universalis.

Leo Lyon Zagami

CIA Chiefs of Section (CoS) in the Vatican from 1948 to 2009*

1948-1951: Felton Mark Wyatt
1952-1959: Gerald M. Miller
1959-1963: Thomas Karamessines
1964-1965: Felton Mark Wyatt
1965-1967: William King Harvey
1967 1969: Seymour Russell
1969-1971: Hugh Montgomery
1971-1975: Howard E. "Rocky" Stone
1979-1981: Duane R. Clarridge
1981-1984: William J. Mulligan
1985-1987: Alan D. Wolfe
1987-1989: John J "Jack" Devine
1990-1998: ???
1998-2003: Jeffrey W. Castelli
2003-2006: Robert E. Gorelick
2006-2007: Anna M. Borg
2007-2009: John D. Peters
2009: ???

(*) This is a list included in the appendix of the 2014 book entitled The CIA in the Vatican, originally titled La CIA en el Vaticano, authored by Eric Frattini of Lima, Peru (born 1963). Frattini is a Spanish essayist, novelist, journalist, college professor, political analyst, and intelligence expert who currently works as an external consultant and lecturer for security forces and intelligence agencies in Spain, Portugal, Great Britain, Romania, and the USA. The omissions from the period 1990-1998, and 2009 to present are for security reasons. Unfortunately, no questions can be asked—that's how it works in the intelligence world.

CLASSIFIED CORRESPONDENCE BETWEEN THE GRAND MASTER OF THE GRANDE ORIENTE D'ITALIA VIRGILIO GAITO (REGULAR ITALIAN FREEMASONRY), CARDINAL SILVIO ODDI AND POPE JOHN PAUL II DURING THE 1990s:

FIG. 48

TRANSLATION:

A∴G∴D∴G∴A∴D∴U∴ *
UNIVERSAL MASONRY- ITALIAN COMMUNION
GRAND ORIENT OF ITALY
THE GRAND MASTER

Pope Francis: The Last Pope?

Holy Father,

It is with profound joy and honour that the here undersigned Cardinal Silvio Oddi and the lawyer Virgilio Gaito, Grand Master of the Grand Orient of Italy of Palazzo Giustiniani make your Holiness aware of the convergence of views reached by us, finding out that in the negative relations that have existed for centuries between Roman Catholicism and Freemasonry, on one side and then the other, that has been attributed with excessive importance to what divides us, neglecting completely the creed which has always united us: the need for Man, amended by vice, to elevate temples to virtue and purity to project himself in the brightness of the celestial spaces.

Opposite fundamentalism has dug a deeper wall that has not benefited anyone. Humanity has dire need of harmony to save themselves from moral destruction before a physical one. On the threshold of the third millennium the increasingly advanced and sophisticated technology, if not driven by enlightened consciousness,** risks to deliver us hopelessly in the hands of Big Brother so lucidly forecasted by George Orwell which advances menacingly into the almost total indifference of a society dominated by hedonism, consumerism and, especially, the ignorance that suffocates and kills freedom.

It therefore appears in all its dramatic urgency that all the Illuminated minds ***, in front of the heavens, with humility accept to march together to send away from the precipice the disbanded flock. We believe this to be, in the year of World Tolerance, the categorical imperative of all those who have the exciting privilege and incommensurable responsibility to the care of souls and moral guidance.

Additional Notes by the author:

* *A.·.G.·.D.·.G.·.A.·.D.·.U.·. are the initials for the Italian words that stand for* **To the Glory of the Great Architect of the Universe** *-Abbreviations of technical terms or of official titles are of very extensive use in Freemasonry.*

** *enlightened consciousness translates in Italian:* coscienze illuminate *a term used by the Illuminati to define themselves.*

*** *Illuminated minds translates in Italian:* menti illuminate *another term used by the illuminati to define themselves.*

FIG. 49

TRANSLATION:

For a long time the Grand Orient of Italy of Palazzo Giustiniani follows with full consent the great and exhausting work that your Holiness, following in the footsteps of Jesus, the truest Messenger of love to appear so far on this Earth. Around the world we are searching for a common language that unites the people, which will restore their dignity and faith in a liberating catharsis which is anxious with human wickedness * or the fragility of our human bodies ** which has made us fear the irreparable for your mission.

So, fully aware of the aims pursued by Universal Masonry, that has always been devoted to the improvement of the individual for the improvement and progress of Humanity that can be reached only through love and tolerance, we feel the time has come to launch a call for reconciliation that will put an end to the secular incomprehension between the Catholic Church and Freemasonry.

In the rest of the world, indeed the latter has always carried out a philanthropic mission (it's enough to remember the International Red Cross was created by Mason and Nobel prize winner Henri Dunant) by establishing hospitals, nursing homes for the elderly, kindergartens,

Leo Lyon Zagami

research centers for cancer, smallpox, polio, tuberculosis, AIDS and the most dangerous social diseases, by being on the side of the underdogs, of the suffering, the oppressed, the downtrodden.

In our country it has been asserted that the Gran Orient of Italy of Palazzo Giustiniani, in addition to intense cultural activities to stimulate the moral progress and strengthen civic consciousness, assists with the foundation of night kindergartens in Turin, available also for anyone who does not have a roof for the night. With the Foundation of the Milanese *Pane Quotidiano* we provide breakfast every morning to all those in need, with the Bolognese *ANT*, we assist cancer patients in the terminal stage, and the Florentine Association we provide care and transportation for the sick. We have sent medicine and rare kinds of comfort to the battered people of former Yugoslavia, we have raised funds and sent through the *Caritas* association aid to the children in Bosnia, we have sent a welcome offer for the reconstruction of the Church of Shkodër in Albania, donated ambulances equipped to various relief Agencies, we have established a network of families who guest in their homes at their own expense for long periods of time the Chernobyl children, saving them from certain cancers.

Additional Notes by the author:

* referring to the attempted assassination of Pope John Paul II.

** referring to the fragility of the Polish Pope in his later years.

FIG. 50

TRANSLATION:

The Grand Orient of Italy of Palazzo Giustiniani is present every day alongside anyone, tried by the vicissitudes of life, yearning for a word of hope and to recover their dignity, a brother among brothers, son of the same Father.

As the ways of Roman Catholicism and Freemasonry are in this direction at least parallel, we, the undersigned, believe that there is today no more reasons for opposition between the two institutions and that, instead, the two by overcoming ancient, bitter, painful disagreements and misunderstandings between them, must reach their hand to make more intense and beneficial for Humanity their work of kindness and charity.

We are in fact convinced that intolerance and fanaticism are the forces of evil against which we can and must mobilize legions of good into a true holy alliance.

This time God really wants it, because the war is not going to be bloody, there will be no burnings, murders, genocide, but we will win by force of example, of the desire to be the best, to give ourselves to others with generosity so that in every corner of the Earth everyone will have respect for themselves and others, with dignity, both conscious of their duties before their rights, will know how to elevate from the miseries of this world to look in the sky which one day will see us all connected in the chain of eternal love.

Agreeing on the analysis accomplished the undersigned submit to the wisdom and farsightedness of His Holiness the evaluation of the possible promotion of bilateral meetings at qualified levels, preceded by a special hearing from you, Holy Father, granted to the Grand Master Virgilio Gaito in the presence of the undersigned Cadinale Silvio Oddi, to concretely start the desired and mature process of rapprochement between the Catholic Church and regular Freemasonry.

Pope Francis: The Last Pope?

FIG. 51

TRANSLATION:

In the year of world tolerance such an extraordinary event would be one of the most comforting in the history of Humanity and we would be particularly happy to see it realized by your Holiness which has all the esteem of regular Masons in Italy and—we are certain—the rest of the world which, together with the undersigned Cardinal Silvio Oddi, wish you to continue for many years in your apostolate of peace.

With deep respect,

SILVIO ODDI
CARDINAL OF THE HOLY ROMAN CHURCH

VIRGILIO GAITO
GRAND MASTER OF THE GRANDE ORIENTE D'ITALIA

HIS HOLINESS
JOHN PAUL II
VATICAN CITY

FIG. 52

TRANSLATION:

A∴G∴D∴G∴A∴D∴U∴.

UNIVERSAL MASONRY- ITALIAN COMMUNION

GRAND ORIENT OF ITALY

THE GRAND MASTER

Rome, 1st of February 1996

Your Holiness,

You would want to allow someone who has the high honor, not disjoint from the great burden, to bear today the gavel of authority* of the Grand Orient of Italy of Palazzo Giustiniani formed in Milan in 1805 and since present with many twists and turns in the history of our beloved country, to extend to your Holiness and to the Catholic Church the warmest greeting for 1996, which bears the wish of harmony and peace to all men of good will as advocated by Christ and all those great Initiates who revealed to the inhabitants of this earth their divine destiny by teaching them the way of purification, of tolerance, of love *which moves the sun and the other stars.*

We often wondered, in studying the relations which existed for centuries between Roman Catholicism and Masonry, if, from one side or the other, they have attributed with excessive importance to what has divided us, ignoring completely what unites us forever: the need for Man, amended by vice, to elevate temples to virtue and purity, to project himself in the brightness of the celestial spaces, the ideal dimension towards which the immense Pythagoras exhorted us to look for the longest time.

Opposite fundamentalism has dug a deeper wall that has not benefited anyone because Humanity has the dire need of harmony to save themselves from moral destruction before a physical one. On the threshold of the third millennium the increasingly advanced and sophisticated technology, if not driven by enlightened conscience, will put us hopelessly into the hands of Big Brother so lucidly forecasted by George Orwell, that advances menacingly with

Leo Lyon Zagami

great steps into the almost total indifference of a society dominated by hedonism, consumerism and, especially, the lack of culture that suffocates and kills freedom.

Additional Notes by the author:

* The importance of the gavel, according to **Joseph F. Ford** in *Early History and Antiquities*: *"Perhaps no lodge appliance or symbol is possessed of such deep and absorbing interest to the craft as the Master's mallet or gavel. Nothing in the entire range of Masonic paraphernalia and formulary can boast of an antiquity so unequivocally remote."*

FIG. 53

TRANSLATION:

It therefore appears in all its dramatic urgency that all the Illuminated minds, facing the heavens, with humility, accept to march together to send away from the precipice the disbanded flock. We believe this to be, in the year of World Tolerance, the categorical imperative of all those who have the exciting privilege and incommensurable responsibility for the care of souls and moral guidance.

For a long time the Grand Orient of Italy of Palazzo Giustiniani follows with full consent the great and exhausting work of your Holiness, following in the footsteps of Jesus, the truest Messenger of love to appear so far on this Earth. Around the world we are searching for a common language that unites people and will restore their dignity and faith in a liberating catharsis which is anxious with human wickedness and the fragility of our human bodies which has made us fear the irreparable for your mission.

So, fully aware of the aims pursued by Universal Masonry, which has always been devoted to the improvement of the individual for the improvement and progress of Humanity which can be reached only through love and tolerance, we feel the time has come to launch a call for reconciliation that will put an end to the secular incomprehension between the Catholic Church and Freemasonry.

In the rest of the world, indeed the latter has always carried out a philanthropic mission (it's enough to remember the International Red Cross created by Mason and Nobel prize winner Henri Dunant) by establishing hospitals, nursing homes for the elderly, kindergartens, research centers for cancer, smallpox, polio, tuberculosis, AIDS and the most dangerous social diseases, by being on the side of the underdogs, of the suffering, the oppressed, the downtrodden.

In our country it's been asserted that the Gran Orient of Italy of Palazzo Giustiniani, in addition to an intense cultural activities to stimulate the moral progress and strengthen civic consciousness and to assist with the foundation of night kindergartens in Turin, available also for anyone who does not have a roof for the night. With the Foundation of the Milanese *Pane Quotidiano* we provide breakfast every morning to all those in need. With the Bolognese *ANT*, we assist cancer patients in the terminal stage, and with the Florentine Association, we provide care and transportation for the sick. We have sent medicine and rare kinds of comfort to the battered people of former Yugoslavia, we have raised funds and sent through the *Caritas* association aid to the children in Bosnia, we have sent a welcome offer for the reconstruction of the Church of Shkodër in Albania, donated ambulances equipped to various relief Agencies, we have established a network of families who guest in their homes at their own expense for long periods of time the Chernobyl children, saving them from certain cancers.

Pope Francis: The Last Pope?

FIG. 54

TRANSLATION:

So we are present each day, even without the beneficiary knowing—just as it is a good rule for each Mason to do, standing next to all tried by the vicissitudes of life, yearning for a word of hope, to recover their dignity, a brother among brothers, son of the same Father. Our roads differ perhaps in this direction or are they at least parallel? Then why not give us a hand to make our work of goodness and charity more intense and beneficial for Humanity?

The greatness of a man is not measured so much by the successes he obtains, but by the humility in recognizing his own mistakes. In the availability of a constructive dialogue with those he considers hostile or unrecoverable. Last year two Illuminated men, Yitzak Rabin and Yasser Arafat, have shown the world how true this appeal was, expressed by your predecessor at the time of the first World War against the unnecessary slaughter, which has been sealed with peace, almost miraculously. Unfortunately, a few days after a murderous hand will turn off the generous existence of Rabin, whom we discovered by obituaries as being a Freemason. Our thoughts went to the dramatic attempt against your life: still intolerance and fanaticism, forces of evil, trying to bring back Humanity to the dark ages.

But we can and we must use in contrast the legions of good in a true holy alliance. This time God really wants it, because the war is not going to be bloody, there will be no burnings, murders, genocide, but we will win by force of example, of the desire to be the best, to give ourselves to others with generosity so that in every corner of the Earth everyone will have respect for themselves and others, with dignity, conscious of your own duties, before your rights, knowing how to elevate from the miseries of this world to look in the sky that one day will see us all connected in the chain of eternal love.

FIG. 55

TRANSLATION:

With this hope, that one day—and it would be one of the most comforting in the history of Humanity—we'd love to see implemented if your Holiness will grant us a hearing, permit us to bestow upon you our esteem from regular Italian Masons, and we are sure—the rest of the world, and to wish you to continue for many years in your apostolate of peace.

Happy New Year, your Holiness, we hope you will accept this with your highest consideration.

VIRGILIO GAITO
GRAND MASTER

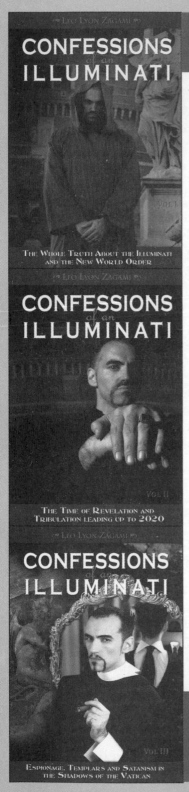